PRAISE FOR *ESSENTIALS* OF *ADVERTISI*

"This is a book I have been waiting for for some time. Most introductions to advertising are either written by communications and psychology specialists with little interest in ethics, culture and history. Other texts indulge in industry critique without paying attention to the perspective of practitioners. Cluley offers a book that can be read by both the uniniti- ated student and the seasoned ad man and ad woman. There are many surprises that await the reader – not least Cluley's answer to the puzzle why the industry survived the much-advertised 'end of advertising'. If you are looking for a one-stop source for both the long view and recent trends in this industry then Cluley's book will be the right choice for you."
Stefan Schwarzkopf, Associate Professor,
Copenhagen Business School

"This innovative textbook takes a fresh look at advertising, making us question many of our preconceived notions about this field of study. Taking the reader on a fascinating journey through various aspects of advertising studies, including historical perspectives, Robert Cluley sheds new light on this important topic in an engaging and informative style."
Pauline MacLaren, Professor of Marketing and Consumer Research,
Royal Holloway, University of London

"A superb introduction to alternative views of advertising which explains its essential features as a means of communication. A major contribution of this text is that it also highlights key issues concerning the role of advertising in business and society with succinctness and great clarity."
Professor Mike Saren, Professor of Marketing,
University of Leicester

Essentials
of Advertising

Essentials
of Advertising

Robert Cluley

KoganPage

First published in Great Britain and the United States in 2017 by Kogan Page Limited

2nd Floor, 45 Gee Street
London
EC1V 3RS
United Kingdom

122 W 27th Street, 10th Floor
New York, NY 10001
USA

4737/23 Ansari Road
Daryaganj
New Delhi 110002
India

© Robert Cluely 2017

The right of Robert Cluely to be identified as the author of this work has been asserted by him in accordance with the Copyright, Designs and Patents Act 1988.

ISBN   978 0 7494 7839 1
E-ISBN 978 0 7494 7840 7

British Library Cataloguing-in-Publication Data

A CIP record for this book is available from the British Library.

Library of Congress Control Number
2017001498

Typeset by Integra Software Services, Pondicherry
Print production managed by Jellyfish
Printed and bound in Great Britain by Ashford Colour Press Ltd.

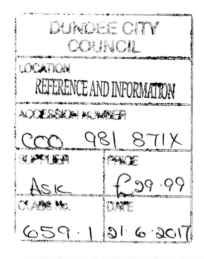

CONTENTS

About the author xi
Acknowledgements xii
About this book xiii

01 **The essentials of advertising: What are advertisements and why should we study them? 1**
Introduction 1
Overview 2
What are we talking about? A definition of advertising 3
The development of advertising over the years 5
Why study advertising? 8
What is advertising studies? 11
How to read this book 13
Summary 15
References and further reading 16

02 **Big questions: Advertising, communication, rhetoric and persuasion 19**
Introduction 19
Overview 20
Communication as a monologue: the transmission model of communication 20
Communication as a dialogue: social constructionism 25
The power of words 30
Rhetoric: the ancient art of persuasion 32
Big questions 36
References and further reading 37

03 **Art or science: What do legendary advertisers think about advertising? 41**
Introduction 41
Overview 42

Two types of theory: espoused theory and theory-in-use 42
Scientific advertising 43
Creative advertising 50
What do contemporary advertising workers think? 56
Summary 58
References and further reading 60

**04   Work, agencies and contexts: Organizational
        perspectives on advertising 63**
Introduction 63
Overview 64
The advertising industry 64
The importance of creativity 71
Industry restructuring 74
Summary 81
References and further reading 82

05   Information and value: The economics of advertising 85
Introduction 85
Overview 86
Advertising and consumers: why do consumers respond
   to advertising? 87
Does advertising improve profit? Advertising and the firm 93
Advertising and markets 96
A welfare view 98
Putting it all together 100
References and further reading 101

**06   The hierarchy of effects: The psychology
        of advertising 103**
Introduction 103
Overview 104
Cognitive psychology 106
Social psychology 113

Depth psychology 118
Divided or united? 124
Summary 126
References and further reading 127

**07   The society of the spectacle: The sociology
of advertising** 131
Introduction 131
Overview 132
Social theory and advertising 133
Does advertising bring us together or pull us apart? 141
Creating acceptable advertising: the licence to operate 145
Summary: what does critical mean? 149
References and further reading 150

08   The magic system: Cultural studies of advertising 153
Introduction 153
Overview 153
Reading ads 154
Symbolic consumption: resistance and avoidance 165
Reading culture through advertising 167
How advertising changes culture: cultivation theory 171
Is advertising culture? 173
References and further reading 174

**09   The medium is the message: Media studies
and advertising** 177
Introduction 177
Overview 177
Differentiating media 178
The medium is the message: media ecology 181
Advertising and the media ecology 185
Advertising and the news 187
Summary 192
References and further reading 193

10   The distorted mirror: Advertising and ethics 195
Introduction 195
Overview 195
The distorted mirror: ethical criticism of advertising 196
Sticking up for advertising 201
The last word: Pollay's response 203
Advertising ethics in practice 205
Advertising for good 209
Whose side are you on? 211
References and further reading 212

11   Where next? The new essentials of advertising 215

Index 217

ABOUT THE AUTHOR

Robert Cluley is an Assistant Professor at the University of Nottingham. He has taught marketing management, advertising and branding to thousands of students in his career as an academic and has seen his students go on to leading jobs at advertising agencies and brands.

His own research has appeared in leading academic journals such as *Marketing Theory*, *Journal of Marketing Management*, *Organization Studies* and *European Journal of Marketing*. He currently sits on the Editorial Board of *Marketing Theory* and is an Honorary Lecturer at St Andrews University.

He lives and works in Nottingham – where he can be found boxing and playing guitar with equal ineptness.

ACKNOWLEDGEMENTS

Thank you to my family, Victoria, Lana and Wren, for their support in the preparation of this book, and to my colleagues and students for challenging me to think differently about advertising.

ABOUT THIS BOOK

Advertising surrounds us. It influences which businesses succeed and which fail. It helps politicians win elections. It creates trends and fashions. It shapes what we all want and what we all spend our money on. Simply put, it is hugely important.

As a result, lots of people have had something to say about advertising. Psychologists try to understand what happens to our brains when we see advertisements. Media practitioners try to understand how to reach their target markets. Business people, for their part, try to figure out whether all the money they spend on advertising is worth it. These are just a few examples. There are many other groups of people who are interested in understanding something about advertising.

The point of this book is to bring these disparate discussions together to try to reduce things down to some essential ideas, concepts and issues. This is a daunting task. There is a lot to cover.

So let me explain quickly how I have approached the problem.

There is a tendency among some academics to write huge textbooks that include everything the authors can think of. The reader then has to figure out what is important to them. As someone said to me recently, this is like trying to include the entire internet in a textbook. It is going to fail.

I have approached the task from a different perspective.

I want to help you to navigate your way through the essentials of advertising. Assuming many of you have access to wider resources such as the internet, I have not tried to include everything. Rather, I have reviewed the main discussions about advertising and separated them into broad areas of interest. I have picked out some of the most well-known and important cases, examples and studies to illustrate how people in each of these areas support their ideas. My hope, then, is that the book will be a springboard for you to jump into the wider area of advertising studies according to *your interests*.

That's the theory at least!

The essentials
of advertising 01

What are advertisements and why
should we study them?

Introduction

A lot of people have thought about advertising. Some explain how
it works to change consumers' decisions. Others are interested in
exploring what kinds of techniques advertisers use. Some people
have looked at the history of advertising or compared advertising in
different cultures. Still others want to discuss the ethics of different
advertising practices.

When we look across all these discussions, we find that there is a
lot of agreement about the essentials of advertising (and, of course,
just as much disagreement). But looking across all these discussions is
difficult. You have to be able to think like a marketer, a psychologist,
an economist, a sociologist, a historian and so on. Consequently, it is
rare for people to do it.

To paraphrase a famous Apple ad from the 1980s, this book will
help you to *think differently* about advertising. It will help you to
think about advertising and to appreciate the wide variety of thinking
about it. So, rather than focusing on the differences between perspectives, I want to help you appreciate the similarities. After all, whether
it comes from psychology, economics, management or marketing,
thinking about advertising shares one very important feature. It is
about advertising.

The basic argument of this book, then, is that we can only get to grips with the essentials of advertising by learning to appreciate *advertising studies* as an area of knowledge. As such, it is a good idea to start by defining what advertising is. This might seem obvious but I bet you have rarely asked yourself what makes something an advertisement. The answer I will offer in this chapter is that advertising refers to *any attempt to change demand through communication.* It might seem obvious to us now that advertising is about selling things, but, as we will see, this was not always the case.

Overview

The chapter proceeds as follows. First, we will explore what advertising is. Here we consider the historical development of the term. After this, we will explore some potential reasons you might be interested in advertising. Some of these might resonate with what you are already thinking. They might be the reason you purchased this book. But there are many reasons to think about advertising and possibly some that you might not have considered yet. We will then sketch out an overview of advertising studies. That is to say, we will briefly think about the different groups of people who have studied advertising. Throughout the chapter, you will see a number of thought boxes, which delve into more detail about a particular issue, topic or debate. You can jump into these as you see fit.

OBJECTIVES

By the end of this chapter, you should be able to:

- define what advertising is;
- describe the development of advertising; and
- outline advertising studies.

What are we talking about? A definition of advertising

Let's start with some basics. What is an ad? It seems like such a simple question that it is almost embarrassing to ask it. Yet, like most simple questions, it is actually quite difficult to answer.

We all see hundreds, if not thousands, of ads on a daily basis and when we see them we tend to recognize that they are ads and not something else (see Thought box 1.1). But what is it that makes something an ad and not news or art, for example? They often look very similar. We will come across them in the same places. Why are they different? It is hard to say.

To make matters worse, if you think about all the ads you see in a typical day, you will notice that ads themselves can be very different. Some of them are funny. Some are serious. Some are glamorous. Some are mundane. Some are memorable. Others annoying. Some explain a product or service in detail and provide you with information about what it does, how it works and how much it costs. But others say nothing about the product at all. Some ads consist of printed words, while others use moving images, sounds, posters, web content and, increasingly, events and experiences.

This leaves us with a basic problem: ads look a lot like things that are not ads and, at the same time, they look very different to other ads. To get around this problem, and to stop us from going mad, I think it is useful to think about *what ads do* rather than *what they look like*. To put it more technically, it is helpful to think about advertising as a verb (something people do) rather than a noun (a name for a set of things). The best way of explaining what ads do that I have been able to think of is to say that ads are *attempts to change demand*. More specifically, they are *attempts to change demand through communication*.

One of the benefits of this way of thinking is that it helps us recognize that there are many different ways that ads work. As the saying goes, there are many ways to skin a cat. The same is true of changing demand. It can be done by offering new information to consumers. But it can also be done by creating powerful brands.

It can be done by segmenting groups of consumers into niche markets. But it can also be done by promoting to a mass market.

Equally, thinking this way about advertising helps us to recognize that there are different ways of communicating. We can talk. We can listen. We can broadcast the same message to lots of people at the same time. We can also speak to individuals separately. We can use technologies to help reach people or speak personally to those around us.

It is my belief that the ways that we *change demand through communication* in any context is determined by three factors:

- Advertising changes because of *real changes* in consumer behaviour, media technologies, markets and cultures.

- Advertising changes because of *perceived changes* in consumer behaviour, media technologies, markets and cultures on the part of businesses, organizations and advertising practitioners.

- Advertising changes because of *theoretical changes* about how consumers, markets and cultures work. These are promoted by academics, researchers and industry experts.

One of the main arguments of this book is that, more often than not, it is our ideas about advertising which shape what we do as advertisers, consumers, organizations, brands and societies – not actual changes in the real world. For now, though, the important point is that ads that look very different all do similar things. This is one reason why we can see examples of ads from ancient civilizations and still understand them as ads. It is no surprise, for instance, that as far back as ancient Mesopotamian civilization, traders and manufacturers used notices, posters and town criers to change demand (Fletcher, 2008). They were advertising even if their ads would not work now.

Thought box 1.1: How much advertising is there?

You might think that someone would keep count of how many advertisements there are. But in reality no one does. There are lots of different estimates. Here is just a sample of them:

- Fletcher (2008) suggests that there are at least 25 million new advertising posters and billboards put up each year in the United Kingdom.

- It has been estimated that half of the mail delivered in the United Kingdom is junk mail.

- In 2013, nearly 100 billion spam emails were sent every day.

- Bogart (1990) calculated that 330 million commercials are broadcast each year on television in the United States.

- In the United Kingdom, 65,000 new television ads are prepared each year.

- Coca-Cola has over 2 billion 'brand communication opportunities' with which to advertise to consumers in the United States each day (Donation: 2004: 31).

- 60 per cent of the pages in all newspapers are ads (Collins and Skover, 1993).

Perhaps you do not think this is a lot of advertising but I think it is. Indeed, each year when I begin teaching a new class advertising I do the same activity. I buy a copy of a random magazine on the morning of the first lecture. In class, I ask the students to guess how many pages of the magazine are ads. They tend to guess between 10 and 25 per cent. Then I start flicking through the pages and call out 'ad' or 'article'. After a few pages, students start laughing as they see how many ads there are. But, by the time we have gone through the first 20 or so pages and seen than the majority of them are ads, their laughs turn to shock!

The development of advertising over the years

It is easy to assume that as long as there have been markets there have been ads. It is obvious to us now that advertising is designed to change demand through communication. But there is actually a precise moment when this way of thinking emerged. It happened in the early 20th century when advertisers started describing their activities as *salesmanship on paper* or *salesmanship in print* (see Thought box 1.2). Prior to this, advertising had a number of uses. It was not just about selling. In fact, it started off not being about selling at all.

According to the *Oxford English Dictionary*, the word 'advertising' entered the English language over 600 years ago through the French word *avertissement*. Originally, the French word referred to a notion of shrewdness, awareness or acumen. It was a little like the modern-day idea of being 'switched on'. It was both an instruction that said 'You should pay attention' and it was a label saying that 'This is important'.

Thought box 1.2: The birth of modern advertising

We can point to a particular moment when advertising practitioners recognized that *advertisements in the world* had changed and that their *advertising theories* were out of date. It happened in 1904 at the office of a US ad agency called Lord and Thomas. An executive was sitting at his desk one day when a messenger brought him a slip of paper that read: 'I am in the saloon downstairs. I can tell you what advertising is. I know you don't know. It will mean much to me to have you know what it is, and it will mean much to you. If you wish to know what advertising is, send the word "yes" down by the bellboy.'

The executive did not bite. But one of his juniors, a man named Albert Lasker, did. Lasker wrote 'Yes' on the note and sent it with the messenger to the note's author. Shortly after, the author of the note, a man named John Kennedy, joined Lasker in his office.

Kennedy asked Lasker what advertising was. Lasker answered that advertising is 'news'. 'No,' said Kennedy, 'it is a very different thing.' He went on to explain that advertising is about giving people a 'reason why' they should purchase a product. He told Lasker that 'advertising is a very simple thing. I can give it to you in three words, it is "salesmanship in print"' (see Cruikshank and Schultz, 2013).

O'Reilly and Tennant help us to see the importance of this distinction: 'All these years later, it sounds ridiculously simple; it's now a given that advertising is about salesmanship. But in 1904 the idea was downright revolutionary. Until then the pioneers of advertising had simply invited or implored readers to visit their shops and buy their products' (2009: XVIII–XIX).

So, from the 15th century, what we would now call the preface of a book was marked 'avertissement'. Equally, in the 17th century it made sense when someone said he 'had advertisement that the person of the said Earl of Glamorgan was arrested'. Still now you might see the French word *avertissement* used on product warning labels.

These examples are clearly not talking about advertising as we understand it. They do not involve changing demand at all. What changed?

Well, first, the term was refined to mean the calling of attention to something through some form of media. Early examples of this use of the term referred to placards, posters and newspapers and the calls of town criers. In 1780, for instance, a newspaper reported: 'Much of the employment a shopkeeper gets, is owing to the attraction of a happy-fancied sign, advertisement, or shop-bill.'

But the term was modified further. By the 20th century, it came to refer primarily to promotional announcements for products and services broadcast through a medium such as television or the press. That is to say, it became linked with selling.

The cultural theorist Raymond Williams (1980) explains this shift by looking at the economic situation at the turn of the 20th century. During the industrial revolutions in Britain and North America, production moved from small-scale manufacturing to expensive large-scale facilities. In these new factories, it was machines rather than humans that made things. Yet, early on, producers found that people were not impressed by the mass-produced products that machines could churn out. Prior to the industrial revolutions, when people made products, they would be unique and customized. Machines, in contrast, could only make basic standardized products. So producers needed to find a way to convince people that mass-produced goods were superior. They needed to find a way to manage demand. Unfortunately, at the time, retailers were also reorganizing their operations. Large-scale retailers and mail-order services replaced smaller independent stores. These new stores were designed to house more products but fewer salespeople (Leiss *et al*, 2005). The idea that you could sell products through printed words was the perfect solution to producers' problems in this context. Williams (1960) suggests that we talk about 'modern advertising' to reflect this new understanding of advertising.

Looking back at the changing meaning of the word 'advertising' in this way not only helps us to define what we are thinking about in this book, it also helps us to see that *advertisements in the world* and *advertising theory* are not always the same. Looking at the history of advertising in this way also shows us that both *advertisements in the world* and *advertising theory* change! As you can see in Thought box 1.2, it was even the case that, as ads were being used to manage demand at the turn of the 20th century, leading advertising agents did not realize it. They thought they were delivering information and news.

Why study advertising?

Now we know what advertising is and we can appreciate how the word itself has developed historically, we can think about why it is important to study advertising. It seems to me that there are five general reasons why people think about advertising (I am not including 'because I have to in order to get course credit' in this list).

1 *Practical reasons to understand advertising.* Some people want to know how to make effective ads so that they can change demand in their favour. They may want to increase their sales, launch a new product, strengthen their brand, win an election or achieve some other practical objective. For them, advertising is a means to an end. Indeed, there are a number people working in an industry dedicated to producing effective advertising who need to know how advertising works. The advertising industry employs around 300,000 people in the United Kingdom alone and over 1 million people in China. People motivated by practical reasons, then, typically want to know how advertising works so they can produce more effective ads.

2 *Personal reasons to understand advertising.* If the people motivated by practical reasons are doing their jobs properly, chances are you will change your behaviour because of ads. The strange thing is, though, you might not feel like advertising affects you. Psychologists tell us that almost everyone refuses to accept that

advertising affects their behaviour. At best, we think that it affects 'other people'. This is called the 'third person effect' (Shin and Kim, 2011; Davidson, 1983). The problem is, we cannot all be right. Advertising cannot only affect other people. So it may be interesting to know how ads work to change what we do and think.

3 *Cultural reasons to understand advertising.* The third set of reasons people tend to be interested in advertising is more cultural. Twitchell, for instance, notes that advertising is 'the dominant culture' (2000: 3). Certainly, there is an awful lot of advertising around us all the time. According to some research, we see up to 5,000 ads each day (see Thought box 1.3). Compare this to the number of works of art, music, film or any other cultural media that people see on a regular basis and it is hard not to agree with Dyer when she describes advertising as 'the "official art" of the advanced industrial nations' (1982: 1). As a result, many people are interested in understanding ads as cultural texts.

4 *Social reasons to understand advertising.* Other people are more interested in advertising for social reasons. They acknowledge that advertising helps to support a range of social interactions. It pays for television programmes, newspaper reporting, web searches and so on. But people motivated by social interests question what else advertising does. Researchers motivated by such social concerns want to explore the role of advertising in society and understand whether the effects of advertising are shared equally across all social groups.

5 *Ethical reasons to understand advertising.* Finally, there is an ethical reason to understand advertising. Advertising is regularly blamed for a range of social, cultural and behavioural problems. In the United Kingdom, for instance, advertising has been named as a cause of riots, underage plastic surgery, decreased attention among children, narcissism and increased materialism. Whether or not these accusations are fair depends, ultimately, on how you think advertising works. This means that many people want to understand advertising to make a decision about what advertisers *should* be able to do and what advertising can be blamed for.

So there are a number of reasons for us to want to understand advertising. But being motivated to do something and doing it are, as any advertiser knows, two different things. Before we set off on our journey through the essentials of advertising, it is probably a good idea to set the scene in more detail.

Thought box 1.3: How much advertising do people see?

While there are a lot of ads around us each day, that does not mean we see or hear them all. Perhaps a better question is, 'How many ads do people actually see?'. Here is a sample of what we know:

- Britt *et al* (1972) modelled the level of ad exposure using computer simulations. They estimated that advertising exposure per day ranged from 117–285 for males and 161–484 for females.

- Kern-Foxworth (1994) estimates that an average American teenager will have watched more than 350,00 of these television commercials by the time they are 18 years old – which is roughly the same as them watching commercials 9 am to 5 pm every day for a year (Plous and Nepture, 1997).

- Twitchell (2000) claims that we see 5,000 ads every day.

- *The New York Times* (2007) reports that over the last 30 years the typical US city resident has seen their exposure to ads rise from 2,000 a day to 5,000 a day.

- *The Guardian* (2005) reports that a resident of London will be exposed to 3,500 ads in a typical day.

- Media Matters estimates that 'today's typical adult gets about 600–625 chances to be exposed to ads in one form or another'.

Clearly, the vast majority of these ads cannot work or we would all be changing our minds and buying new products hundreds of times every day. But does that mean that none of them work? Indeed, as we will see later in the book, for some thinkers these figures prove that we are better off thinking about the effects of 'advertising as a whole' rather than thinking about any given ad in isolation.

What is advertising studies?

There are many different groups of people who have essential knowledge about advertising that can help you to understand it better. The point of this book is to introduce you to them. Hopefully, once you have read this book, you will be able to understand the different interests people have when they study advertising and how these differences shape what they say about it. Here is just a selection of the groups of people who have studied advertising that we will look at in this book:

- marketing and business researchers;
- advertising practitioners;
- sociologists;
- psychologists;
- geographers;
- cultural critics;
- historians;
- political activists;
- consumer groups; and
- economists.

These groups tend to work separately from one another. This means that while they speak about the same thing, they rarely speak to each other. It also means that, while there may be disagreements and uncertainties in one area, they may have been settled elsewhere. I believe this problem is caused by the different backgrounds and interests people have before they study advertising. There is no reason this has to continue.

Developing your knowledge of advertising should, I believe, involve an engagement with all of these different ways of thinking about it. This does not mean that you have to become a fully trained psychologist, historian and so on. Rather, it means you should understand why psychologists or historians are interested in advertising and what they can tell you about it. For instance,

Table 1.1   Big questions across advertising studies

How advertising works
How does advertising communicate with consumers?
Is advertising an art of a science?
Is the advertising industry well organized?
What is the relationship between advertising and consumer behaviour?

The side effects of advertising
Does advertising help consumers make better decisions or not?
Does advertising have social and cultural effects?
How can advertisers balance their moral duties to their own ethics, their clients and their organizations?

sticking with this example, psychologists have attempted to explain how advertising changes peoples' purchasing behaviours, attitudes towards brands and motivations. This has been incredibly powerful in developing advertising practice. However, one criticism of psychological research is that it does not account for the changing nature of advertising or consumption. While this might be true, psychologists would respond that they are not trying to do this. That is what historians should do. Understanding something about both of these perspectives means you can, hopefully, take the best from both of them.

Across these different ways of thinking about advertising, there are some common issues – or what I call 'big questions' (see Table 1.1).

Each area of advertising studies has its own answers to these questions and their own ways of supporting their arguments. Unfortunately, though, the answers they propose often differ as do the ways they justify them. In fact, within many of the disciplines that make up advertising studies, there are different answers to these questions as well (see Thought box 1.4).

Ultimately, then, I think that it comes down to two essential issues, which unite all thinking about advertising. First, is advertising good or bad? Second, can advertising be managed or not? I do not have the answers to these questions but I hope that by the end of this book you will be able to develop your own answers.

How to read this book

To help you to think differently about advertising, the book takes us on a journey through the different areas of advertising studies.

Accepting our definition of advertising as any *attempt to change demand through communication*, we will start off by thinking about what communication is. This will help us to get to grips with one of the most profound 'big questions' at the heart of advertising studies: How does advertising communicate with consumers? In Chapter 2, we will see that there are two broad perspectives here. There are those who believe that advertising changes demand by providing information. They tend to think about communication as a 'monologue' through which advertisers transmit information to consumers. In contrast, there are those who think advertising is more about persuasion. They tend to think about communication more as a 'dialogue' between advertisers and consumers.

From here we will think about how these two perspectives inform what advertisers themselves think. In Chapter 3, we will explore what legendary advertisers have to say about advertising. In this chapter we will be introduced to an ongoing debate among advertising workers: is advertising a science or an art? As we will see, the scientific perspective draws on a 'monologue' view of communication while the artistic perspective is grounded in a 'dialogue' view. We will then think about how advertising actually gets made. This is the topic of Chapter 4. In this chapter, we will look at the advertising industry and the organization of advertising work. We will consider whether the advertising industry is well organized.

Following this, we will step outside of the narrow concerns of advertising organizations to think about the relationship between advertising and consumers. We will explore the economics of advertising in Chapter 5 and the psychology of advertising in Chapter 6. Here, too, we will see how researchers can be divided into two broad categories. There are those who think advertising transmits information to consumers that helps them to make better decisions. But there are others who see advertising as a dialogue through which sellers persuade consumers to want things they do not necessarily need.

Thought box 1.4: How advertising changes demand – the economists' views

- *Informing consumers – a positive view of advertising.* Advertising rebalances 'information asymmetries' that exist in markets. All purchases involve risks and consumers often minimize their risks by purchasing whatever they have bought before – even if it wasn't the perfect solution to their problems. Advertising allows consumers to find out about new products, services and brands and reduces the risks of making a new purchase. Advertising, therefore, makes a positive contribution to society. It helps us to allocate our resources efficiently.

- *Increasing competition – a positive view of advertising.* Advertising lowers a very important barrier to entry – existing behaviours. This makes it possible for new entrants to compete with established firms. It allows innovative manufacturers to explain the benefits of a new product or service to consumers. As such, advertising not only changes the level of demand for products, it also changes what products we demand. This not only helps consumers to make better choices it also encourages innovation and competition.

- *Persuading consumers – a negative view of advertising.* Ads rarely present us with facts. They make more emotional appeals than rational ones. They make us *want* to try a new product, switch to a different offering, go to a new store, even if it is not in our best interests to do so. Ads, then, allow brands to persuade us. They make it harder for us to allocate our resources efficiently.

- *Creating brands – a negative view of advertising.* Advertising changes what we think about products. It makes us care more about the brand rather than the product itself. Steven Heyer, former President of The Coca-Cola Company, summarized this view nicely when he said 'Coca-Cola isn't black water with a little sugar… It's an idea' (Donation, 2004: 29). As such, advertising raises barriers to entry as new entrants cannot compete with established firms in terms of their brand values. Advertising, therefore, decreases competition and makes markets worse.

From here, in Chapters 7, 8 and 9, we will venture outside the consumer's head. We will think about the effects of advertising on society, culture and the media. There is quite a lot of cross-over among the topics in these chapters, but I have separated them out because I think lumping them together can be confusing. What brings these areas together, though, is a shared belief that advertising has aggregate effects outside of markets.

This brings us to the question of ethics. As we will see in Chapter 10, advertising involves a number of ethical considerations. Advertisers themselves know this only too well. So we will think about where ethical challenges come from and consider how advertisers deal with them.

Each chapter begins with some key questions for you to keep in mind as you read through it. These point out some of the big debates that motivate researchers in each area. I do not have answers to these questions. In fact, I am not even sure that some of the big questions can ever be answered properly. But I would encourage you to make your own mind up about these key questions as you read through each chapter.

You will also see that each chapter includes a number of thought boxes. These are designed to go into a bit more detail about a particular case, example, model or theory. You can hopefully read the book and understand the essentials of advertising without look-ing into them. But if you want to understand a bit more about the background or context for a topic, I would recommend you have a look into them. Finally, each chapter closes with some suggestions for further reading and lists other interesting sources. These include the texts I have referenced in the chapter but also a number of other sources that I think could be useful to you.

Summary

As you can see from this introduction, advertising is incredibly important in most developed economies. Not only is it a key industry in its own right, it is an essential part of most other industries. It is, in many ways, the oil that keeps markets moving.

Yet it can be difficult for us to fully appreciate the role of advertising in our lives because we tend to limit ourselves to thinking about whether or not advertising affects us individually in our purchase decisions. Advertising, though, has a number of different functions for people, businesses and societies. The challenge of studying advertising is, at heart, then, the challenge of understanding what many different groups of people have to say about it.

That is to say, to understand the *essentials of advertising* we have to learn how to *think differently* about advertising.

Some other interesting sources

The History of Advertising Trust is a great source on the development of advertising in the United Kingdom. Details are available here: www.hatads. org.uk/

There are a number of interesting exhibitions and museums documenting the changing nature of advertising around the world. For example:

- The Museum of Brands in London (www.museumofbrands.com/).

- The Advertising Archives (www.advertisingarchives.co.uk/).

- The Musée de la Publicité in Paris.

- The National Museum of American History (http://americanhistory. si.edu/).

References and further reading

Collins, R K L and Skover, D M (1993) Commerce and communication, *Texas Law Review*, **71**, pp 697–746

Cowell, A (2001) Advertising, rhetoric, and literature: A medieval response to contemporary theory, *Poetics Today*, **22** (4): 795–827

Cruikshank, J L and Schultz, A W (2013) *The Man who Sold America: The amazing (but true!) story of Albert D. Lasker and the creation of the advertising century*, Harvard Business Review Press, Boston

Donation, S (2004) *Madison & Vine: Why the entertainment and advertising industry must converge to survive*, McGraw-Hill, New York

Dyer, G (1982) *Advertising as Communication*, Routledge, London

Fletcher, W (2008) *Powers of Persuasion: The inside story of British advertising*, Oxford University Press, London

Kern-Foxworth, M (1994) Aunt Jemima, Uncle Ben, and Rasus, in *Blacks in Advertising Yesterday, Today and Tomorrow*, Greenwood Press, Westport

Leiss, W, Kline, S, Jhally, S and Botterill, J (2005) *Social Communication in Advertising: Consumption in the mediated marketplace*, 3rd edn, Routledge, Abingdon

O'Reilly, T and Tennant, M (2009) *The Age of Persuasion: How marketing ate our culture*, Counterpoint, Berkeley

Plous, S and Nepture, D (1997) Racial and gender biases in magazine advertising, *Psychology of Women Quarterly*, **21**, pp 627–44

Schwarzkopf, S (2009) What Was Advertising? The Invention, Rise, Demise, and Disappearance of Advertising Concepts in Nineteenth- and Twentieth-Century Europe and America, *Business History Conference, Business and Economic History On-line: Papers Presented at the BHC Annual Meeting*, 7: pp 1–27. Wilmington: Business History Conference

Twitchell, J (2000) *20 Ads that Changed the World*, Three Rivers Press, New York

Williams, R (1960) The Magic System, *New Left Review*, I/4 (July–August), pp 27–32

Williams, R (1980) Advertising: The magic system, in *Problems in Materialism and Culture*, Verso, London

Big questions   02

Advertising, communication, rhetoric and persuasion

Introduction

If we accept that advertising is an attempt to change demand through communication, one of the first things we need to think about is what we mean by communication. As we will see in this chapter, this is one of the foundational topics in advertising studies. It fuels one of the most fundamental debates throughout advertising research.

There are two broad theoretical perspectives we need to consider here. The first takes a very literal view of communication. It sees it as a process of transmitting information from one person to another much like a monologue. The second perspective takes a more iterative approach. It views communication as a process through which meaning is created between people through dialogue. The debate between these two positions lies in the background of many of the other theoretical discussions we will explore in this book.

One solution to this debate has been for advertising researchers to accept that advertising is a unique form of communication. This allows researchers to park the bigger debates about communication and focus more specifically on advertising itself. In this regard, researchers agree that advertising is primarily concerned with persuasion – that is, convincing people to change what they demand. This has led them to engage with a very old idea about communication known as rhetoric. Rhetoric is the study of persuasive techniques and has been employed productively in advertising studies.

Overview

The chapter starts with the idea that advertising is a form of communication that involves transmitting information to consumers. This is commonly known as the 'transmission model of communication'. As we will see, this idea relies upon a number of assumptions about the nature of communication and language. After highlighting some of the challenges to this perspective, we will turn to a competing theory of communication known, broadly, as 'social constructionism'. This is a theory of communication as a two-way process in which meaning is created through dialogue. From here, we will look at the idea that advertising is not just communication but a very specific form of communication known as persuasion. Here, we will explore advertising rhetoric studies.

By the end of this chapter, you should be able to:

- describe the transmission model of communication and social constructionism;
- evaluate the strengths and weaknesses of monologue- and dialogue-based theories of communication; and
- highlight rhetorical devices used in advertising.

Key questions to keep in mind

- Is advertising a monologue or dialogue?
- Do words and images contain meaning?
- Is advertising communication or persuasion?

Communication as a monologue: the transmission model of communication

In the first half of the 20th century, there was a growing need to understand the communications process. New media such as the telegraph, the telephone and the radio allowed people to communicate in new ways. But they had significant technical issues. For instance, telephones were originally purchased in pairs that could only call each other (Wu, 2012). Unsurprisingly, people wanted to be able to call more than one other telephone so they modified their phones into complex circuits. To take advantage of this demand, phone companies changed how telephones worked but they had to deal with crossed wires, delays, and distortion. The first theory of how communication works was developed to help solve these problems.

To understand why communications broke down, scientists, mathematicians and engineers were employed to investigate the physical limits of different communications technologies. The work of Claude Shannon marks a key starting point here (see Thought box 2.1). Shannon was an American mathematician and electrical engineer. He worked on and researched a range of issues brought together under the topic of the 'transmission of intelligence' (Gleick, 2011: 187). Shannon argued that any problem of communication could be understood as the problem of taking a message from one point and reproducing it exactly at another. It did not matter what the message was about or even what form it took, communication was a process of transmission. Whether we are talking to someone in the same room, sending a Morse code message across continents, speaking on the telephone to our neighbour, or broadcasting an ad on TV, the problem remains the same: how can we take information from one point and reproduce it at another?

Along with his co-author Warren Weaver, Shannon (1949) worked this idea into a model communication now known as the 'transmission model' (see Figure 2.1). This tells us that there are five steps to communication:

1 An information source or sender must select a message to transmit.

2 The message must be encoded into a signal that can be sent through a transmitter or communication technology.

3 The transmitter sends the messages to the correct destination. In so doing, it might introduce noise into the signal.

4 Once it has been received, the signal must be separated from any noise. It must then be decoded into the original message so that it can be understood.

5 The destination or receiver has a copy of message and the communication process is complete.

Let's look at a real-world example. When we type an email, we encode what we want to say into words, images, emojis and so on. These are then automatically encoded by our computer into a stream of zeros and ones which are then packaged into a signal that can be sent over fibre-optic cables and routed through the various tubes of the internet. When they reach their destination they have to be decoded back into zeros and ones, then words, images, emoticons and so on and finally into the message we wanted to communicate to our contact.

Unfortunately, as well as the encoded signal, the signal that arrives at the destination often includes noise that was not in the original message. Noise is anything that is added into the message as part of the communication process that makes it hard to decode the signal back into the original message. For example, when the wind blows into your mobile phone, it creates noise that makes it hard for the person listening to you to hear what you are saying. Equally, if you are speaking to someone in a crowded bar, the noise of other people talking can lead to confusions and misunderstandings. Of course, these people are probably having their own conversations – you are noise as far as they are concerned. This is precisely the problem Shannon wanted to solve for communications systems. Signals are also noise.

Shannon argued that man-made communications media, such as the telephone system and the internet, must also include feedback loops to help reduce the effects of noise (see Figure 2.2). He spent a great deal of his life helping to develop them. If you have ever received an automatic email saying that an email you sent was 'undeliverable', you have experienced a feedback loop influenced by Shannon's work.

Figure 2.1   The transmission model (adapted from Shannon and Weaver, 1949)

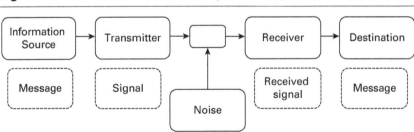

Shannon noted that in everyday communication people rely on natural feedback mechanisms. For instance, you might ask the person you are talking to on your mobile phone to repeat themselves if the wind adds noise to their signal. If you are listening to someone in person, you might nod along or mutter 'yes... hmmm... oh right... got you...' to feedback to them that you are following what they say. If you receive a message that does not make sense, you might say 'What!?!!?'. These signals do not send new information but help to make sure that the signal containing the information is distinguishable from the noise inherent in the communication channel.

The beauty of this perspective is that it allows the communications process to be calculated mathematically. If we are not concerned with the meaning of a message but simply the amount of information it contains, we can use mathematics to figure out the most efficient way to transmit a message, the necessary level of 'redundancy' or repetition that ensures that noise does not interfere with the message but does not waste too much capacity of the channel. We can, simply put, calculate how much information comes out the other end of the transmission system and compare it with how much went in.

But the model has been used much more widely. As the economic historian Mirowski (2002) details in his book *Machine Dreams*, Shannon's perspective on communication has had profound effects on the understanding of humans as communicators within the academic disciplines of psychology and economics. Researchers here have been particularly inspired by the idea that humans act as 'information processors'.

This was not the most thoroughly worked part of his theory but Shannon argued that for communication to work in everyday situations humans must possess a great deal of mathematical knowledge and undertake a great deal of statistical processing. When we are sending messages, he argued, we must implicitly know how much redundancy is expected for a receiver to accurately comprehend our message. And, as receivers, we must be able to decode messages, distinguishing the signal from noise, and filling in errors based on our knowledge of the statistics of language and interpersonal

Figure 2.2   The transmission model with a feedback loop (adapted from Shannon and Weaver, 1949)

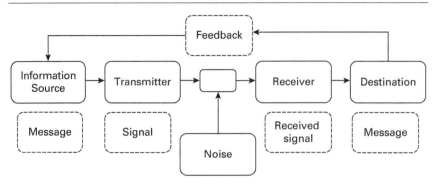

communication. For this reason, we do not have to finish our sentences exactly in spoken speech and we can understand a sentence even if there is a spelling mistake. As Shannon puts it: 'Anyone speaking a language possesses, implicitly, an enormous knowledge of the statistics of the language. Familiarity with the words, idioms, clichés and grammar enables him to fill in missing or incorrect letters in proofreading, or to complete an unfinished phrase in conversation' (Gleick, 2011: 229).

Thought box 2.1: Claude Shannon

Shannon realized how important it was to distinguish a signal from noise from his work in the Second World War. Along with mathematics and engineering, Shannon was an enthusiastic cryptographer – a code-breaker. During the war, he worked to decode enemy messages that the Allies intercepted. He saw similarities between the processes through which code-breakers decoded messages and the process through which, for example, telegraph operators decoded the series of dots and dashes sent over the telegraph into messages that communicated some information. Shannon tells us: 'a secrecy system is almost identical with a noisy communication system' (Gleick, 2011: 216). In each case, the communication process was enabled by systems for encoding and decoding the message shared by the source and the destination and by the ability of someone at the destination to distinguish noise from the message.

Communication as a dialogue: social constructionism

For Shannon and Weaver, the semantic content of a message (how and why particular words or images had certain meanings) was not really important. As Weaver put it, they were 'not at all directly concerned with the meaning of individual messages' (1949: 14). For them, communication involves sending information. It is just new data (see Thought box 2.2). In fact, their model only works by ignoring the question of meaning and the interpretation of messages.

But although Shannon and Weaver were not interested in semantic issues, as the transmission model of communication has been applied in practical areas such as advertising studies, researchers had to address the question of meaning. Initially, researchers viewed information as the possession of particular codes (words and images). A brand name, for example, was seen as a code that represented information about the origin and quality of a good. Indeed, the American Marketing Association still defines a brand in this way as: 'A name, term, design, symbol, or any other feature that identifies one seller's good or service as distinct from those of other sellers.'

This idea links into a particular theory of meaning sometimes called 'the container theory of language' or 'the picture theory of language'. No matter which term one prefers, the basic assumption is that words and images contain their meaning and create a picture of the world. Reddy (1979) describes these approaches as adopting a 'conduit' perspective on meaning. They assume that words, images, sounds and so on are able to deliver the same messages in every context irrelevant of who is speaking, when they are speaking or how they are speaking. According to this view successful communication, consequently, involves selecting the right codes to transmit your meaning. The people who receive the messages do not have to do anything – they will automatically know the meaning of the message.

It is here, though, that Shannon and Weaver's model starts to encounter problems. Think about it: when you say 'I'm sorry', are you always sorry? Of course not! Words and phrases are polysemic – they can mean lots of different things. In fact, they can mean the exact opposite in different contexts. How many times have you said you were sorry as a way to show you were not sorry? Probably you can think of at least one example!

Thought box 2.2: The meaning of information

According to Mirowski, 'Shannon's information concept has to be one of the most misunderstood notions on the planet' (2002: 70). For Shannon, information is linked with uncertainty. The more uncertainty there is, the more information there is too.

So, if the letter 't' is followed by the letter 'h' in English, not much information is conveyed by the letter 'h' because most words beginning with 't' also begin 'th'. Indeed, in this case, I could get away without using the second letter. 'Tats amzng', for example, is most likely read as 'That's amazing'. This is the logic behind auto-fill forms on websites and search engines and predictive text on mobile phones.

When a message includes additional components that do not convey a great deal of information, such as the letter 'h' from the example above, they are said to be 'redundant'. As Gleick (2011: 230) explains: 'If a letter can be guessed from what comes before, it is redundant; to the extent that it is redundant, it provides no new information.'

Although we might think that redundant components of a message are useless, for Shannon they are actually really important. Redundancy corrects errors. It is a feedback mechanism. Shannon estimated that English, for example, has a 'built-in redundancy' of around 50 per cent (Gleick, 2011: 229). That is, half of what we say contains no new information (like this sentence). Instead, it simply reproduces what has already been communicated in a new way to ensure that there were no errors in the reproduction of the message from one point to another (like this sentence).

The amount of information in a message is, then, an abstract quantity. It is calculated in 'bits' or 'bytes' (this is why we talk about computers being able to process or store an amount of information in 'bytes' irrelevant of what the information is about). If only one message is possible on channel, there is no information. If there are two messages, then there is a bit of information. For instance, a light switch can be used to communicate one bit of information. It is either 'on' or 'off'. Each of which could stand for anything we wanted such as 'I'm awake' and 'I'm asleep', '1' and '0' or 'Thieves beware' or 'Burgle this house'. Although there are two possible messages, there is only one bit of information. Put differently, how much new data do I have if I know the state of the light-bulb? One bit. In contrast, a light-bulb that is always off communicates no information. No matter what the signal meant, if you told me the light-bulb was off I would not know anything new.

So how do we know what the meaning of a word is? The answer for other theorists is not to look in the dictionary but to understand the context in which it has been used. This leads us to a second theory of communication known as social constructionism.

Social constructionism is a theory of communication based in the concept of dialogue. It tells us that meaning is constructed between senders and receivers. As such, social constructionism tells us that we need to look at the wider social context around communication. We need to consider who is speaking to whom and the linguistic context around a message such as the other words or images that a message draws on.

Let's look at these in more detail.

Social context

Ethnographers tell us that words can completely change their meaning depending on the social situation that they are used in. In a famous example, a researcher who was studying family life came across the phrase 'Sit in the apple juice chair'. Technically, this does not make sense. It is impossible to sit in a chair made of apple juice. In fact, it is impossible to have a chair made of apple juice. (One exception, of course, is if the apple juice is frozen. But even here it would only be accurate if someone said 'Sit in the frozen apple juice chair'). Yet, the family involved in the study did understand this sentence. The reason was because, over time, they had come to refer to a specific chair at their dining table as the 'apple juice' chair. It was where they would sit to drink apple juice. In this case, then, the words only had meaning in a very specific context: one family's home. The meaning of the words, we might say, was constructed between this group of people. The words did not contain their meaning. Rather a group of people had agreed that they meant specific things.

Linguistic context

Another element of social constructionism is the idea that the meaning of words changes given the other words and images that surround them. Within behavioural economics, for instance, researchers have illustrated that we can shape what information is transmitted by framing it with different types of words. In one study, participants were asked to imagine that an unusual disease threatened to kill 600 people. They were asked to choose between two alternative programmes which could combat the disease. In the first case, participants were offered the following choice:

> If Programme A is adopted, 200 people will be saved.
>
> If Programme B is adopted, there is 1/3 probability that 600 people will be saved, and 2/3 probability that no people will be saved.

In this study, 72 per cent of the participants chose Programme A. This was no doubt because they preferred the thought of saving 200 people rather than risking saving no one. That is to say, when faced with these choices people tended to be 'risk averse'. As the researchers conclude: 'the prospect of certainly saving 200 lives is more attractive than a risky prospect of equal expected value' (Tversky and Kahneman, 1981: 543).

However, a second group of participants was offered a different choice. They were offered the following options:

> If Programme C is adopted 400 people will die.
>
> If Programme D is adopted there is 1:3 probability that nobody will die, and 2:3 probability that 600 people will die.

In this case, participants tended to be more willing to take a risk. In fact, in this study 78 per cent of participants chose the more risky option (Programme D, if you hadn't guessed).

But look closely at the four programmes. Do they look similar? They should. Each programme is 'effectively identical' (Tversky and Kahneman, 1981: 543). The only thing which differs is the linguistic context of each option. When the information was presented positively – in terms of saving lives – people were less willing to take a risk. But when the choice was framed negatively – in terms of people dying – people were willing to take risks. This shows us the power of framing. Even when the information transmitted does not change, if we choose particular words to frame it in a certain way, we drastically change the message that is received. Tversky and Kahneman explain: 'Choices involving gains are often risk averse and choices involving losses are often risk taking' (1981: 543).

Taking this idea further, Lakoff and Johnson (2003) argue that we must consider words as metaphors. That is to say, in many cases the meaning of a word is not contained in that word itself but is embedded in a network of associations with other words. For example, take the word 'argument'. In English, this word has several connotations. We typically think of an argument as a dispute between two conflicting sides. Watch a debate on the evening news to see this. One side is trying to defeat the other. Often arguments are hostile and, in some cases, violent. As such, they are something we should avoid. But in other cultures arguments have different associations. In some cultures, an argument is treated as a game in which two competitors test their ability to creative a persuasive account. It is seen more as a dance between partners than a battle. As such, to understand the meaning of a word we also need to take account of the associations it has for particular groups of people (see Thought box 2.3).

Thought box 2.3: The associations of advertising

In the 1940s James Vicary, a notable advertising researcher credited with discovering the power of subliminal advertising, wanted to demonstrate the power of word associations to marketers. As he put it: 'If we could find a standard method of measuring the content, emotion and stability of words as symbols, we could more clearly understand the meaning of answers to poll questions and the motivations of people in the selection of words to express their thoughts in open interviews' (1948: 81).

The problem, Vicary (1948) observed, is that words do not exist in isolation. Rather, they exist in clusters of meaning. If a word in a cluster changes, it can affect the meaning of the rest of the words in that cluster. Equally, if a word moves from one cluster to another, it can change its meaning as well as the meaning of the old cluster and the new cluster. The causes of these changes are incredibly complex. They are historical, cultural and sociological. But their effects are very pertinent for marketing. Pick a word as your brand name without understanding its association with other words, Vicary argued, and you are asking for trouble.

To demonstrate the power of associations, Vicary (1948) decided to study a word most marketers are interested in: advertising. He interviewed 162 New Yorkers and asked them to list the first four words that came to mind when they thought about advertising. From these lists he discovered that many of the associations offered linked advertising with manipulation and persuasion. At the extreme, they associated advertisers with 'Hucksters'. Interestingly, this was the title of a successful movie about advertising that did not paint advertising in a positive light. Indeed, Vicary argued that it is only by clustering word associations together that we can start to appreciate whether a word is generally taken to be positive or negative, whether it has a personality or gender or any other pertinent associations that could inform marketing practice.

The power of words

Social constructionism also suggests that the world as we know it is constructed through language. It is through our concepts that we define the world around us and, according to this theory, through such concepts that we act on the world. For instance, when we have the concept of a mountain, we can identify a piece of the earth as a mountain and try to climb it. Yet even though the word 'mountain' suggests that a mountain is a discrete entity with a beginning and end, in reality this is not the case. A mountain is more of a social construction than a physical fact. Social constructionism, thus, turns the notion that language reflects the 'real world' on its head. It is, for social constructionists, because we have a concept of mountain that we can find mountains – not the other way around. As such, for social constructionists, pretty much all action is fundamentally shaped by our language.

Figure 2.3 The cyclical model of brands (adapted from De Chernatony and Dall'Olmo, 1998)

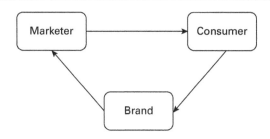

So, rather than view advertising as a monologue whereby brands communicate messages to passive audiences, practitioners, theorists and researchers informed by social constructionism emphasize that brands and consumers engage in dialogues (see Figure 2.3). In this regard, De Chernatony, McDonald and Wallace tell us that, 'while marketers instigate the branding process' through their ads, 'it is the buyer or the user who forms a mental picture of the brand' (2011: 30). To recognize this, brand researchers distinguish between the brand identities organizations hope to create, the fluctuating images consumers perceive in the marketplace and the relatively stable reputation of a brand that persists over time (De Chernatony, 1999). Ignore these differences, brand research shows us, at your peril. It is tempting to think what a consumer hears and what a brand says are the same but this is rarely true.

In contrast to the transmission of communication, then, social constructionism tells us that there is much more to the process of communication than sending a message from one point to another. Rather than seeing meaning as contained within a message and encoded through words and images, social constructionism tells us that senders and receivers construct meaning between them. To put this simply, we can distinguish between these two theories by comparing a monologue with a dialogue. A monologue involves one person speaking to another – like a lecture or speech. The transmission model is based on this style of communication. A dialogue is more like a conversation in which the line between speaker and listener is blurred (see Figure 2.4). Social constructionism is based on this style of communication.

Figure 2.4   Monologue and dialogue images of communication

Monologue: sender transmits a message containing meaning to a receiver

Dialogue: both sender and receiver construct meaning

Rhetoric: the ancient art of persuasion

One solution to the debate between the monologue and dialogue approaches to communication has been for advertising researchers to think about advertising as a specific, potentially unique, form of communication. Namely, they have focused on understanding advertising as persuasive communication rather than relating it to communication more generally. This makes sense, of course, if we accept that advertising is an attempt to change demand through communication (see Chapter 1). Here, researchers have turned to a very old set of concepts developed in the study of rhetoric.

Simply put, rhetoric is the technique of persuasion. It is based on the idea that there are particular ways of communicating that are persuasive and differ from other type of communication. As Pracejus, Olsen and O'Guinn put it: 'Advertising tries to convince consumers to do something, typically to buy something. Thus, advertising is merely rhetoric in the service of selling' (2006: 82). As such, advertising researchers who have adopted a rhetorical approach have attempted to set out what persuasive techniques advertisers use (Scott, 1994a). The popularity of this approach cannot be underestimated. According to Cowell, 'virtually all recent studies of advertising as a cultural phenomenon could be considered broadly rhetorical in approach' (2001: 797).

The study of rhetoric, though, dates back to ancient Greece and the ideas of Aristotle. He wrote one of the earliest theories of persuasion and, it is widely agreed, he set out many of the tools and techniques that politicians, business people and advertisers still use every day.

Figure 2.5   Aristotle's rhetorical triangle

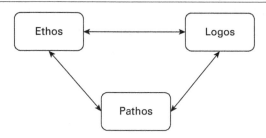

His book dates from the 4th century BC and is still in print! It is, then, surely worthwhile exploring Aristotle's ideas about rhetoric as an essential introduction to advertising rhetoric.

For Aristotle, rhetoric is the ability to spot the means of persuasion in any given situation. The basic building blocks of persuasion are consistent but, for him, how we use them depends on the situation we are in. These building blocks are ethos, pathos and logos. The concept of ethos tells us that persuasion occurs when we build a sense of belonging with those we are trying to persuade. We should, first, convince our audience that we are worth listening to. The requirement for pathos tells us that we should use our audience's emotions to persuade them. For instance, using extreme cases and striking images to tug on an audience's heartstrings is particularly persuasive. Finally, we also need to convince our audience that we know what we are talking about. That is to say, we need to be able to present a coherent and supported argument. This forms the requirement for logos. These building blocks are interrelated and are sometimes known collectively as the rhetorical triangle (see 'Aristotle's rhetorical triangle').

According to Aristotle and subsequent rhetoricians, there are a range of tools through which we can craft these building blocks. These include the following:

- A strong introduction attracts the audience's attention and asserts the speaker's credentials. While it is generally considered bad to set out what will follow in too much detail, the introduction does offer the opportunity to set the terms of what will follow.

- Narration allows us to frame the facts as we see them. This might involves presenting a part of some occurrence as the whole fact, using spurious correlations to imply cause and effect or selecting powerful metaphors. Strong speakers are able to convince the audience that the story they narrate is the truth, the whole truth and nothing but the truth. After all, you can't argue with the truth.

- Through division a speaker is able to acknowledge that some people might disagree with their story but do so in a way that convinces their audience that these disagreements are not valid. Persuasive communicators make sure they pick on weak points in their opponent's arguments – the ones that they can respond to.

- Through the use of proof, persuasive communicators can not only reiterate why they are right but also disprove those who disagree with them.

- By using refutation persuasive communicators attack those who disagree directly rather than focusing on their arguments. For example, politicians often point to each other's past mistakes in an attempt to refute current disagreements.

- Persuasive communicators will offer a strong conclusion that leaves their audience in no doubt that they have been convinced and in doubt what they should do going forwards.

Outside of advertising studies, researchers have used these ideas to explore political rhetoric and the rhetoric of successful leaders. The important point from this for advertising studies is that persuasion involves the use of specific tools and techniques. In this regard, researchers have explored the rhetoric techniques (sometimes called 'rhetorical devices') employed in modern advertising.

Researchers such as Mulvey and Medina (2003), Phillips and McQuarrie (2002), Scott (1994a, 1994b) and McQuarrie and Mick (1992) have paid particular attention to the use of images in advertising – often basing their studies on print advertisements. The central thrust of this research has been to uncover the visual 'templates' used, uniquely, by advertisers (Phillips and McQuarrie, 2004: 114). Others have noted the use of drama and storytelling in advertising (Woodside, Sood and Miller, 2008; Deighton, 1985).

Table 2.1   Rhetorical focus of 2,000 ads in leading US magazines, 1900–1980

	1990s	1910s	1920s	1930s	1940s	1950s	1960s	1970s	Total
Rhetorical focus									
Ethos	11%	7%	14%	24%	18%	8%	5%	8%	12%
Pathos	27%	25%	30%	42%	50%	42%	44%	37%	37%
Logos	62%	68%	56%	35%	52%	49%	50%	54%	51%
Tactics									
Competitive standing	28%	21%	24%	22%	27%	39%	29%	23%	27%
Premiums	46%	42%	37%	25%	10%	12%	14%	14%	25%
Coupons	18%	20%	38%	27%	7%	7%	18%	30%	20%
Demonstration	7%	8%	16%	20%	20%	25%	22%	20%	17%
Tangential	16%	9%	6%	6%	16%	9%	7%	11%	10%
Testimonials	10%	6%	11%	23%	14%	8%	7%	6%	11%
Before/After	3%	2%	1%	13%	6%	3%	2%	2%	4%
Humour	2%	0%	0%	5%	7%	1%	3%	5%	3%
Contests	2%	0%	0%	4%	1%	1%	2%	1%	1%
Editorial	1%	1%	2%	0%	0%	1%	1%	2%	1%

(Adapted from Pollay, 1985)

Deighton, Romer and McQueen, for example, argue that a dramatic rhetoric 'draws the viewer into the action it portrays... When a drama is successful, the audience becomes "lost" in the story and experiences the concerns and feelings of the characters. When an argument is successful, the audience weighs the evidence and then yields to it' (1989: 335). In contrast, other researchers chart the changing rhetoric of advertising. Here, Pollay (1985) tracks the rhetoric focus of 2,000 US magazine ads from the 1900s to 1980s and notes an increase in the use of pathos matched by a decrease in the use of ethos and logos (see Table 2.1).

To pick one example of work in this area, let's return to Pracejus, Olsen and O'Guinn (2006). They chose to investigate the meaning of white spaces in contemporary advertising. From a transmission model perspective, white space is meaningless. Yet they note that many advertisers choose to include a lot of white space in their ads. Indeed, they often pay for a lot of it. So what does it communicate?

Based on interviews with advertising agents and consumers, they find that there is a broad agreement about the meaning of white space. White space communicates elegance, power, leadership, honesty, trustworthiness, a modern nature and refined tastes. It has acquired these meanings, Pracejus, Olsen and O'Guinn (2006) argue, through cultural changes including the development of minimalist art and architecture. As such, they conclude that rhetorical conventions used in advertising must always been understood as 'a matter of history. Things mean what they mean not due to some inherent quality of a string of letters or any other symbol but rather through agreement by social actors and publics that certain linguistic forms mean certain things. Producers and receivers come to agree upon linguistic and rhetorical meanings over time' (2006: 83). Their study, in other words, supports a dialogic or social constructionist view of communication.

The rhetorical study of advertising, though, gets around the question of communication. It is less interested in understanding the communication process than understanding how advertisers create persuasive messages that change what people demand. That is not to say, though, that researchers in this area pay no attention to theoretical issues. Often they set out their assumptions about these issues explicitly. But their interests lie elsewhere.

Big questions

The ideas we have explored in this chapter lie in the background of many of the debates we will look at throughout the rest of this book. Unfortunately, though, I have not come across a truly compelling account which answers the question 'what is communication?' once and for all. Ultimately, I think it is up to us as individuals interested in advertising to decide where we stand on this debate.

Sometimes it is certainly easier and more convenient to assume that advertising is a monologue. But, in reality, this gets brands into all sorts of trouble. It is very easy to design ads assuming they will be understood by consumers and that this will motivate them to change their behaviours. If this were the case, advertising would be a lot simpler. Sadly, it is not the case. It is a difficult, perhaps impossible, task to select the perfect codes to transmit a message and it is probably even more difficult to ensure that a message will move people to change what they demand.

Does this mean that social constructionism is the answer? In theory, maybe. But in the reality of advertising studies, social constructionism can be incredibly difficult to investigate. If a brand, for example, is the result of a cyclic process between marketers and consumers where do you start looking if you want to understand what your brand means?

Despite these complexities, though, it is really useful to understand that when people talk about, practice and research advertising, they are not necessarily looking at the same thing. For some, their focus is on advertising as a monologue in which brands transmit information to consumers. For others, it is a dialogue where meaning is co-produced by marketers and consumers. For others still, it is neither. It is a set of techniques and devices that, irrelevant of issues of meaning and information, persuade people to change what they think and what they do. The next chapter picks up this theme. It explores the techniques and devices that prominent advertising practitioners champion.

Some other interesting sources

If you are interested in rhetorical devices, there are a range of excellent and practical talks which may help you to improve your powers of persuasion:

- Matt Abrahams' 'Think Fast, Talk Smart' (https://youtu.be/HAnw168huqA).
- Will Stephen's 'How to sound smart in your TEDx Talk' (https://youtu.be/8SOFDjFBj8o).
- Gordon Kangas' 'Giving Presentations Worth Listening To' (https://youtu.be/NUXkThfQx6A).

References and further reading

Aristotle (1991) *The Art of Rhetoric* (trans H C Lawson-Tancred), Penguin Books, London

Cowell, A (2001) Advertising, rhetoric, and literature: a medieval response to contemporary theory, *Poetics Today*, **22** (4), pp 795–827

De Chernatony, L (1999) Brand management through narrowing the gap between brand identity and brand reputation, *Journal of Marketing Management*, **15** (1–3), pp 157–79

De Chernatony, L and Dall'Olmo Riley, F (1998) Defining a 'brand': beyond the literature with experts' interpretations, *Journal of Marketing Management*, **14** (5), pp 417–43

De Chernatony, L, McDonald, M and Wallace, E (2011) *Creating Powerful Brands*, 4th edn, Butterworth-Heinemann, London

Deighton, J (1985) Rhetorical Strategies in Advertising, in *Advances in Consumer Research*, eds Morris B Holbrook and Elizabeth Hirschman, **12**, pp 432–36, Association for Consumer Research, Provo, UT

Deighton, J, Romer, D and McQueen, J (1989) Using drama to persuade, *Journal of Consumer Research*, **16**, pp 335–43

Lakoff, G and Johnson, M (2003) *Metaphors We Live By*, 2nd edn, University Of Chicago Press, Chicago

McCracken, G (1987) Advertising: Meaning or information, in *Advances in Consumer Research* eds. Melanie Wallendorf and Paul Anderson, Association for Consumer Research (**14**) pp 121–24, Provo, UT

McQuarrie, E F and Mick, D G (1992) On resonance: a critical pluralistic inquiry into advertising rhetoric, *Journal of Consumer Research*, **19** (2), pp 180–98

Mulvey, M S and Medina, C (2003) Invoking Rhetorical Power of Character to Create Identifications, in *Persuasive Imagery: A consumer response perspective*, eds Linda M Scott and Rajeev Batra, Erlbaum, Mahwah, NJ

Phillips, B J and McQuarrie, E F (2002) The development, change and transformation of rhetorical style in magazine advertisements, 1954–1999, *Journal of Advertising*, **31** (Winter), pp 1–13

Phillips, B J and McQuarrie, E F (2004) Beyond visual metaphor: a new typology of visual rhetoric in advertising, *Marketing Theory*, **4** (1–2), pp 113–36

Pollay, R W (1985) The subsiding sizzle: a descriptive history of print advertising, 1900-1980, *Journal of Marketing*, **49** (3), pp 24–37

Pracejus, J W, Olsen, G D and O'Guinn, T C (2006) How nothing became something: white space, rhetoric, history, and meaning, *Journal of Consumer Research*, 33, pp 82–90

Reddy, M J (1979) The conduit metaphor: a case of frame conflict in our language about language, in *Metaphor and Thought*, ed A Ortony, Cambridge University Press, Cambridge

Scott, L M (1994a) The bridge from text to mind: adopting reader-response theory to consumer research, *Journal of Consumer Research*, 21 (December), pp 461–80

Scott, L M (1994b) Images in advertising: the need for a theory of visual rhetoric, *Journal of Consumer Research*, **21** (September): 252–73

Shannon, C E and Weaver, W (1949) *The Mathematical Theory of Communication*, University of Illinois Press, Chicago

Tversky, A and Kahneman, D (1981) The framing of decisions and the psychology of choice, *Science*, **211** (4481), pp 453–58

Vicary, J M (1948) Word association and opinion research: 'advertising' – an illustrative example, *Public Opinion Quarterly*, **12** (1), pp 81–98

Art or science   03

What do legendary advertisers think about advertising?

Introduction

In the previous chapter, we saw how advertising researchers have attempted to understand the types of rhetorical devices and persuasive techniques that advertisers use. In some cases, these studies have been used to make grand conclusions about the nature of communication. But they have also been of great interest to advertisers looking to learn the tricks of the trade.

Indeed, if we want to understand what advertising does, surely it makes sense to look at what people involved in producing advertising say about it rather than just look at academic studies of what people do. Practitioners, presumably, know something. The advertising industry is unique here. There is a rich tradition of leading practitioners setting their thoughts down on paper. Every leading advertising agent, it seems, is an aspiring writer too.

This chapter will explore these works. We will look at how, when advertising practitioners put their ideas about advertising down on paper, they tend to support one of two contradictory explanations about how advertising works. One group of writers has argued that advertising is a form of science. Others, in contrast, argue that advertising must be a creative art. In this chapter we will investigate some of the leading practitioner-authors whose ideas have shaped these two perspectives. In particular, we will look at the work of Claude Hopkins, Rosser Reeves, Bill Berbach and Mary Wells Lawrence. As we will see, broadly speaking, the view of advertising as a science draws on the transmission model of communication for theoretical support. The artistic perspective is grounded in social constructionist ideas. Although, it is worth noting that practitioners rarely address such theoretical issues head on.

Overview

The chapter proceeds as follows. First, we will set out a conceptual vocabulary to help us make sense of practitioner theories by developing the ideas of 'espoused theory' and 'theory-in-use'. These ideas have been used to make sense of the ways business people across a range of sectors speak about what they do. We will then explore the development and central tenets of the scientific perspective on advertising. After this we move to review the creative perspectives of advertising. We close by exploring empirical studies that look at the theories current practitioners draw on when developing advertising.

By the end of this chapter, you should be able to:

- distinguish espoused theory from theory-in-use;
- describe scientific advertising and creative advertising and
- evaluate the role of espoused theory and theory-in-use in contemporary advertising practice.

Key questions to keep in mind

- Is advertising a science?
- Is advertising an art?
- How do advertising workers balance competing theories in practice?

Two types of theory: espoused theory and theory-in-use

Before we start talking about particular practitioner theories, it is useful to set out some concepts that will help us in this chapter.

In this regard, management and organization theorists have studied how business practitioners explain what they do. They tell us that people tend to offer two conflicting explanations when asked to describe how they work. These are distinguished as espoused theory and theory-in-use.

Espoused theory is the name for the ideas people say they believe in. When an advertising practitioner writes down their theory of advertising, some of which we will explore shortly, they are offering their espoused theory. One of the benefits of espoused theory is that people get to really think through important issues and difficult problems. As such, espoused theory can be very persuasive. It often makes a lot of sense.

However, it turns out that while espoused theory looks great on paper, in the real world it is less effective. Indeed, researchers tell us that when they observe business practitioners at work, whether that is producing ads or conducting any other business function, they rarely stick to their espoused theories. It becomes far more important to make things work. Here, they tend to rely on different explanations which researchers call theory-in-use. Espoused theory is theory in an ideal world. Theory in use is theory in the real world (see Binet and Field, 2009 for a study into advertising practitioner's theory-in-use).

Keep in mind that, in this chapter, we are going to look primarily at espoused theories. It is important to note that many of the leading advertising agents who set down these theories of advertising broke their own rules (see Thought box 3.3 for an example). The espoused theories we will review, though, do still tell us something about how advertising works. They also tell us how advertisers want it to work. Towards the end of the chapter, we will pay some more attention to exploring current theories-in-use.

Scientific advertising

In Chapter 1, we saw that advertisers started to think about advertising as salesmanship in print at the start of the 20th century. One implication of this shift that we have yet to explore is what it means to sell. Of course, selling means getting someone to buy something but, at the time that advertisers started thinking about their work as salesmanship, there was a well-established way of thinking about sales.

For the best part of 25 years before advertisers thought about themselves as salespeople, the sales process had been understood through a simple acronym developed by an advertising worker and salesman called Elmo St Lewis: AIDA (Strong, 1925). To sell, the acronym states, you must lead a consumer through a four-stage journey (sometimes called 'the funnel'):

1 You must get someone's *attention*.

2 You must *interest* them in your offer.

3 You need to create a *desire*.

4 You must encourage them to a specific *action*.

Understanding that advertising was a form of sales meant that advertising, too, should work through set rules. This kicked off a search to discover those rules. It was against this background that the scientific theory of advertising emerged. It was brought together in the most popular advertising book ever was published: Claude Hopkins' *Scientific Advertising*. It sold 8 million copies and changed the face of advertising. It also made Hopkins rich and famous.

Hopkins made his name as a copywriter specializing in highly effective sales promotions. He believed that effective advertising involved using 'fixed principles... from which you never swerve (1967/1997: 192). In his autobiography, he explains how he came to this perspective. Working originally as a booker-keeper, he saw that manufacturers were increasingly turning to advertising to grow their businesses. He spied an opportunity. The company he worked for had hired a leading advertising agent but he proved unsuccessful. Hopkins offered to fill in. His employers were sceptical. But he convinced them to let him try. He wrote a letter promoting a new model and sent it to thousands of existing customers. Hopkins' letter set out the benefits of the product and offered customers the chance to try it for free if they took their letter to a store. Hopkins collected these letters from storekeepers. This meant he could prove that customers had read his letter and had gone to a store to try the product.

Based on this success, Hopkins soon took on more responsibility for producing sales promotions. In each case he adopted the same approach. He invested in small-scale trials in what he called 'test markets' to identify the best way to promote a product. Based on the results of these tests, he would amend and improve the advertising until he was sure that it was worth releasing it more widely (see Thought box 3.1). Hopkins explained: 'Almost any question can be answered, cheaply, quickly and finally, by a test campaign. And that's the way to answer them – not by arguments around a table. Go to the court of last resort – the buyers of your product' (1967/1997: 294). Here, we can

Thought box 3.1: Remember those coupons your Grandma was always collecting?

In order to measure the performance of an ad – whether that is in a test market or not – Hopkins argued that it was essential to trace the results. He would make sure that he knew what objectives an advertising campaign was designed to achieve and, once he knew what the desire outcome was, he would find a way to quantify it. Based on the AIDA model, Hopkins focused his efforts on achieving action. His favoured method was the use of coupons which required the consumer to take some small step in order to redeem a benefit – such as cut out a coupon and take it to a shop.

Coupons are great for consumers. They save them money and let them try new products. But they are also great for advertisers. Coupons can be 'keyed' to allow advertisers to calculate exactly how many ads had changed demand. A key is just a reference number that allows the advertiser to identify which ads the consumer had seen and taken the coupon from. Armed with this information, an advertiser could be certain that their investment in advertising produced a positive return. With keyed ads it was easy to compare the cost of producing an ad with the amount of coupons that were redeemed. This meant companies could calculate the cost of buying a new customer through their advertising. Put simply, the lower the cost of producing an ad and the higher proportion of coupons redeemed, the better the ad. As Hopkins summarized: 'Your object in all advertising is to buy new customers at a price which pays a profit. ... Learn what your consumers cost and what they buy' (1967/1997: 302).

see Hopkins' implicit reliance on the transmission model of communication we discussed in the last chapter. He does not believe that context has any effect. If an ad communicates its message in a test market, it will have the same effect, he believes, everywhere else.

Hopkins' successes meant that he soon moved into the advertising industry proper. In fact, he was hired by Albert Lasker at Lord & Thomas – the same man who had been convinced that advertising was salesmanship in print just a few years earlier. Now working full time in advertising, Hopkins devoted his time to finding advertising techniques that worked no matter what product, service or brand he was promoting. He explained: 'There are exceptions in business, but not in advertising' (1967/1997: 4).

The laws he discovered included:

- *Be natural and simple – never try to show off.* Hopkins did not approve of ads that bore the stamp of a particular advertiser. He did not believe that an advertising agent should work to create their own style. Ads should promote products not advertising agents. All an advertising agent should do is apply the fundamental laws of advertising. 'Brilliant writing,' he wrote, 'has no place in advertising. A unique style takes attention from the subject. Any apparent effort to sell creates corresponding resistance. ... Anything which suggests an effort to sell on other lines than merit and service is fatal' (1967/1997: 181).

- *Offer service.* Just as Hopkins warned against obvious sales techniques, he believed that humour 'has no place in advertising' (1967/1997: 183). 'Spending money,' he explained, 'is usually serious business' (1967/1997: 183). Instead of frivolous jokes, advertisers should make consumers' lives better by providing them a service – primarily information that helps them to spend their money more effectively.

- *Aim to get action.* Hopkins felt that new customers needed to reduce the risk of buying a different product. Giving them samples and discounts helped here. Moreover, getting a consumer to cut out a coupon was investment on the part of the consumer that, no matter how small, is essential to selling. It is an action.

- *Give actual figures and state definite facts.* Hopkins believed that ads should be specific. No consumer believes an advertiser when they describe a product as 'the best'. General superlatives are a waste of time. Indeed, Hopkins explained: 'No generality has any weight whatever. It is like saying, "How do you do?" when you have no intention of inquiring about one's health. But specific claims when made in print are taken at their value' (1967/1997: 253). Hopkins did not approve of advertising campaigns that provided information to consumers on a piecemeal basis. He thought that ads 'should tell the full story' because consumers do not read ads 'in series' (1967/1997: 187). If something is important enough to motivate consumers it should be included in every ad.

A notable revision to Hopkins' theory came in the early 1960s after television had overtaken newspapers and magazines as the dominant advertising media. In 1961, an advertising executive called Rosser Reeves published a short manual that he had prepared for his colleagues at the Ted Bates agency. It was called *Reality in Advertising*.

Like Hopkins, who he described as 'one of the advertising immortals' (1961: 55), Reeves believed that if you have enough data you do not need to treat advertising as 'a mysterious vortex into which millions of dollars are poured every year' (1961: 11). With enough data, patterns 'begin to emerge; the patterns shape themselves into principles; the principles, tested and retested by further observation, begin to appear as laws of reality in advertising' (1961: 23). So, like Hopkins, Reeves argued that you can discover 'the laws of cause and effect' in advertising (1961: 23).

But Reeves did not focus on sales as the ultimate aim of advertising. Reflecting changes in consumer psychology which we will explore in Chapter 6, he argued that the consumer 'carries a small box in his head for a given product category' (1961: 39). The advertisers first job is to own 'a bit of space in the box' (1961: 39). He called this 'penetration'. Advertising campaigns with a high level of penetration are those that transmit their message to the most number of people.

The most obvious way to increase penetration is to create more advertisements. But ads do not exist in a vacuum. Penetration is a finite resource within a given market or product category. As Reeves puts it: 'As your penetration goes up, your competitors' tends to go down' (1961: 37). Moreover, as brands compete to get their message across, there is a risk that consumers will not listen to anyone.

Better than creating more advertising, then, is creating better ads. Reeves called this the 'the pure power of copy' (1961: 41). An effective message can change people's behaviour without the need for promotions, special offers or deals. It does so by offering a strong claim which differentiates the product from the competition' and explains to the consumer the product's primary benefit. Reeves famously called this the Unique Selling Proposition or USP. To establish which ad was best, Reeves measured the proportion of people who remembered an ad and started to use the product. He called them 'the pulled'. He then compared this to the proportion of people who saw the same ad, remembered it but did not start using the product. He called this group 'the unpulled'. Split the difference between them and you can calculate 'how many have been pulled over to the usage of our product by your advertising' (1961: 10). The best ads are those that pull the highest proportion of people (see Thought box 3.2).

While Hopkins argued that anyone could produce great ads by following his rules, Reeves was clear advertisers still needed advertising agents. Reeves explained: 'When an agency turns loose a group of qualified scientists, when broad-scale, open-end research and testing are started, it is astonishing how many radical differences come swimming to the top – difference either in the product, or in the use of the product, which had not been suspected before' (1961: 54). Indeed, despite his admiration for Hopkins, Reeves said himself that you should 'not believe an advertising agent who tells you he has a foolproof method. He is like the man who wants to sell for $100 a machine that makes authentic $20 bills' (1961: 94).

Hopkins' and Reeves' espoused theory, then, was based on the idea that advertising could operate with complete certainty. This was an extremely attractive idea and has proven an attractive theory ever since. Although some of the science behind Hopkins' approach has been disproved, other forms of scientific knowledge have replaced it. Recently, for example, we see neuroscientists claiming that they have discovered a 'buy button' in the human brain and charging brands a fortune to test their ads using brain-scanning imagery to see if they activate it. I am sceptical they have really made this discovery but they all follow Hopkins' fundamental theory.

Thought box 3.2: The cost of bad advertising

For Reeves, sales are rarely determined by advertising alone. The weather, for instance, can have much more effect on the sales of many products than ads. So attributing sales to an ad will inevitably include erroneous data. Moreover, it might hide more important insights. As we will see, Hopkins discovered that advertising can drive people away from a brand. He explained that 'the people who read and remember your advertising may buy less of your product than people who are not aware of your advertising at all. Your advertising, in other words may, literally, be driving away customers' (1961: 7–8). If you simply attribute all sales to advertising, you might overlook the reality that it is people who have not seen your ads who buy the most of your products and, conversely, that the people who have seen your ads do not.

Armed with these concepts, Reeves discovered that bad advertising had effects that Hopkins had not even considered. Hopkins simply considered an ineffective ad as one that did not pull consumers to your offering. Reeves discovered that it might also drive them away. If you have high penetration for a bad message, one that does not pull consumers, you will persuade a lot of people not to purchase your brand. Rather than miss out on new customers, this means an ad might also drive away existing customers. Equally, if your USP is not unique, if it simply copies features or benefits of your rival, your campaign might well end up benefiting your rival. It may convince consumers of the benefit but not your offering.

Counter-intuitively, then, bad advertising is not only a waste of money. It drives your sales down and your competitions' sales up. Reeves concluded: 'A company with a strong message may get its story into the heads of only a few people, and become rich. Conversely a company with a bad message may get its story into all the heads, and become bankrupt' (1961: 18).

Creative advertising

Reading the works of Hopkins and Reeves, it is easy to think that all the problems of advertising were solved over a 100 years ago. Yet, at around the same time as Albert Lasker was learning that advertising was salesmanship on paper, other practitioners were developing some different perspectives on advertising. Rather than model themselves on salesmen or scientists, they thought that advertising could be an art.

A forerunner of this approach was Thomas Barrett – a marketer for the British soap company Pears during the late 19th century. As makers of an industrial mass-produced item, Pears needed to sell their soap in large volumes to generate a profit. Based on the notion of English colonialism, they had built a reputation as a producer of soap for the upper classes. But this market was small and offered few opportunities to grow. So Barrett tried to reposition Pears as the soap of the people.

First, Barrett tried to build Pears' market by distributing samples. Pears sent out free trials to parents of new-born babies. They also cajoled doctors, actresses and professors to endorse the product. These appeals had limited success. Pears' breakthrough came when they adopted a more artistic approach to advertising. At the time, British newspapers and magazines would build their circulation by including images and art that readers could pull out and display in their homes. Barrett encouraged Pears to adopt the same approach. He bought the rights to a famous painting called 'A Child's World' by the then-renowned artist Sir John Millais. Millais had sold this painting to the *Illustrated London News*, who printed it as a full-page illustration in their 1887 Christmas issue. Thinking that they had extracted as much value from the painting as possible, the *Illustrated London News* sold it to Barrett.

Barrett had the idea to add a cake of Pears soap to the painting and continue to give away free copies. He convinced Millais to edit the picture with a bar of Pears branded soap on the understanding that in so doing he would help his art reach an entire new audience. True to his word, Barrett bombarded the British Empire with free copies of the painting – now retitled 'Bubbles'. Pears spent a reported £3 million 'saturating the British Empire' with the painting (Twitchell, 2000: 45).

Barrett's idea was that whenever someone put the painting up in their home they would, literally, be putting up an ad for Pears. And, more importantly, they would be welcoming the brand into their homes. No longer would it be the soap of the few. Now it would be the brand of the many. Pears would cease to be a product for the upper classes and become a product for everyone. Advertising, Barrett believed, could show its message. It did not always have to say it explicitly in a USP.

This more artistic approach to advertising gradually fell out of favour as scientific advertising rose to prominence. But it returned in the 1950s and 1960s. This was thanks, in no small measure, to the influence of Bill Bernbach, who was born in New York in 1911 and worked as a copywriter and creative director at an agency called Grey Advertising.

Bernbach grew increasingly concerned with the preference for scientific advertising. The problem, as Bernbach saw it, was that scientific advertising looked good on paper but did not work in reality. Scientific methods meant that agencies were 'turning their creative people into mimeograph machines' (Tungate, 2013: 45). Every ad produced according to scientific advertising, he argued, would start to look the same. For brands, this meant it was almost impossible to market their product. They could not differentiate themselves. Bernbach later explained, 'when everybody says the same thing, you don't stand out' and people stop listening.

The best way to get them to listen to you is not to repeat yourself again and again as Reeves and Hopkins advised. You have to be artistic. As Bernbach puts it:

> The truth isn't the truth until people believe you, and they can't believe you if they don't know what you're saying, and they can't know what you're saying if they don't listen to you, and they won't listen to you if you're not interesting, and you won't be interesting unless you say things imaginatively, originally, freshly. (Sullivan, 2008: 5)

He set his concerns down in the following letter that he sent to the agency managers at Grey Advertising:

> There are a lot of great technicians in advertising. And unfortunately they talk the best game. They know all the rules. They can tell you that

people in an ad will get you greater readership. They can tell you that a sentence should be this short or that long. They can tell you that body copy should be broken up for easier reading. They can give you fact after fact after fact. They are the scientists of advertising. But there's one little rub. Advertising is fundamentally persuasion and persuasion happens to be not a science, but an art.

It's that creative spark that I'm so jealous of for our agency and that I am so desperately fearful of losing. I don't want academicians. I don't want scientists. I don't want people who do the right things. I want people who do inspiring things.

In the past year I must have interviewed about 80 people – writers and artists. Many of them were from the so-called giants of the agency field. It was appalling to see how few of these people were genuinely creative. Sure, they had advertising know-how. Yes, they were up on advertising technique.

But look beneath the technique and what did you find? A sameness, a mental weariness, a mediocrity of ideas. But they could defend every ad on the basis that it obeyed the rules of advertising. It was like worshiping a ritual instead of the God... Let us blaze new trails. Let us prove to the world that good taste, good art, and good writing can be good selling. (Bernbach and Levenson, 1987)

Unfortunately, Bernbach was not persuasive enough. Grey Advertising were unconvinced. So, in 1949, along with a college from Grey called Ned Doyle and an independent advertiser called Mac Dane, he started his own agency called Doyle Dane Bernbach (DDB). His aim was simple: instead of employing 'routinized men who have a formula for advertising', DDB would 'stand out'. He wanted the agency itself to develop 'a distinctive personality'. He wanted to produce advertising that was bold and brave. Rather than interrupt and annoy consumers, this advertising would entertain and engage them. Such work would not be produced by technicians but creative people with 'a deep insight into human nature'. In fact, he encouraged his colleagues to read Aristotle's work on rhetoric which we discussed in the last chapter. He described him as the world's greatest ever salesman.

Bernbach, though, did not set down his ideas in print as Hopkins and Reeves had. We can understand why he did not by returning to his 1947 letter to Grey Advertising. There he stated that he believed advertising workers should be free to develop their own ideas and 'not have the advertising philosophy of others imposed on us'. We can piece together his ideas by looking at his work. In this regard, there is a plethora of text which explore the campaigns and advertisements created at DDB. In addition, his colleagues recorded some of Bernbach's ideas in two books: *Bill Bernbach Said* and *Bill Bernbach's Book*.

Bernbach's approach to advertising is best illustrated in his most famous campaign for the Volkswagen Beetle (although it should be noted that Bernbach himself did not write this advertisement). The first ad in this campaign, 'Think Small', was a direct challenge to the consumer to think. It presented the Beetle as a product with a personality. As Twitchell puts it, in the 'Think Small' ad we see 'vast amounts of blank space with just a postage stamp of a car. We have to work to see it... Unlike other ads of the time, they were not billboards passing at warp speed. These were like homework assignments; you had to spend time with them... they didn't behave like advertising copy' (2000: 115).

At the time of this ad, car ads were notable for three characteristics: the cars were big, the ads included men driving fast and they included attractive women. In contrast, in the 'Think Small' ad, the car is shown free from any adornments, surrounded by white space – which, as we discussed in the last chapter, has some powerful rhetorical effects. Indeed, rather than use camera tricks to direct the consumer's attention and close-ups to magnify the car, the Beetle, a small car, is made even smaller in the ad.

As such, the ad takes ownership of the product's perceived weakness and it turns this weakness into a strength. The copy reads: 'once you get used to some of our economies, you don't even think them anymore / Except when you squeeze into a small parking spot.' The ongoing appeal of this creative approach is illustrated by UK advertiser John Hegarty. He observes: 'Bernbach showed us that the truth is the most powerful strategy you can employ in advertising... creativity could be inclusive and inspiring as well as intelligent – it didn't have to be patronizing to succeed and it demonstrated that humour was an incredibly powerful tool' (2011: 19).

If Bernbach had a rule, it was that 'the most important aspect of advertising is how you say what has to be said'. He felt that, in most cases, it was easy enough to find out what had to be said. Consumers tend to want the same USP. Indeed, market research produced by all the brands in a product category will, he explained, find the same things motivate consumers. Successful ads have an impact because they communicate their messages in an engaging way. They stand out. As Bernbach put it: 'The essence of impact is saying things the way they were never said before.' Bernbach's influence was, in this sense, to give birth to a so-called 'creative revolution' in advertising in which creativity and individual talent formed the basis of success.

Instead of leaving behind a set of principles, Bernbach's influence spread through his work, the people he worked with and through the people who were inspired by his approach. His colleague, Mary Wells Lawrence, for instance, pushed Bernbach's ideas forwards. Wells Lawrence thought that advertising could be a cutting-edge commercial art form. Unlike Bernbach, she took this approach to the advertising agent as well. While Bernbach was an unimpressive figure, Wells Lawrence was glamorous. She went to parties and knew rock stars and millionaires. Moreover, she saw this as part of her training. As she explained: 'Awareness is at the very core of the advertising business, you have to be aware of what is happening today, now, this minute, to be connected, to be effective, not only about the issue but also about style, trends, art' (2003: 123).

Thought box 3.3: Scientific advertising in action

Although Hopkins' theory was remarkably popular in his lifetime and has been incredibly influential ever since, Feldwick (2015) highlights a fundamental flaw in his logic. If Hopkins had discovered the laws of advertising which could be apply by any skilled technician, and if he had summarized them in his book, why would anyone need to hire an advertising agent to help them in the future? Moreover, why would anyone need to hire Hopkins who was the most expensive agent in the world?

For Feldwick (2015), we must appreciate that Hopkins' book was an elaborate sales pitch for his agency and an elaborate sales pitch for advertising in general at a time when business thinking was increasingly preoccupied with rational decision making. The title, *Scientific Advertising*, for example, clearly references Frederick W Taylor's *Scientific Management* – a best-selling management book that revolutionized the organization of production. Indeed, Feldwick argues that many of the fundamental principles Hopkins draws on come from Taylor's work. He tells us that 'Scientific Advertising created a powerful belief that good advertising could be defined in terms of Taylorian efficiency – that with enough measurement and experimentation, we could arrive at rules of what works best and progressively eliminate trial and error and the wastefulness' that many managers accused advertisers of' (2015: 46).

Perhaps, Feldwick (2015) suggests, in reality things were not as straightforward as Hopkins suggested in his espoused theory. In fact, when we look at Hopkins' theory-in-use, we quickly see that he broke many of his own rules. While he said that advertising should be truthful, exact and offer a service for the consumer, this did not mean that Hopkins did not go in for some good old-fashioned salesmanship. Quite the opposite.

Wells Lawrence's approach to advertising was grounded in her training in the theatre. She thought that advertising should be a theatrical performance. A good ad, for Mary Wells Lawrence, dramatized a product and romanticized a brand. A good campaign, for its part, created an exciting spectacle where consumers would anticipate the next ad much like they might wait eagerly at the doors of the theatre – this, of course, was a direct rejection of one of Hopkins' fundamental laws of advertising or Reeves' belief in repeating a single message over and over again.

Her approach to advertising, then, involved imbuing products and brands with consumers' emotions. She would place them into consumers' lives using references and situations that consumers could relate to. Wells Lawrence went as far as convincing advertisers to rethink their entire brand strategy to fit with her advertising ideas.

Her work for Alka Seltzer illustrates this well. Alka Seltzer was an indigestion relief tablet – it was largely considered a medicine. Wells Lawrence thought it could be repositioned as a lifestyle product.

For Wells Lawrence anyone living in the 1960s could not avoid an upset stomach. There was so much going on: the hard work of a booming economy, the hard partying supported by mind-bending drugs, the hard-to-digest food new immigrant communities had brought to the United States and the hard-to-digest art of the bohemian avant-garde. As she explains in her autobiography, in her head Alka-Seltzer was 'bumping up against Vietnam, the Kennedy assassinations, Martin Luther King and Neil Armstrong padding around in moon dust – not to mention Andy Warhol, Alice Cooper and what had become of Abbie Hoffman' (2003: 123). Out of this soup, working with colleagues, she developed a campaign that dramatized Alka-Seltzer around the tagline 'Plop, Plop, Fizz, Fizz'.

This line not only focused consumers' attention on taking two tablets – and therefore instantly doubled sales as previously Alka-Seltzer directed consumers to take a tablet one at a time – but it sent consumers back to that point of relief after the late night party or meal. Like a scene from a movie or a song lyric, it was evocative. It did not tell the consumer about the product, it showed the benefit. Supporting this, Wells Lawrence convinced Alka-Seltzer to change its marketing strategy. They developed portable foil packs that held two tablets and offered them in bars, restaurants and newsagents rather than the pharmacists.

We can see, then, how different the creative or artistic approach to advertising is from the scientific approach set out by Hopkins and Reeves. Whereas they believed that advertising could be engineered to produce predictable results and minimized the role of individual advertising agent, the creative approach tells us that advertising is mysterious. Rather than follow rules, it sees advertising agents in dialogue with consumers, creating drama and personalities out of products. In other words, it is grounded in a social constructionist or dialogic theory of communications.

What do contemporary advertising workers think?

According to Feldwick, these two espoused theories of advertising have dominated the advertising industry throughout its history. As he puts it: 'There has been a rumbling debate for well over a hundred years now as to whether advertising should be considered an art or a science' (2015: 21). It is certainly tempting to think you have to pick one side in this debate. However, it is worth remembering that while espoused theory might make the world seem black and white, theory-in-use deals in shades of grey.

Indeed, research tells us that within contemporary advertising agencies these two perspectives can exist alongside each other (Kover and Goldberg, 1995). Hackley (2000), for instance, argues that these different approaches to advertising have traditionally co-existed within advertising agencies as different departments have been set up around their own perspectives. Accounts managers, he tells us, 'are supposed to be mature and business-literate… and keep every-thing on schedule'. They are the scientists of advertising. Planners are 'boffins' who spend 'a lot of time wading through research data to distill essential marketing and consumer information' (2000: 239). They too adopt a scientific perspective. Creatives, in contrast, 'do not have to be mature all the time but… must be disciplined enough to come up with good ideas from scratch, to a deadline'. Do not worry if you do not know what these terms mean yet. We will look at them in more detail in the next chapter.

As we will also see in the next chapter, though, the advertising industry has come to operate through a project-form of working. Advertising agents come together in ad hoc teams depending on the needs of their clients. In order to work effectively, they need to be able to communicate with each other. This means that it is increas-ingly difficult for advertising workers from different departments to rely on clear functional divisions.

According to Nyilasy and Reid, the result of these changes is that advertising practitioners have come to possess a 'sophisticated and complex set of native theories about how advertising works' (2012: 38). This set of ideas has much in common with the view of advertising as an art but also integrates many of the scientific advertising ideas popularized by Hopkins. Across a series of in-depth interviews with experienced ad workers, they find that advertising practitioners generally believe that creativite work best. But, while they emphasized the importance of finding creative and original ways to get attention, raise brand awareness and influence attitudes, in keeping with the scientific approach to advertising, advertising practitioners also pointed out the importance of rational appeals and behavioural responses.

According to Nyilasy and Reid (2012, 2009), current practitioners feel that the need for certainty – that is, proof that advertising is working – comes largely from their clients. In order to keep their clients happy, and paying their bills, they need the ability to switch from creative to rational appeals and from the development of personal style to the ability to conform with the client's ideas. Put otherwise, they need to be able to switch between scientific and creative advertising. Rather than follow a particular theory dogmatically, practitioners reported that they would change their theory-in-use depending on the situation. Practitioners explained that understanding consumer attitudes within the context of a particular market, taking account of current fashions and historical trends and exploring consumers' familiarity and resistance to particular advertising appeals, was the key ingredient in producing successful advertising. The practitioners they interviewed did not believe that there was a correct way to produce advertising or a correct way to persuade consumers. They only believed in what worked in a given context.

So, according to Nyilasy and Reid's work, modern advertisers must switch between scientific and artistic ideas of advertising when they deem it necessary. While, logically, these ideas might be contradictory, advertisers refer to a higher-order justification. The success of advertising depends on the context of the advertising. As Nyilasy and Reid explain: 'To practitioners, advertising is situational and different situations may make basic theories work in different ways – in short, when it comes to regularities of advertising effectiveness, "it all depends"' (2012: 40).

Summary

In this chapter, we have explored practitioner theories of advertising. We have compared scientific theories of advertising – notably Hopkins' notion of scientific advertising and Reeve's reality perspective – with creative approaches. Here, we focused on Bill Bernbach.

Using the conceptual tools of espoused theory and theory-in-use, we have seen that contemporary practitioners are willing to switch from one perspective to another depending on the situation. This, I think, marks an important distinction. Just because someone says that advertising works a certain way, does not make it so. If anything, these espoused theories tell us something about the desires and wishes of advertising practitioners.

Some practitioners like the idea that advertising is predictable. It lets them feel secure that they are selling an expertise to their clients. Others like the idea of uncertainty. If advertising is an art, you have to accept that it can go wrong and that there are no quick and easy solutions to advertising problems. This also provides a persuasive sales pitch for the advertising agent. Indeed, for me, what is interesting is how the science versus art debate has shifted over the years. In the next chapter, we will look at changes in the advertising industry. I believe that you can only understand why a particular approach is popular at any given time if you understand this wider context.

Some other interesting sources

The radio show 'This American Life' has an interesting story about the history of Bernbach's most famous campaign for VW. It questions whether Bernbach gets too much credit for this ad. It is available here: www.thisamericanlife.org/radio-archives/episode/383/Origin-Story

There are a range of interviews with Bill Bernbach available on YouTube. I recommend these from the American Association of Advertising Agencies (AAAA): https://youtu.be/vUs5-3Y6vxM and https://youtu.be/4lhXh-loeKs

There are also a range of presentations and interviews with advertising practitioners who worked with Bernbach. I recommend this interview with George Lois: https://youtu.be/-92PkAXJlqQ. And this Ted Talk: https://youtu.be/fzHlZOnCQLc

If you are interested in some new forms of scientific advertising, Patrick Renvoise's talk on neuromarketing entitled 'Is There a Buy Button Inside the Brain' is an interesting watch. It is available here: https://youtu.be/_rKceOe-Jr0

References and further reading

Alvesson, M (1993) Organizations as rhetoric: knowledge-intensive firms and the struggle with ambiguity, *Journal of Management Studies*, 30 (6), pp 997–1015

Applegate, E (ed) (1994) *The Ad Men and Women: A biographical dictionary of advertising*, Greenwood Press, Westport

Argyris, C and Schön, D A (1974) *Theory in Practice: Increasing professional effectiveness*, Jossey-Bass, San Francisco

Bernbach, E and Levenson, B (1987) *Bill Bernbach's Book: A history of advertising that changed the history of advertising*, Villard Books, New York

Binet, L and Field, P (2009) Empirical generalizations about advertising campaign success, *Journal of Advertising Research*, 49 (2), p 130–133

Cruikshank, J L and Schultz, A (2013) *The Man Who Sold America: The amazing (but true!) story of Albert D Lasker and the creation of the advertising century*, Harvard Business Press, New York

Fox, S (1984) *The Mirror Makers: A history of American advertising and its creators*, William Morrow, New York

Hackley, C (2000) Silent running: tacit, discursive and psychological aspects of management in a top UK advertising agency, *British Journal of Management*, 11, pp 239–54

Hegarty, J (2011) *Hegarty on Advertising: Turning intelligence into magic*, Thames & Hudson, London

Hopkins, C (1966/1997) *My Life in Advertising & Scientific Advertising*, McGraw-Hill, London

Kover, A J and Goldberg, S M (1995) The games copywriters play: conflict, quasi-control, a new proposal, *Journal of Advertising Research*, 35 (4), pp 52–68

Nyilasy, G and Reid, L N (2012) Agency Practitioners' Theories about Advertising, in *Advertising Theory*, eds S Rodgers and E Thorson, Routledge, London

Nyilasy, G and Reid, L N (2009) Agency practitioner theory of how advertising works, *Journal of Advertising*, 38 (3), pp 81–96

Ogilvy, D (1963) *Confessions of an Advertising Man*, Atheneum, New York

Ogilvy, D (1983) *Ogilvy on Advertising*, Guild Publishing, London

Pratt, A C (2006) Advertising and creativity, a governance approach: a case study of creative agencies in London, *Environment and Planning A*, 38, pp 1883–99

Reid, L N, King, K W and DeLorme, D E (1998) Top-level agency creatives look at advertising creativity then and now, *Journal of Advertising*, 27 (2), pp 1–16

Strong, E K (1925) *The Psychology of Selling and Advertising*, McGraw-Hill, New York

Stuhlfaut, M W (2011) The creative code: An organisational influence on the creative process in advertising, *International Journal of Advertising*, 30 (2), pp 283–304

Tungate, M (2013) *Adland: A global history of advertising*, Kogan Page, London

Twitchell, J (2000) *20 Ads that Changed the World*, Three Rivers Press, New York

Wells Lawrence, M (2003) *A Big Life (in Advertising)*, Simon & Schuster, London

Work, agencies and contexts 04

Organizational perspectives on advertising

Introduction

In the last chapter we saw how two very different espoused theories exist side by side in the advertising industry. We closed by acknowledging that the changing nature of the advertising industry may help us to explain which theory is most popular at any given time. In this chapter, we will pay more attention to these changes.

It turns out that there is an organized system that produces most of the advertising and marketing communications we see. It is commonly called the 'advertising industry'. In this chapter we will explore how this industry works. As we will see, for many years, it has operated through a simple structure. But, in response to a range of business trends, technological developments and entrepreneurial inventions, this structure has come under sustained pressure in recent decades. As a result, new players have emerged and established organizations have fallen by the wayside. Although the basic features of the industry remain, they now fit into a much more complex production chain.

As well as describing the nature of these new advertising industries, in this chapter we will also explore organizational and management research. Researchers in these disciplines have found advertising organizations to be a rich site for understanding changes in working life, business relationships and creativity. From the perspective of advertising studies, this helps us to understand how the careers and working practices of advertising agents and the structure of advertising agencies shape the advertising we see around us.

Overview

The chapter proceeds as follows. First, we will explore the development of the advertising industry. We will see how advertising agencies emerged to sell space to advertisers and later developed creative expertise. We will then explore some of the common organizational features and working practices in the advertising industry. After this, we will move on to explore recent trends in the industry that have added additional complexities to the ways advertising gets made.

OBJECTIVES

By the end of this chapter, you should be able to:

- describe the role of advertising agencies;
- recognize common functional departments and working practices in the advertising industry; and
- contextual industry developments such as networks, specialists and intermediaries.

Key questions to keep in mind

- Is the advertising agency necessary to the production of advertising?
- How can advertising agents demonstrate their expertise in creativity?
- How has the relationship between advertisers, agencies and media providers changed?

The advertising industry

The advertising industry is composed of three types of companies and is sometimes described as a 'tripartite industry' (Fletcher, 2008). Let's look at each in turn:

- The production of advertising starts with advertisers (also known as 'clients' or 'accounts'). These companies have a particular problem they want to solve through advertising.

- Advertisers hire advertising agencies (also known as 'shops') to design and produce effective advertising for them.

- Agencies, in turn, commission media producers (also known as 'content providers') to distribute the ads to a target market.

While these three roles fit together neatly, they have changed over time and are continuing to change. One area of tension is the role of the agency. It is, after all, entirely possible for advertisers to produce their own ads and distribute them to potential customers. In fact, this was how advertising started and, to this day, many companies still produce and distribute ads themselves. This relation is illustrated in 'The Direct Era' (see Figure 4.1).

So where did agencies come from and how did they come to occupy their position in the middle of the advertising industry?

As modern advertising was beginning to take shape media providers stepped up to help advertisers communicate with larger audiences. This relation is illustrated in 'The Mediated Era' (see Figure 4.1). Media providers would sell space in their newspapers, pamphlets and magazines to commercial organizations on an individual basis. Over time though, this model proved limited. It was especially constraining for larger companies who wanted to advertise across multiple markets. Making deals with numerous publications in each location was inefficient and ineffective. In response, entrepreneurial individuals started to broker the relationship between advertisers and media providers. They purchased space in multiple outlets and offered advertisers a single point of contact – a one-stop shop where they could buy lots of advertising space in different media outlets. As such, the industry moved into the 'Agency Era' (see Figure 4.1).

These entrepreneurs soon found that they could negotiate preferential rates from media providers. They could block buy space from media providers at a discount and sell it on to advertisers at full cost. At this early stage, then, agents were essentially wholesalers. They traded space in the media. Indeed, even today we hear advertising agencies being described as 'shops' because originally that is what they were.

Figure 4.1 The development of the advertising industry

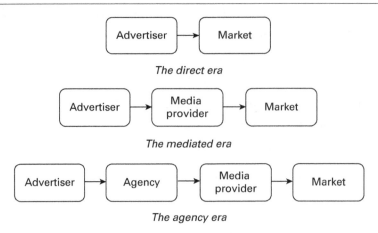

The direct era

The mediated era

The agency era

They were shops that sold advertising space. Equally, we hear of advertising space being described as 'inventory'. It is the product that is sold by these shops. The entrepreneurs themselves became known as agents because they acted as sales agents for media providers.

Soon the wholesalers began to actively seek advertisers in order to push up the price of the media space they owned. Indeed, while there may be some debate concerning who the first advertising agent was, we do know that as early as 1786 a UK-based advertising agent called William Taylor advertised for his own services as an agent (Fletcher, 2008). As such, agents increasingly moved from 'space selling' to 'space brokerage' (Williams, 1980: 216). They actively encouraged advertisers to buy advertising space and encouraged media providers to produce it.

To help do this, agents started to add additional services to their offering. They started to offer advice and guidance to advertisers. For example, they realized that advertisers would be more willing to advertise in an outlet if they knew lots of people read it or if the right kind of people read it. So, agents asked media providers to provide information about their circulation and audiences. This allowed advertisers to calculate, albeit quite crudely, the cost to reach their target audiences. They could, for example, calculate the CPM (cost per thousands) of a particular audience by dividing the cost of the advertising space by the number of people the newspaper or magazine reached. This measure has remained a key measure for the efficiency of advertising (Jeffries, 2012).

In addition to providing information, agencies increasingly started to advise their clients on the types of advertising they produced. This meant that instead of bringing an ad to an agent, advertisers could approach agents with a problem and let agents design a solution. At this point, then, agents moved from brokering space to offering a specialist business service. It did not matter what the product was. Agents claimed they knew how to advertise it. Indeed, because media space was really a commodity that any agent could buy and sell, the best way to differentiate themselves from other agencies was to emphasize this creative service. In fact, this is one of the reasons advertising agents like Hopkins and Reeves were so keen to set their theory of advertising down on paper. It helped them to sell their style of advertising. Their theories are sales brochures.

This focus on creating ads has profoundly shaped the advertising industry ever since. This means that, more often than not, what an advertiser says to consumers is chosen by their advertising agency. As a result, agencies have to have an in-depth understanding of the business. They need to know when the client is going to launch a new product, when it is suffering bad fortunes and its long-term plans. For this to work, the relationships between agencies and clients have tended to become institutionalized with particular agencies being synonymous with particular clients. Indeed, the average relationship between an advertiser and an agency lasts over 7 years in the United Kingdom, and 10 years in the United States.

To facilitate these relationships a number of conventional working practices have developed in the advertising industry. Established working practices allow clients to move agencies easily without having to set up new procedures and vice versa. It also allows agencies to work with different media outlets when necessary. Let's look at some of these standard working practices in more detail:

- To ensure that a prospective agency understands their business, clients invite agencies to pitch for the account. This involves a presentation by key staff about the agency covering its work and its personnel and its ideas for the client. The pitch is the chance for an agency to show that it understands the client and has the creative capacity to produce effective solutions to their market-ing problems. Illustrating the importance of shared cultures, some pitches are called 'chemistry meetings' as they are designed for an advertiser and an agency to feel whether they have the right 'chem-istry' to work together.

• To guide the agency that wins an account, clients produce a docu-ment known as a creative brief. It sets out the client's needs, their budget and some of the constraints that the agency must work within.

• Some agencies work for a single client. But it is more typical for them to work with multiple clients. This is known as the agen-cy's roster. Managing a roster is not easy. It is generally accepted that agencies will not work with multiple clients operating in the same market. Such competitors are thought to have conflict (or 'conflicts of interest'). Consequently, sometimes agencies 'resign' from accounts in order to work with another advertiser operating in the same industry as their previous client.

• Clients provide the revenue for the advertising production chain. Typically, agencies earn their money from a commission they charge on any media space they purchase for their clients. Traditionally, this was set at a standard rate of 15 per cent. In other words, if an agency billed a client for £100,000 of media space, they would only purchase £85,000 of media space and would keep the £15,000 that was left over. In some cases, they might also be able to bill clients for the costs of producing ads. For this reason, agencies have tended to favour 'above the line' or 'paid' forms of advertising that allow them to charge commission. Occasionally, media providers might even offer an agency a rebate to encourage them to use their services – although this is a controversial practice and is considered unethical in some national advertising industries (Fletcher, 2008).

• Clients occasionally put their account under review. This means the incumbent agency that holds their account will have to justify their costs. Often the incumbent agency will be asked to pitch (or repitch) again for the business against other agencies. Clients might focus their review on particular aspects of the relationship or look to improve their advertising in particular areas. For example, in procurement-led reviews accounts are reviewed in terms of costs and quantifiable outcomes rather than marketing strategy or the branding needs of an organization.

The range of services agents offer their clients means that they are large and diverse organizations. They might have begun as shops but, as they began to offer production, strategy and research, agencies became much more complex. They became 'idea factories'. Typically, agencies now share some common features:

- *Account management.* The account management function manages the relationships between clients and agencies. Account managers listen to a client's marketing needs and report these back to the agency. They are sometimes described as 'suits'. They need to have intimate knowledge of their client's key people, strategy, objectives and marketing needs. White (2000: 13) describes them as 'business associates for the client'. In some cases, they even help the client to formulate their marketing strategy.

- *The creative department.* The creative department takes information from the account team and uses it to produce a 'concept' for an ad or campaign that will help the client to meet their marketing objectives. A concept is the key idea behind an ad. It is a translation of the marketing objectives into a persuasive message that will appeal to consumers. It is reported back to the client by the accounts team and, if the client is happy, they commit to cover the costs of making the concept a reality. The technical name for these is 'executions'. The creative department is a space for artistic experimentation. Creatives are typically organized in pairs known as 'teams' comprising an artist and a writer.

- *Account planning.* Account planning is responsible for ensuring the agency has a detailed understanding of consumers based on market research, experience and intuition. They feed this to account managers to help develop client briefs. For example, they may help to define the target audience for a campaign or craft the most attractive strategy for reaching a target audience. According to White: 'Planners have to combine a good knowledge of research techniques and interpretation with a more or less magpie mind and the ability to empathize, and argue, with the creatives' (2000: 13).

- *Media planning and buying.* Media planning and buying departments organize for ads to appear in particular media outlets. Their job is to ensure that media providers produce content that will attract the right audiences to help advertisers meet their marketing objective. They also work to secure the most cost-effective media space for an advertiser. They have to keep on top of changes in the media landscape and new technologies.

- *Management and administration.* Management and administration departments deal with day-to-day affairs such as HR and budgeting. They ensure that clients pay their bills and that the agency pays theirs too.

Agencies that offer all of these services are known as 'full service' agencies (see Figure 4.2). This was the dominant form of advertising agency until the late 1960s and is still the dominant mental image many people have when they think of an advertising agency. One explanation for this is that US advertising agencies, which tended to be structured in this way, exported this organizational structure, business models and working practices around the world (Wing, 2008; Anderson, 1984).

This is not to say, however, that the history of the advertising industry is simply a tale of Americanization or even that it would be a bad thing if it were. The development of account planning, for example, was a British phenomenon (Fletcher, 2008). US agencies focused on account management. Their account executives were little more than salesmen who maintained close personal relationships with key personnel in client organizations. Account planners in Britain saw their role differently. They worked as marketing consultants – helping clients to identify marketing needs, focus on particular marketing strategies and provided marketing research as part of their service (see Feldwick, 2000). One consequence of this expanded remit of accounts planners has been that full service agencies have added market research teams (or 'consumer insight', 'data analysis', 'analytics', 'big data' or whatever the latest buzzword happens to be). The

Figure 4.2 Full service agency structure (adapted from White, 2000)

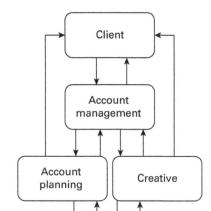

role of this function is to crunch data to improve the development of marketing strategy, produce effective concepts and executions and prove the effectiveness of advertising campaigns.

We can see, then, how agencies have come to occupy centre stage in the production of advertising. It is still possible to produce advertising without them. But they have become a linchpin in the production of advertising. They have become integral not simply to the production of advertising but also to the business model of many media providers. In addition, although they are, in essence, simply selling a commodity, they have created expert knowledge and influence for advertisers. They play a key role in shaping the ads we see.

The importance of creativity

Although account executives win business, the role of creativity in the advertising industry cannot be underestimated. It is, in many ways, the foundation of agencies' claims to expertise. Up to the 1970s agencies were almost expected to offer a full service for their clients. These agencies tended to differentiate themselves through key accounts, global reach or their particular approach to the creative function. Indeed, 'creative' was really the only part of the advertising business that could not be replicated by any agency a client could work with. Marking this, up to the 1970s most agencies were named after their creative talent (Tungate, 2013). For example, Bill Bernbach, the influential creative talent from the 1950s whom we discussed in the last chapter, gave his name to Doyle Dane and Bernbach (DDB). This is precisely why almost all the practitioner writings we have looked at focus on how best to produce effective advertising and not, for example, on how to manage advertising organizations.

This brings us to one of the enduring problems for advertising agencies. How do they show their clients that they are more creative than other agencies? They cannot rely on formal qualifications in the same way other professional business services such as accountancy and law can. Creativity cannot be taught. Rather, advertising agents have to learn on the job. They pick up skills by working with experienced colleagues and by building their own experiences. In fact, Pratt (2006) reports that advertising workers even 'hop' from one agency to another just to work with a particular advertising agent or a prestigious client. It is, in this sense, extremely important that advertisers spent time talking about advertising and the industry. It is 'a way in which tacit "ways of doing" and "ways of being" are passed on' (Pratt, 2006: 1894). Indeed, according to Grabher (2001), as much as periods of productivity help advertising agents to learn new skills, 'periods of idleness' allow more senior advertising agents to show junior workers how the industry works.

Advertising agents, then, have produced 'impression of professionality' because they lack professional qualifications (Alvesson, 1994: 545). Individual agents contribute to this by looking, acting, dressing and speaking like the right sort of creative person. They earn the respect of their clients by displaying their creativity, imagination and cultural distinction. Alvesson (1998), for instance, emphasizes the importance of looking like an advertising worker in the recruitment of new staff to an advertising agency. Women, he tells us, should be young, attractive and fashionable. Men should be healthy, approaching middle age, rugged but well groomed.

More generally, agencies themselves must also do this work. This is why agency offices tend to be designed more like contemporary art galleries. It is for the benefit of clients. It demonstrates that agencies are creative and that they are different types of organizations who are able to do something different from the client. Another way agencies can demonstrate their creative skills is through awards. The ad industry is geared up around a series of award ceremonies that celebrate creativity and establish the effectiveness of advertising for businesses. Leading awards include: Cannes Lions, D&AD, IPA Effectiveness Awards and the Clios. These allow agents to define what creative advertising looks like. Often these award ceremonies take place in exotic and glamorous locations. Ultimately, they allow advertisers to set their own definition of what constitutes good work. However, researchers have yet to confirm whether winning awards is a good thing for clients. Research suggests that many awards focus too much on artistic innovation and overlook the contribution of advertising to business.

However, while researchers suggest that a great deal of the efforts in the advertising industry can be understood as attempts to establish creative expertise, ironically, true creativity is not part of this. Hackley (1999), for instance, argues that individuality is frowned upon in many agencies (see Thought box 4.1). Instead, agents are expected to conform to industry norms concerning the ways they dress and act at work. One of the first informal rules we can observe in the advertising industry concerns space. While advertisers must be creative, they tend to be located in a small number of locations. In North America, the industry is primarily concentrated in Madison Avenue, New York. In Europe, it is concentrated, primarily, in Soho, London. These areas are ad villages (see Thought box 4.2).

We can see, then, how the focus on creativity emerged thanks to the place of advertising agents in the production of advertising. We can also see how this has presented some unique organizational challenges to advertising agents and agencies. Agents need to demonstrate both that they conform to the expectations of a professional business service. That is to say, that they can do a good job. But part of this involves presenting themselves as maverick and innovative individuals. For agencies, too, there is delicate balance that needs to be struck between being professional and innovative. Get the balance wrong and an agency risks looking either unprofessional or ineffective.

Thought box 4.1: Diversity in the advertising industry

Despite the professed desire among agencies for 'individuals', an ongoing issue for the advertising industry is the lack of diversity among advertising workers.

Although a recent survey by the IPA and *Campaign* suggests that there is no real gender basis among advertising workers with roughly 50 per cent of all advertising workers being female, things are less positive when you look at senior positions in the industry. *Campaign* reports that even though 'women account for 56.1 per cent of the junior agency roles, this drops to 39.2 per cent at the head of department level and 30.5 per cent in leadership positions'.

Indeed, things are not as rosy when we look from the perspective of ethnicity. Here *Campaign* reports that '13.1 per cent of the industry is from a BAME background – slightly lower than the 14 per cent share of the UK population. It is, however, far below that of London, where most of the big agencies are based'. BAME stands for 'black, Asian and minority ethnic'. Things get even worse from an ethnicity perspective when we consider seniority. *Campaign* tells us that 'BAME employees make up 10.8 per cent of those at the most senior level in creative agencies, but only 2.9 per cent at media agencies'.

See www.campaignlive.co.uk/article/adland-16-part-two-ethnicity/ 1380162 www.campaignlive.co.uk/article/adland-16-part-one-gender/1379217

Industry restructuring

In spite of these standardized working practices, since the 1960s the industry has slowly restructured. In the 1960s many agencies floated on the stock market. This meant they could be bought and sold. And this is exactly what happened (see Tungate, 2013). The shock waves these mergers and acquisitions sent through the industry led to a range of innovations which we are still working through to this day. Three notable trends have been the rise of 'the network', 'the specialist' and 'the intermediary' as new links in the advertising production chain. These have brought with them new working practices.

Thought box 4.2: Inside the ad village

Advertising agencies tend to be clustered in a small number of centres. Each has their own working practices and advertising styles (see Tungate, 2013). US advertising, for example, has a reputation for being results-driven and utilitarian – with advertising copy staying close to 'the product'. The United Kingdom, in contrast, has a reputation for irreverent and self-depreciating humour.

Pratt explains that there is a 'need for close and frequent relationships between the advertiser and the agency to negotiate the content of advertisements and campaigns. In order to be more creative, agencies have needed to gain the trust of advertisers (and autonomy). In part, physically close linkages and frequent contacts achieve this' (2006: 1897). But, he argues, there are also 'a number of organisational and labour-market factors that may account for the extreme proximity' between agents and advertisers (2006: 1883). Ad villages act as nodes drawing in creative talents. This makes them centres of excellence and specialist skills. The technical term for this is 'agglomeration'. Researchers have found that advertising agents 'need constantly to check and update what is "good", checking the output of others, as well as the career progress of peers or superiors' (Pratt, 2006: 1892).

However, while some 'people in the advertising business talk about spatial proximity to supplying services in terms of convenience', ad villages also allow the industry to act as a community (Grabher, 2001: 367). Indeed, they have their own newspapers, blogs, hashtags and bars. Success as an advertising agent is dependent, then, not only on performing for a client but also for others in one of these communities. This is how agents can get ahead in advertising.

Concentration allows practitioners to hang out in 'communities of peers [which] serve as a sort of informal educational system for disseminating knowledge' and popularize 'particular language and dress codes and, more generally, the code of conduct and habitus' of the advertising industry (Grabher, 2001: 368). This high level of socialization means that advertising practitioners can easily work together in bespoke teams as they can assume a high degree of 'rules and protocols of shared understanding' will be present (2001: 354).

Networks

One of the most obvious changes to the advertising industry since the 1960s has been the rise of 'networks' that own many different agencies such as the UK-based WPP. These new holding companies emerged in the 1960s as the advertising industry entered a period of mergers and acquisitions. There are a number of reasons why this happened. Here are a few:

- In some cases founders of agencies realized they could make a fortune by 'going public' – that is to say, incorporating their part-nerships and selling their shares in their companies to private investors.

- At the same time, during the post-war consumer boom, as coun-tries such as Britain, France and Germany began to recover, larger international agencies started to buy out smaller local ones. This was often done to acquire key accounts and creative expertise or enter new markets (US agencies, in particular, often felt the need to follow their clients as they moved into new territories – believing that physical proximity was an essential ingredient for their relationship to stay secure). Marion Harper, head of the agency McCann-Erickson, was a key leader in this regard.

- Strategically, while some agencies sought to differentiate themselves through their international or global perspectives, others felt that certain functions performed within full-service agencies could be streamlined. Building larger advertising conglomerates would allow them to exploit cost-saving synergies as administration and other functions could be performed just as well across agencies. Thus, large networks had economies of scope and scale. This allowed them to compete on the basis of both creative talent and price.

- By keeping agencies as separate entities, networks could get around the problem of conflict. That is to say, while conflict meant that an agency could not work with a client and its competitor, there was no such rule for a network. Within a network, different agen-cies could work with both a client and their competitor without the fear that their business secrets would be shared. But the profit would all go to the same place: the network.

As a result of these benefits, networks have come to dominate the advertising industry – adding another layer to the traditional tripartite structure of the industry. Indeed, despite the plethora of advertising agencies around the globe, Tungate quotes an industry insider as saying: 'Almost everyone in advertising works for one of five different companies' (2013: 149). Those five companies serve to illustrate that the advertising industry is far from the US-dominated industry some think it is. They are: WPP (UK), Omnicom (USA), Publicis (France), Interpublic (USA) and Dentsu (Japan).

Specialists

One side effect of the rise of the network has been the emergence of the 'independent agency' as a category. Networks were not the only organizations to realize that there were potential opportunities in combining specific functions. Smaller more entrepreneurial organizations also saw this as an opportunity. Unlike networks, who sought to exploit the opportunity through expanding their scale, these organizations looked to do so by limiting what they did. That is to say, they became specialists.

For example, we saw the rise of the 'creative boutique' at around the same time as the networks began to grow. These, typically smaller, agencies would only perform creative functions such as concept development and execution. In a break with traditional ways of working creative boutiques could not rely on generating revenue through commission on media sales. Thus, they were happy to work for flat fees, cost-plus arrangements and in some cases performance-related pay. One of the first such boutiques grew into the famous UK agency Saatchi and Saatchi.

In contrast to creative boutiques, which have largely remained small-scale, a second example of a specialist agency illustrates a real area of growth for the advertising industry: the media-buying agency. As we have seen, traditionally, advertising agencies covered their costs and earned their profit through a commission on the media space they purchased for their clients. Shrewd observers spotted an opportunity here. Why not specialize in this function – given that it was the only bit of the advertising business that actually made money!

To make things even more attractive, as this was part of the advertising business that simply involved trading a commodity – media space – it was sometimes more acceptable for media specialists to ignore the issue of conflict. Media specialists, such as ZenithOptimedia, also found that they could cut out many of the costly business functions of full service agencies such as account planning and creative, and as they could bulk-buy media space at an even bigger discount than full service agencies, they could also offer lower commission rates. As such, it is now common for media commission rates to be far lower than 15 per cent – in some cases, they may now be as low as 2 per cent.

More recently we have seen other specialists emerge such as account planning specialists and companies specializing in particular industries, consumers and media types. As a consequence of the rise of specialists, the production of advertising has become more fragmented and complex than ever before. It is possible for a client to put together teams of specialists from a range of agencies for particular projects and reconfigure them for others. As Thought box 4.3 explains, this has had an important effect on the working practices in the industry. Notably, it has meant that advertising agents have to be both unique but interchangeable and able to slot into teams without the ability to 'storm' or 'norm'.

Intermediaries

The relationship between an advertiser and an agency is key to the advertising industry. Traditionally, these relationships were serviced by accounts executives whose job involved keeping abreast of personnel changes at an advertiser and maintaining close personal relations with key decision makers. However, as the production of advertising has grown increasingly complex with advertisers able to assemble teams of specialists, it has become increasingly costly and time consuming.

It took several years for this model to take off. The rise of networks and specialists were largely responsible for it doing so. Indeed, since the idea of intermediaries was first put forward, there has been a tenfold increase in the number of agencies competing for advertisers' business. It has even been reported that marketing officers at some advertisers field as many as 20 cold calls from agencies pitching for their business each day!

Table 4.1 Main intermediaries in the United Kingdom

Name	Founded	Activities
Oystercatchers	2007	Agency search and selection, evaluation, training and coaching
The Observatory	2006	Agency selection, relationship management, procurement and skills development
Creative Brief	2003	Agency selection, relationship management, procurement and skills development
Agency Insight	1991	Agency search and selection, relationship management and strategic consultancy
Agency Assessments International	1988	Agency search and selection, re-muneration negotiation, relation-ship management
AAR	1975	Agency selection, relationship appraisal, commercial evaluation and benchmarking

(Adapted from www.campaignlive.co.uk)

Equally, the focus on cost-accounting and data-driven marketing has encouraged advertisers to rely on new forms of accountability. Whereas strong personal friendships and congenial account executives may have been enough to keep a client happy in the past, now they are much more demanding. They want to see results and demonstrable performance.

The result has been that more intermediaries have opened in recent years (see Table 4.1). As *Campaign* summarizes: 'Today, an oversupplied advertising market and the growing complexity of pitches are the main reasons why consultants continue to play such a pivotal role, handling between 35 and 40 per cent of the 400-plus pitches taking place each year.'

So, we can see how the industry is changing with new layers of complexity being added to what has been, traditionally, a fairly simple production chain. As a result, there are now much more diverse relationships and working practices in the industry and new skill sets are developing all the time. In particular, we have seen a trend for clients to not only demand more accountability from their agencies but to work with different agencies for different purposes (see Thought box 4.3). They might work with a network for some campaigns but used media specialists or insight specialists to help them develop their understanding of the market. They might even create ad hoc teams comprising staff members from several agencies to work on a specific campaign.

Thought box 4.3: Projects and new working practices

As a result of the disintermediate of the industry, clients have far more flexibility in how they work with agencies. As such, it is typical for large clients to operate their own 'roster' of agencies. Some might bring different areas of expertise in terms of media or function. Some might be knowledgeable about a particular market or location. But some might be added to a roster to keep other agencies on their toes. Clients, in short, compile rosters of different agencies into 'trading zones' offering them 'different business models, organizational philosophies, and worldviews' (Grabher, 2001: 354).

Consequently, those working within the advertising industry no longer find themselves confined to the walls of their own agencies. Teams from different agencies work on projects for particular clients even though they might be competing against each other to win accounts at other times. Each project brings together unique constellations of individuals, professions and organizations to work towards a shared goal. They are unpredictable and contingent and have meant that advertising agencies have had to developed sophisticated management practices.

For Grabher, this means the industry is highly diverse and constantly drifts 'between the poles of rigid order and excessive disorder' (2001: 354). Such 'diversity enlarges the 'genetic pool' for the evolution of new organizational mutations… [and] broadens the scope for the new entrepreneurial activities' (2001: 363). It also makes the industry highly competitive. Personal and organizational rivalries are welcomed. Indeed, 'errors are considered inevitable and something to be assimilated and incorporated into the performance' and not something that should be repressed or embarrassing (Grabher, 2001: 368). New ways of working also make the industry highly reflexive. The industry, put simply, thinks about itself a lot. There is an expectation that practitioners will 'radically question the appropriateness of the assumptions of one's own organisational behaviour' (Grabher, 2001: 354).

Summary

In this chapter we have seen that the advertising industry is set up to capitalize on creativity. Practitioners must balance sound business skills with imagination and the working practices, training and management styles developed in the industry all work to achieve this aim. However, as an industry that is not only open to innovation but welcomes it, the advertising industry has undergone a number of

---

Some other interesting resources

The Institute of Practitioners in Advertising has a range of guides available on its website covering topics such as how to find an agency, remuneration, creating effective briefs for agencies and developing sustainable relationships between clients and agencies. They are available here: www. ipa.co.uk/. The 4As also has information on its website: www.aaaa.org/

There are a number of good advertising industry magazines, blogs and podcasts. Personally, I recommend:

Advertising Age (www.adage.com)

AdWeek (www.adweek.com)

Campaign (www.campaignlive.co.uk)

The Drum (www.thedrum.com)

The Digiday podcast series is a particularly good deep dive into client, agency and media perspectives. Details are here: www.digiday.com

A number of advertising awards offer archived of successful advertising campaigns. For examples, see:

Cannes Lions (www.canneslions.com)

The Design and Art Direction Awards (www.dandad.org)

The Clios (www.clioawards.com)

---

changes over time. The rise of networks and specialists, for example, has meant that the industry is now more professional and draws on experts from a range of business functions like never before. The role of the agency is, itself, constantly changing.

Perhaps because of this constant change, the advertising industry has been a favourite hunting ground for researchers from management and organization studies. They have investigated how the advertising industry works, how creative talents can be channelled for the benefit of clients and how new forms of governance help to control and empower workers. Indeed, it is common for researchers in these areas to argue that advertising is at the vanguard of changes in management and the knowledge economy. This leads us nicely into the next chapter where we will look in more depth at the economics of advertising.

References and further reading

Alvesson, M (1994) Talking in organizations: Managing identity and impressions in an advertising agency, *Organization Studies*, **15** (4), pp 535–63

Alvesson, M (1998) Gender relations and identity at work: a case study of masculinities and femininities in an advertising agency, *Human Relations*, **51** (8), pp 969–1005

Anderson, M H (1984) *Madison Avenue in Asia: Politics and transnational advertising*, Fairleigh Dickinson University Press

Boddewyn, J J (1989) Advertising self-regulation: true purpose and limits, *Journal of Advertising*, **18** (2), pp 19–27

Brown, A (2006) Advertising regulation and co-regulation: the challenge of change, *IEA Economic Affairs*, June: 31–36

Cronin, A M (2004) Regimes of mediation: Advertising practitioners as cultural intermediaries?, *Consumption Markets & Culture*, **7** (4), pp 349–69

de Waal Malefyt, T and Morais, R J (2010) Creativity, brands, and the ritual process: confrontation and resolution in advertising agencies, *Culture and Organization*, **16** (4), pp 333–47

Duhan, D F and Sandvik, K (2009) Outcomes of advertiser–agency relationships: the form and the role of cooperation, *International Journal of Advertising*, **28** (5), pp 881–919

Feldwick, P (2000) *Pollitt on Planning*, NTC Publications, London

Fletcher, W (2008) *Powers of Persuasion: The inside story of British advertising, 1951-2000*, Oxford University Press, Oxford

Grabher, G (2001) Ecologies of creativity: the village, the group, and the heterarchic organisation of the British advertising industry, *Environment and Planning A*, **33**, pp 351–74

Hackley, C (2000) Silent running: tacit, discursive and psychological aspects of management in a top UK advertising agency, *British Journal of Management*, **11** (3), pp 239–54

Hackley, C (2002) The panoptic role of advertising agencies in the production of consumer culture, *Consumption Markets & Culture*, 5 (3), pp 211–29

Hackley, C and Kover, A J (2007) The trouble with creatives: negotiating creative identity in advertising agencies, *International Journal of Advertising*, 26 (1), pp 63–78

Heath, R and Feldwick, P (1999) Fifty years using the wrong model of advertising, *International Journal of Market Research*, 50 (1), pp 29–59

Jeffries, M (2010) *Data-driven marketing: The 15 metrics everyone in marketing should know*, John Wiley & Sons, London

Kenny, K and Euchler, G (2012) 'Some good clean fun': humour, control and subversion in an advertising agency, *Gender, Work & Organization*, 19 (3), pp 306–23

McFall, L (2002) What about the old cultural intermediaries? An historical review of advertising producers, *Cultural Studies*, 16 (4), pp 532–52

Moeran, B A (1996) *Japanese Advertising Agency: An anthropology of media and markets*, Curzon, London

Moeran, B (2009) The organization of creativity in Japanese advertising production, *Human Relations*, 62 (7), pp 963–85

Morais, R J (2007) Conflict and confluence in advertising meetings, *Human Organization*, 66, pp 150–59

Packard, V (1957/1981) *The Hidden Persuaders*, Penguin, London

Pratt, A C (2006) Advertising and creativity, a governance approach: a case study of creative agencies in London, *Environment and Planning A*, 38, pp 1883–99

Sasser, S L and Koslow, S (2008) Desperately seeking advertising creativity: engaging an imaginative '3Ps' research agenda, *Journal of Advertising*, 37 (4), pp 5–20

Tungate, M (2013) *Adland: A global history of advertising*, Kogan Page, London

Turnbull, S and Wheeler, C (2015) The advertising creative process: a study of UK agencies, *Journal of Marketing Communications*, pp 1–19

West, D C, Kover, A J and Caruana, A (2008) Practitioner and customer views of advertising creativity: same concept, different meaning?, *Journal of Advertising*, 37 (4), pp 35–46

Williams, R (1980) *Advertising: The magic system, problems of materialism and culture*, Verso, London

Information
and value

05

The economics of advertising

Introduction

We closed the last chapter considering the importance of advertising work when it comes to understanding the knowledge economy. This offers us a nice way to step outside of the advertising industry itself to think about the essentials of advertising more generally. In this chapter, we will pick up the economic theme and explore the economics of advertising.

As a body of research and theory, economics explores how people allocate scare resources. Predominantly, it focuses on the ways that buyers and sellers decide on the correct price for a product or service. However, economic ideas have informed discussions in other areas. They have, for example, been used to explain how people allocate their time and attention. Levitt and Dubner's (2006) bestselling *Freakanomics* is perhaps the most recent example of this trend.

Surprisingly, given this focus on consumer decisions, for a long time mainstream economic research overlooked advertising. It was assumed that 'there is no purpose' in advertising in competitive markets (Pigou, 1924: 173–74). If sellers wanted to increase the quantity they sold, they simply needed to lower the price of their offering. Buyers weighed up the benefits of an offering against the price and, if they found the price reduced, would buy more of the product or service. There is no need for rhetoric or persuasion.

However, with the growth of modern advertising, economists started to realize that advertising does affect consumers. The question they still needed to answer is how it does so. In this regard, economists have explored the effects of advertising on individual consumers, firms and markets. As we will see, though, despite nearly a century of work in this area, they have yet to agree on the effects of advertising. For some, it makes markets more competitive and improves consumers' abilities to make decisions. For others, it has the opposite effect.

Overview

The chapter proceeds as follows. First, we will review economic research that explores the effect of advertising on consumers. Here we highlight three arguments that have been put forward to explain how advertising causes consumers to change their decisions. Second, we will review the economic research which investigates the effects of advertising on firms. We will see that advertising has different effects on established firms and new entrants. Third, we turn to wider economic discussions about the impact of advertising on markets. We will then consider whether advertising improves or damages the competitiveness of markets. Finally, we will ask whether the economic study of advertising is able to prove whether advertising is good or bad.

OBJECTIVES

By the end of this chapter, you should be able to:

- describe advertising as persuasion, information and value;
- highlight the economic effects of advertising on firms;
- appreciate the relationship between advertising and market variables such as price and profit; and
- recognize implicit assumptions within economic research.

Key questions to keep in mind

- Does advertising help consumers to make better or worse choices?
- Does advertising affect the performance of firms?
- Does advertising improve or damage the competitiveness of markets?
- Can we ever prove that advertising has an overall economic impact?

Advertising and consumers: why do consumers respond to advertising?

A starting point for economic research into advertising focuses on the possible effects of advertising on demand – that is, the choices consumers make. Traditionally, economists have assumed that consumers seek to maximize the benefits they get from the products and services they purchase and will search for the best quality goods at the lowest prices (see Thought box 5.1). It is here that economists have been interested in advertising. Some think advertising can help consumers to make better decisions – others disagree. There are three broad explanations that have been put forward to support these views. Let's look at each in turn.

Advertising as persuasion

In some of the earliest work on the economics of advertising it was argued that advertising could make consumers over-value products and services. This is illustrated in the first demand curve in Figure 5.1. It shows how the post-advertising price increases as a result of successful advertising. This means consumers pay more for the same good or service as a result of advertising even though the benefits of the product or service are no different.

Implicit in this perspective is a criticism of advertising. It suggests that advertising has no real economic value for consumers. Instead, it allows sellers to artificially inflate the price of their goods and services. As we will see below, this is typically done by promoting them in terms of brand's reputation rather than the price or quality of product or service itself. As Robinson puts it, advertising enables firms to win customers by bringing their goods to a consumer's 'notice in a more pleasing and forceful manner' than the competition (1933: 5). But, by focusing consumers' attention on reputation over price and quality, it makes consumers scared to switch to new brands. Put technically, according to this perspective advertising makes demand inelastic.

Thought box 5.1: Thinking like an economist

In their popular economics textbook, Mankiw and Taylor (2011) tell us that to think like an economist we need to accept 10 principles. The first four of these principles set the scene for rational model of consumer behaviour. They lay at the heart of a branch of economics looking at individual consumers and organizations known as microeconomics. So let's look at them in a little more detail:

- *People face trade-offs.* Put simply, this means that to get one thing we always have to give up something else. For every benefit, there is a cost.

- *The cost of something is what you give up to get it.* The cost of something is not just the price. There are 'opportunity costs' which we incur by choosing one benefit over another. Consumers 'engage in activities that require both time and goods for their realization' (Ghez and Becker, 1975: xiv). So, for every hour your spend reading this book, you have one less hour to do other things. Just like money, you cannot spend your time more than once.

- *Rational people think at the margin.* Consumers rarely face 'all or nothing' decisions. Instead of choosing between fasting or eating as much as we can, we tend to only consider a smaller range of choices such as whether to buy a large drink or smaller one. Economists call these 'marginal' benefits and costs. Mankiw and Taylor point out: 'A rational decision maker takes an action if and only if the marginal benefit of the action exceeds the marginal cost' (2011: 7). For example, if you have been at university for two years and are thinking of quitting, you want to consider the costs and benefits of an additional year.

You do not want to consider the costs and benefits of the first two years in your decision.

- *People respond to incentives.* If the costs or benefits of a decision change, rational consumers will reconsider whether they have made a good choice. Generally, economists assume that the quantity demanded of a good will fall when the price of the good rises (this is known as the law of demand). This is shown in the demand curves included in Figure 5.1. The demand line on these charts indicates a hypothetical trade-off between price and quantity. This tells us that as price goes up, the quantity demanded goes down and vice versa.

This allows established firms to charge higher prices and reduce their levels of innovation safe in the knowledge that consumers will be unlikely to switch to other brands. Illustrating this perspective, Kaldor (1950) argues that advertising has a 'concentration effect' on markets. It tends to encourage consumers to concentrate on a small number of offerings from established brands.

Advertising and information

Later contributions to the economics of advertising – notably associated with the influential 'Chicago School' – contested the view of advertising as persuasion. Picking up on a theme first put forward by Marshall (1919), they argued that advertising can help consumers to make better choices. It does so according to Marshall by informing consumers about the existence of products and conveying important information to consumers that reduces the risks of switching to a new brand.

One flaw in this perspective, though, is that a great deal of actual advertising does not include such information (see Thought box 5.2). This issue was addressed head on by Nelson (1974, 1970). He argues that advertising provides a range of information to consumers. It provides *direct* information about the existence, function and price of offerings. But it also provides *indirect* information or signals that consumers can use to inform their choices. For example, advertising may suggest to consumers that a brand is

Figure 5.1   Economic perspectives on advertising and consumption

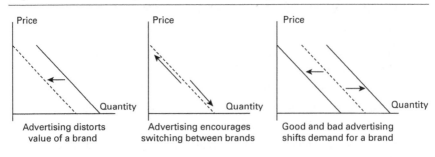

Advertising distorts value of a brand	Advertising encourages switching between brands	Good and bad advertising shifts demand for a brand
Advertising as persuasion	*Advertising as information*	*Advertising as value*

successful. This, in turn, may 'signal' that the brand is big enough to benefit from economies of scale and, as such, offer high-quality products at a low price.

Nelson (1970) suggests that these two types of information have the same effect. They help consumers to make more informed choices. But they have these effects in relation to different types of products and services. There are some produces and services – he calls them 'search products' – which can be evaluated prior to consumption. Direct information is useful to consumers when assessing such goods. There are others products and services that can only be assessed after consumption – Nelson calls them 'experience goods'. Indirect information is useful when assessing these goods.

Implicit in this perspective is a positive view of advertising. It tells us that most consumer markets offer consumers less information than they need to make full use of their resources. The technical name for this is imperfect consumer information. Advertising is a market mechanism that helps to overcome this imperfection. It makes consumers more likely to switch brands and helps new entrants to enter a market. The result of advertising is, then, that demand becomes more elastic and markets become more competitive (and to operate more 'perfectly'). This is shown in the second demand curve in Figure 5.1. It shows how a consumer might change the quantity they are willing to buy or the price they are willing to pay as a result of advertising but the underlining value of the offering remains unaffected.

Advertising as value

Finally, some economists argue that advertising is something that is consumed too. Irrelevant of whether it improves the operation of markets for other goods, it is a product in and of itself. Certainly, advertising is often consumed separately from products and services. For instance, when we watch commercials in between TV shows, we can consume ads without paying for a product. So advertising, in this view, has a *direct value*.

The reason for this is that consumers find value in a range of things. They want social status, celebrity associations and cultural references to help them express who they are. These are rarely contained in products. More often they are associated with them through advertising (Becker and Murphy, 1993).

As such, we can distinguish between the value of good ads and bad ads. Good ads have a positive value for consumers. Put simply, consumers would be willing to pay to consume them. Bad ads, in contrast, have no value or even a negative value for consumers. So consumers must be paid to watch them. This helps us to understand why advertising is often bundled in for free with other goods such as the commercials before and after a TV show. Audiences would be unwilling to watch the ads alone and are paid to watch them with a show.

The key for an advertiser is finding a way to capture the values they create for consumers in the pricing of their products and services. This is shown in the third demand curve in Figure 5.1. It shows how a demand line can shift from good advertising to allow brands to command a higher price. It also shows how a demand line can shift as a result of bad advertising to erode the price a brand can charge even though the underlying product or service remains fundamentally the same.

Based on this perspective, Stigler and Becker (1977) argue that even in a perfectly competitive market where consumers can switch easily from one brand to another and have all the information at their disposal, firms will still advertise. In particular, for markets involving extremely similar and easily substitutable goods, the value delivered to consumers through advertising may be the only competitive activity for firms. Firms in these markets will distinguish themselves through their ability to produce the best advertising. Indeed, more generally, it makes sense for all firms to advertise because it can deliver more value for consumers than it costs to produce for a firm.

These three economic perspectives on advertising emphasize three very different effects on consumers. If advertising is persuasion, it makes consumers want things they do not truly want. According to the economist Galbraith, this creates a *dependency effect* where people end up consuming more and more things but becoming less and less happy. Although they have more stuff, they do not have anything they truly want. But, if advertising provides information, it should have the opposite effect. It should make it easier for consumers to figure out what they want and to find a product that meets their needs. As we will see throughout this chapter, the debate between these two positions informs much of the economic literature. Indeed, it relates to some of the overarching discussions across all the disciplines that contribute to advertising studies. One unique idea which economics adds is the notion that advertising can be a 'good' in its own right. When we look at the ways that people consume advertising in Chapters 6, 7 and 8, we will see how this works in reality. What I find fascinating, though, is the idea that while some advertising is a good, other ads are 'bad'. They are products people must be paid to consume. There are not too many other products that exist in this category!

Thought box 5.2: Is there information in advertising?

In a foundational study, Resnik and Stern (1977) evaluated the extent to which television ads are informative. They defined 14 evaluative criteria which they used to define an ad as informative. These represent 'information cues which could potentially be used in intelligent decision-making' (1977: 51). In their original study, Resnik and Stern conclude:

> Even the most favorable results of this study point to the fact that television commercials have room for improvement in providing useful informational cues to the consuming public. On an overall basis, the study's findings paint a gloomy picture in that less than half of the

sample's advertisements met the liberal criteria of possessing useful informational cues. (1977: 52)

Their coding scheme has subsequently been used to analyse the amount of information in ads across a range of different media and market contexts (see Madden, Caballero and Matsukubo, 1986; Stern, Krugman and Resnik, 1981). Abernethy and Franke (1996) offer a meta-analysis of nearly 60 published studies using the Reskin and Stern scheme. They demonstrate that advertising might include more information than Reskin and Stern originally thought. But they confirm that ads include less information than some economists seem to assume.

Does advertising improve profit? Advertising and the firm

From a firm's perspective, competition is not necessarily a good thing. It depends on the market power of the firm. For established brands, competition can be bad. They would much rather operate without it. Competition, in theory at least, makes demand more elastic. That is to say, it makes a consumer more likely to switch brands and makes it easier for new players to enter a market.

Table 5.1 The benefits and costs of advertising for firms

Benefits	Costs
Advertising increases differentiation between similar offerings	Advertising increases the 'selling costs' of a product and can inflate prices
This produces more loyal customers and reduces consumer switching	At a certain point, advertising becomes less effective as the most responsive buyers are already consuming the brand
This allows firms to exploit economies of scale in production	So, after a while, advertising becomes ineffective and wasteful even for established brands

(Continued)

Table 5.1   *(Continued)*

Benefits	Costs
This allows firms to lower their prices and attract new consumers from weaker brands	
Simultaneously consumer loyalty allows successful firms to increase prices.	
Thanks to economies of scale in the production of advertising, successful firms see great returns on advertising investments	

If advertising can help make a market less competitive, then, it might make sense for a firm to do it. As Robinson puts it, if an established firm 'finds the market becoming uncomfortably perfect (i.e. more competitive) it can resort to advertisement and other devices which attach customers more firmly to itself' (1933: 101). In harmony with this view, Chamberlin (1933) set out some of the costs and benefits of advertising for established firms in one of the earliest contributions to the economics of advertising (see Table 5.1).

From Chamberlin (1933), then, we inherit a 'U-shaped' understanding of the benefits and costs of advertising. For established brands, effective advertising has significant benefits. It allows them to win new customers, retain existing customers, charge higher prices and decrease the number of competitors operating in their market. As a result, 'firms that have some monopoly power are more likely to advertise because they can obtain most of the increased sales stimulated by their advertising' (Telser, 1964: 551).

But, at a certain point, advertising loses its effectiveness for these firms. They must still advertise to maintain their position but no longer see growth through advertising alone. After a while, each firm will have advertised the market into distinct inelastic segments. Ozga explains that 'as more and more of the potential buyers become informed of what is advertised, more and more of the advertising effort is wasted, because a greater and greater proportion of people who see the advertisements are already familiar with the object' (1960: 40).

In contrast, for weaker firms or new entrants, advertising has an opposite 'U-shaped' set of benefits and costs. For new entrants to compete, they must advertise even more than the established players. But, lacking the reputation of established brands, their advertising will be less effective. They will see smaller returns on their advertising investments. As Braithwaite explains, since new entrants 'have to create reputation in the face of one already established, the probability is that their advertisement costs will be heavier than those of the original manufacturer' (1928: 32).

Only once they have established a market presence can new entrants hope to see the benefits of advertising enjoyed by established brands. But this is made even harder as, when new entrants attempt to advertise their way into a market, incumbent market leaders might respond by increasing their own level of advertising. For instance, Thomas (1999) shows how market leaders in the ready-to-eat cereal industry responded to new entrants by increasing their level of advertising.

So, when economists have looked at the effect of advertising on firms rather than consumers, they have discovered that advertising is neither just 'a good' nor 'a bad'. It can be both. It depends on the context. For established firms, advertising can have significant benefits. This is especially true when they can shift the market to focus on reputation – a resource they have in abundance. For new entrants, advertising could be a way to win customers. However, because they do not have an established reputation, they have to create one through their advertising. This can involve a huge investment and is not guaranteed to work.

A point to think about here is how these accounts fit into the economics of advertising and consumers discussed above. If we assume that advertising provides information that helps consumers to make better choices, it is difficult to support the idea that it would stifle innovation and concentrate market power among a small number of established firms. But, if we accept that advertising is persuasive, the economics of advertising and firms starts to make much more sense.

Advertising and markets

While some economists have attempted to explain how advertising affects consumers and others have looked at the effects of advertising on firms, others have investigated the effect of advertising on markets themselves. They have sought to explore the relationship between higher levels of advertising and sales, profit and price and the structure of markets.

Advertising and sales

There are two key questions regarding the relationship between advertising and sales. First, and most obviously, does increased advertising lead to more sales? The general answer put forward here is that advertising does have a positive effect on sales but this effect may be short-lived. Low quality products cannot win out over high quality equivalents through advertising alone. Second, economists have attempted to establish whether advertising grows the total demand in a market or simply redistributes existing demand among firms. Here, they have distinguished between 'constructive advertising' which can expand a market and 'combative advertising' which firms employ to win customers from the competition. They argue that the effects of advertising differ across industries but that, overall, much advertising is combative rather than constructive.

Advertising, profit and price

Economists have tried to prove whether advertising has an effect on the profit firms generate. Many early contributions suggested that the level of advertising is strongly related to the level of profitability in an industry. In keeping with the persuasion view, it was assumed effective advertisers would shift consumer demand so that firms could charge higher prices for their goods. However, more recent work has found that this is not universally true. In some industries advertising does allow firms to charge a higher price and produces greater profits but not in others. According to Porter, for instance, 'advertising is a more powerful influence on the rate of return for products sold through convenience outlets than for those sold through non-convenience outlets' (1974: 425).

Some recent contributions caution that, even when higher levels of advertising are linked with larger profits, it is a mistake to think one causes the other. Correlation, the famous saying goes, is not causation. It might be the case, instead, that advertising helps brands gain power over retailers. This power, rather than advertising itself, allows brands to negotiate preferential treatment with retailers that directly impact profitability.

Indeed, counter-intuitively, research suggests that in some industries heavily advertised goods command lower prices *and* higher profit margins. The reason for this is that well-known brands are a draw for consumers. In order to entice consumers into their stores, retailers will discount these brands. The hope being that these 'loss-leaders' will encourage more consumers to buy more products in the store (see Nelson *et al*, 1992). This not only increases the sales for a manufacturer and allows them to exploit economies of scale but does so without affecting the price retailers pay them.

Advertising, concentration, entry and market share

Some economists suggest that advertising persuades consumers to gravitate to well-known brands. As a result, they argue, advertising leads to more concentrated markets in which a small number of firms dominate thanks to their 'reputational monopolies'. Safe from the threat of new entrants, they can then charge higher prices and reduce their investments in innovation. So, on this view, advertising makes a market less competitive (or 'imperfect').

But this is far from certain. Influenced by the advertising as information perspective, Telser argues that rather than blocking new entrants, advertising is 'frequently a means of entry and a sign of competition' (1964: 558). Indeed, studying the US pharmaceutical industry, Scott Morton concludes 'that brand advertising is not a barrier to entry' (2000: 1103).

To establish which perspective is true, economic research has analysed data across a number of industries and contexts. But this body of research has yet to conclusively demonstrate that advertising stabilizes market shares over the long term. It does in some industries but not in others. Generally, though, it can be said that advertising tends not to stabilize market share significantly nor does it consistently lead to high levels of concentration in markets.

Bringing together these studies, we can say that economic research reveals some important relationships between advertising and market factors. However, it is wrong to think that these relationships hold for all markets and all contexts. They do not. In some markets, advertising can help to concentrate demand and improve profitability. In others, it has the opposite effect. It is essential, then, from an economic perspective, to understand what is true for a market you are interested in rather than looking for fundamental laws of the marketplace as proponents of scientific advertising like Hopkins and Reeves argued (see Chapter 3).

A welfare view

Behind each of the discussions we have looked at so far, there are two more subjective – even ethical – views of advertising and markets. One is positive. It theorizes that advertising makes markets work better for firms and consumers. That is to say, it improves social welfare. The other view says the opposite. It suggests that advertising makes markets less competitive and allows a small group of firms to win out at the expense of consumers and other firms. On this view, advertising damages social welfare.

Table 5.2 Some good and bad things about advertising according to economists

Some good things about advertising...	Some bad things about advertising...
Advertising provides direct and indirect information	Advertising creates spurious differentiation between products
Advertising allows new entrants to compete with incumbent firms	Advertising increases barriers to entry

(Continued)

Table 5.2   *(Continued)*

Some good things about advertising...	Some bad things about advertising...
Advertising decreases market concentration	Advertising allows larger firms to win customers from small firms
Advertising makes demand more elastic	Advertising makes demand inelastic
Advertising forces firms to remain competitive	Advertising adds to firm profitability at the expense of consumers
Advertising adds value to products	Advertising is a selling cost which consumers are forced to pay
Advertising makes products more affordable (eg TV shows)	Advertising is forced onto consumers
Advertising forces firms to innovate to win and keep customers	Advertising discourages innovation and new entrants into markets

As is clear from Table 5.2, the positive and negative views of advertising are both built on a number of mutually supportive propositions. But they each adopt polar opposite perspectives. The positive view says, for instance, that advertising makes it easier for consumers to switch brands, which encourages new entrants to challenge existing firms, which forces existing firms to remain competitive with their pricing and offerings. The negative view, in contrast, tells us that advertising makes markets less competitive by encouraging consumers to be loyal to brands, which makes it harder for new entrants to challenge existing firms, which allows those existing firms to exploit uncompetitive practices such as over-pricing.

Clearly only one of these perspectives can be true. But which one? It is here that we might reach the limit of economic research. While it provides powerful empirical insights concerning particular market contexts, the debate ultimately returns to one of the big questions we looked at in Chapter 2: does advertising transmit information to passive consumers or do consumers use advertising to make their lives better? Put simply, do we think that advertising is a good thing or a bad thing? As far as I can tell, this tends to influence the types of conclusions that economists draw. Pollay, for instance, argues that: 'The economists' conception that "advertising is (only) information" is surely simplistic… [To argue that] advertising is information because it selectively contains some is tantamount to claiming that war is peace because of interludes between battles' (1987: 106). However, others tell us that the idea that advertising is pure persuasion inflates the power of advertising change demand. In reality, writers like Holbrook (who we will cover later in the book) argue that advertising fails to affect demand far more often than it succeeds.

Putting it all together

In closing this chapter, then, I would suggest that it is best to appreciate both of these perspectives and to understand how they might colour the types of conclusions economists draw from their data. If you want to find evidence that advertising is persuasion – you can. Equally, if you want to find evidence that it is information – you can as well. Indeed, to date, economic research in to advertising has been unable to prove conclusively that advertising has consistent effects across different time periods or across different markets. It is useful to bear this in mind. As we will see later in the book, much of the discussion about advertising is shaped not just by what is true but by what people want to be true about advertising. Ultimately, the truth of the matter is probably that advertising is both persuasion and information. Adopting this perspective is useful, I think, because it helps us to take some of the essential things from economics and apply it to our understanding of advertising without having to stick dogmatically to one perspective.

Some other interesting sources

In his TED Talk entitled 'Can advertising save the world?' Jeff Rosenblum argues that in the modern world advertising has to provide information to consumers – because they can find it themselves through a simple web search. As a result, he argues that advertising is increasingly working to make consumers lives better and to help make markets work more efficiently. It is available here: https://youtu.be/SvbcbEizCBY

If you are interested in the limitations of economic models to describe how people actually behave, Rory Sutherland's presentation entitled 'What is Value?' is worth a watch. He promotes the idea that numbers and quantitative analysis preferred by most economists are an inappropriate way to understand value. It is available here: https://youtu.be/3CjjHsE133w. He offers a longer version of his ideas here: https://youtu.be/TPENgRDsN_Q

References and further reading

Abernethy, A M and Franke, G R (1996) The information content of advertising: A meta-analysis, *Journal of Advertising*, **25**, pp 1–17

Becker, G S and Murphy, K M (1993) A simple theory of advertising as a good or bad, *Quarterly Journal of Economics*, pp 942–64

Bloch, H (1974) Advertising and profitability: a reappraisal, *Journal of Political Economy*, **82** (2), pp 267–86

Braithwaite, D (1928) The economic effects of advertisement, *Economic Journal*, **38**, pp 16–37

Chamberlin, E (1933) *The Theory of Monopolistic Competition*, Harvard University Press, Cambridge, MA

Ghez, G R and Becker, G S (1975) *The Allocation of Time and Goods Over the Life Cycle*, National Bureau of Economic Research, Columbia University Press

Kaldor, N V (1950) The economic aspects of advertising, *Review of Economic Studies*, **18**, pp 1–27

Levitt, S D and Dubner, S J (2006) *Freakanomics*, Penguin, London

Madden, C S, Caballero, M J, and Matsukubo, S (1986) Analysis of information content in U.S. and Japanese magazine advertising, *Journal of Advertising*, **15** (3), pp 38–45

Mankiw, N G and Taylor, M P (2011) *Economics*, Hampshire: Cengage learning

Marshall, A (1919) *Industry and Trade: A study of industrial technique and business organization; and of their influences on the conditions of various classes and nations*, MacMillan and Co, London

Nelson, P (1970) Information and consumer behavior, *Journal of Political Economy*, **78**, pp 311–29

Nelson, P (1974) Advertising as information, *Journal of Political Economy*, 82, pp 729–54

Nelson, P, Siegfried, J, and Howell, J (1992) A simultaneous equations model of coffee brand pricing and advertising, *The Review of Economics and Statistics*, 74, pp 54–63

Ozga, S A (1960) Imperfect markets through lack of knowledge, *Quarterly Journal of Economics*, 74 pp 29–52

Paton, D (2002) Advertising, quality and sales, *Applied Economics*, 34 (4), pp 431–38

Paton, D and Fraser, S (2003) Does advertising increase labour supply? Time series evidence from the UK, *Applied Economics*, 35, pp 1357–1368

Pigou, A C (1924) *Economics of Welfare*, 2nd edn, MacMillan and Co, London

Porter, M E (1974) Consumer behavior, retailer power and market performance in consumer goods industries, *The Review of Economics and Statistics*, 56, pp 419–36

Resnik, A and Stern, B L (1977) An analysis of information content in television advertising, *Journal of Marketing*, 41 (1), pp 50–53

Robinson, J (1933) *Economics of Imperfect Competition*, MacMillan and Co, London

Scott Morton, F M (2000) Barriers to entry, brand advertising, and generic entry in the U.S. pharmaceutical industry, *International Journal of Industrial Organization*, 18, pp 1085–1104

Stern, B L, Krugman, D M and Resnik, A (1981) Magazine advertising: an analysis of its information content, *Journal of Advertising Research*, 21 (2), pp 39–44

Stigler, G J and Becker, G S (1977) De gustibus non est disputandum, *American Economic Review*, 67, pp 76–90

Telser, L G (1964) Advertising and competition, *Journal of Political Economy*, 72, pp 537–62

Thomas, L A (1999) Incumbent firms' response to entry: price, advertising and new product introduction, *International Journal of Industrial Organization*, 17, pp 527–55

The hierarchy   06
of effects

The psychology of advertising

Introduction

As we saw in Chapter 5, if we want to understand the effects of advertising on markets and firms we need to agree on how it affects individuals. Does it, for instance, provide us with information that helps us to make better decisions? Or does it persuade us to over-value established firms at the expense of innovative new products?

The purpose of this chapter is to expand our understanding of the effect of advertising on individual consumers by looking at psychological studies of advertising. Psychological theory is the most prominent academic discipline within advertising studies. Indeed, researchers reviewing the theories discussed in academic advertising research between 1980 and 2010 found that over half of the top 30 concepts were first developed in psychology (see Table 6.1). Put simply, it focuses on how advertising affects individual people's behaviours. But psychologists, themselves, do not necessarily agree on how this happens. To this end, throughout the history of advertising studies, researchers have argued for various models which provide us with step-by-step guides explaining what happens inside people's minds when they see advertising.

In this chapter we will review three dominant psychological approaches used in advertising studies: cognitive, social and depth psychologies. As we will see, each of these theories not only tells us something different about the effects of advertising, they all start with very different assumptions about consumers and decision making. As such, the popularity of particular models at any given time tells us as much about what people want to be true as it does about what they think is true.

Overview

The chapter proceeds as follows. First, we will review cognitive psychology. This is the dominant psychological perspective on advertising. Here we will cover two models: the information processing model and the elaboration likelihood model. We will then explore social psychology. Finally, we will turn to depth psychology. This approach was extremely popular in the 1950s and 1960s but has fallen out of favour with academic researchers. Yet many of the ideas and assumptions it developed continue to influence advertising practice. Finally, we will tie these different explanations together into an integrative psychological perspective.

OBJECTIVES

By the end of this chapter, you should be able to:

- describe the basic structure of the information processing and elaboration likelihood models;
- distinguish cognitive and social psychological explanations of advertising;
- contextualize key concepts in depth psychology; and
- synthesize the psychology of advertising through the hierarchy of effects.

Key questions to keep in mind

- Does advertising affect consumers' memories, feelings or understanding of products?
- Are consumers affected by advertising unconsciously?
- Can a single model explain the workings of all ads for all consumers no matter what the product?
- Are psychological theories of advertising compatible with each other?

Table 6.1 Top 30 theories in advertising research between 1980–2010

	Theory/framework/construct	Originating discipline
1	Dual-process models (eg ELM)	Psychology
2	Involvement	Psychology
3	Information processing models	Psychology
4	Interactivity	Communication
5	Source credibility	Psychology
6	Congruity theory	Psychology
7	Cultural dimensions	Anthropology
8	Hierarchy of effects	Advertising
9	Attitude toward advertising	Advertising
10	Brand equity	Marketing
11	Attribution theory	Psychology
12	Integrated marketing communications	Marketing
13	Classical conditioning	Psychology
14	Cognitive response model	Psychology
15	Learning theory	Psychology
16	Uses and gratifications	Communication
17	Media models	Communication
18	Schema theory	Psychology
19	Semiotics	Sociology
20	Social judgment theory	Psychology
21	Advertising effectiveness models	Advertising
22	Alienation	Sociology
23	Balance theory	Psychology
24	Distinctiveness theory	Psychology
25	Theory of double-jeopardy	Marketing
26	Means-end theory	Marketing
27	Perceived risk	Psychology
28	Persuasion knowledge model	Psychology
29	Social comparison theory	Psychology
30	Social learning theory	Psychology

(Adapted from Kim *et al*, 2014)

Cognitive psychology

Cognitive psychologists are interested in understanding how we think. They explore the workings of mental processes such as memory, perception and problem-solving. This approach has been used within advertising studies to understand how people extract product information from ads that can inform their purchases and how ads can affect people's attitudes towards brands. As we will see in this section, advertising researchers have used cognitive psychology to develop models that offer step-by-step descriptions of our engagement with ads.

Information processing model

The information process model (IPM) was the earliest application of cognitive psychology to advertising. Building on the economic perspective that focused on the importance of information, researchers sought to explain how consumers could extract information from ads and store it in their memory for use in subsequent purchase decisions (Bettman, 1979). The IPM was their answer. It is based on the assumption that behaviours are, ultimately, the result of information. If we have new information, we will make different decisions when buying a product, choosing a brand, considering who to vote for and so on. What is important, then, is to understand how information is stored, retained and acted on.

The basic structure of the information processing model can be summarized through five steps (see Figure 6.1). Let's look at each in turn:

1 *Exposure.* The IPM tells us that the most important factor that determines whether an advertisement will affect a consumer is whether or not the consumer has seen or heard it. While this might seem obvious to us now, this idea has been hugely influential. It suggests that one way to improve the impact of an ad is, simply, to increase the number of times people are exposed to it.

2 *Attention.* Just because someone is exposed to an ad, it does not mean they will be affected by it. For that to happen they must also pay some attention to it. If not, the ad will not affect them.

3 *Perception.* Once someone pays attention to an ad, they must make sense of it. In other words, they must perceive or comprehend the message of the ad correctly. If they do not perceive the message correctly, they may take the wrong information from the ad.

4 *Acceptance.* Next, they must compare this information to what they already know. It is not always the case that new information is consistent with existing ideas and it may be rejected if people think it is unbelievable based on what they know. As Scholten explains, people with 'a greater ability to support prior beliefs on the issue and to refute arguments discrepant with those beliefs' may reject advertised information (1996: 101).

5 *Retention.* If people accept the information as true and useful, they will retain it in their memory. It can then inform subsequent product choices.

Throughout this step-by-step process, information that is already stored in a consumer's memory can have an impact. In this regard, cognitive psychologists tell us that we organize what we know into mental frameworks known as 'schema'. These influence how we react to new information. Indeed, if we can position new information within an existing schema it is very likely that we will retain it. If not, we tend to forget it.

Figure 6.1   Information processing model (adapted from Engel, 1993)

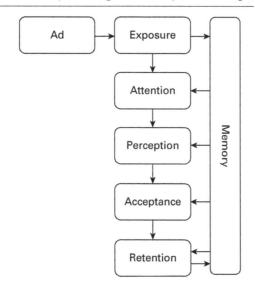

To illustrate this, consider the following passage from a famous cognitive study. Your task is simple. Try to remember as much of it as you can:

> The procedure is actually quite simple. First you arrange items into different groups. Of course one pile may be sufficient depending on how much there is do. If you need to go somewhere else due to a lack of facilities, then this is the next step; otherwise, you are pretty well set. It is important not to overdo things. That is, it is better to do too few things at once than too many. In the short run, this may not seem important but complications can easily arise. A mistake can be expensive as well. At first, the whole procedure will seem complicated. Soon, however, it will become just another facet of life. It is difficult to foresee any end to the necessity for this task in the future, but then, one can never tell. After the procedure is completed, one arranges the materials into different piles again. Eventually they will be used one more and the whole cycle will then have to be repeated. However, that is part of life. (Bransford and Johnson, 1972: 722)

Chances are you do not remember much of this. The reason for this is because you probably did not engage the correct schema to make sense of it. Once you know that it is a description of washing clothes, it should start to make sense. In fact, in a famous study in cognitive psychology, researchers found that they could vastly increase people's retention of information from this passage by telling them what it was about.

In general, the impact of the IPM on advertising practice cannot be underestimated. The focus on memory has influenced standard measures for advertising effectiveness such as 'recall' and 'recognition' tests (see Thought box 6.1). For their part, academic researchers have used the model to uncover how different forms of media, copy and art can improve the transmission of information through ads. They have found, for instance, that consumers can be distracted from engaging with ads when they are occupied with other tasks (sometimes called 'cognitive load'). They have also found that ads can interfere with each other. Consumers can be overloaded with information in environments that suffer from advertising clutter. Researchers have explored how different design features can impact on perception.

They have also looked at the effect of contextual variables (known as 'situational variables' or 'antecedent factors').

Elaboration likelihood model

Unfortunately, though, it turns out that in reality consumers rarely go through the processes in the IPM model. Indeed, as we saw in the last chapter, ads rarely include any information at all! Yet ads still affect us. In fact, research that relied on IPM has produced contradictory and strange results. In an attempt to sort out these contradictions, Petty and Cacioppo (1981) produced an influential 'dual process-ing' model to track some different ways that advertising might affect people. They called it the 'elaboration likelihood model' (or 'ELM').

The fundamental idea behind the ELM is that persuasion depends on the extent to which someone thinks (or elaborates) about a message. Someone might think about a particular ad a lot but other ads might interest them less. Surely, Petty and Cacioppo (1981) argue, this will have some effect on the ways they process the ad. In order to explain what causes different levels of engagement, they followed developments in consumer psychology and shifted the focus from the information in an ad to the attitude of the consumer to that informa-tion (Azjen and Fishbein, 1977). In other words, they acknowledged that people interpret, rather than receive information. They moved from a model based in the transmission model of communication to a more social constructionist perspective.

Thought box 6.1: Measuring recall, recognition and persuasion

The IPM tells us that good advertising increases the amount of consumers who know an ad. A popular way to test this is known as a *recall test*. Here, audience members who have been exposed to an ad asked to list the ads they have seen in a given period of time (the last day, week, month and so on). If a brand's ad is on this list, they can probe to find out what the consumer has learned about the product from the ad. Technically, then, the recall test requires participants to verbalize their learning/memory that resulted from advertising exposure. It requires them to access information in their memory and recode the information back to the interviewer. As such, in this test, effective advertising is assumed to be advertising which has been 'learned' by consumers. But emotional ads that lack a single, rational, verbal (and easily decoded) message are less likely to be recalled. As a result, another method for testing consumer learning has been put forward. It is called a *recognition test*. Here, participants are shown ads, and are asked to indicate whether they have seen it. Often, they are asked to think about the ads they have seen during a particular time period and in a particular context. They might also be shown a series of ads with pertinent information missing (such as the brand name, logo and so on) and asked to complete the missing information or identify a particular brand's ad from the selection. In recognition tests, effective ads are those that are correctly identified. It is worth noting that, according to some researchers, recognition tests are too easy. People often claim to have seen bogus ads that have been made up solely for the purpose of the research at the same level as they claim to have seen genuine ads.

In keeping with the ELM, another set of tests focuses on the extent to which consumers feel persuaded by an ad. Consumers are asked to report their brand preferences (or intent to purchase) before and after exposure to an ad. This test does not measure the effect of an ad on memory, then, but on the consumer's attitude towards a brand or product. Effective ads will lead to large swings in favour of the brand.

Based on this, the ELM traces two ways that advertising can influence consumers:

- *The central route*. The central route looks very similar to the IPM (see Figure 6.2). It describes instances where a consumer pays attention to an ad, explores it for information and evaluates that information in keeping with their current mental schema, knowledge, beliefs and attitudes. The main difference from the IPM is the focus on attitudes. According to the ELM, a consumer's existing attitudes will influence what information they extract from an ad. Celebrities, images, music or humour can all help here. If, for example, an ad features a celebrity we like, that attitude will influence our level of engagement.

Figure 6.2 The central route

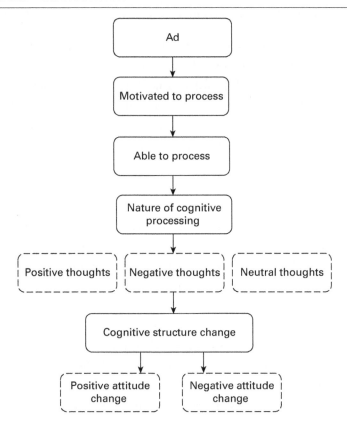

- *The peripheral route.* The second way that advertising can influence consumers according to the ELM is through the peripheral route (see Figure 6.3). Here, the message is not investigated for information and the viewer pays a small amount of attention to it. They might pick out some basic cues but not enough to inform a fully involved choice. For example, MacInnis and Jaoworski offer this example of the peripheral route for a Nike ad: 'consumers involved in a conversation while watching TV may notice that the TV screen contains something gray, but may be unable to determine whether this feature belongs to an identifiable cue such as a basketball shoe or a T-shirt, or even whether it is part of an advertisement' (1989: 6). These cues have an important effect, though. Over time, they might impact someone's motivation and ability to elaborate more fully on the ad. This is known as a peripheral attitude shift. The result of a peripheral attitude shift may be that some follows the central route when they see the ad at a later point.

The ELM tells us that two factors influence which route a message will follow (see Figure 6.4). First, a consumer needs to have the *ability* to process the ad. If, for example, you do not speak the same language as an advertisements you are literally unable to elaborate on it through the central route. Similarly, if you do not have sufficient product or brand knowledge some of the information in an ad might not make sense to you. Likewise, if you do not have much time or are distracted by another task you may only be able to absorb a few features of an ad. You might be able to pick out peripheral cues, such as colours, the attractiveness of models and so on but not much more. Second, a consumer needs to have the *motivation* to engage with the ad. Motivation variables that have been uncovered include involvement with the product or brand and individual differences such as the 'need for cognition' – a concept that tells us that some people enjoy thinking more than others.

One significant benefit of the ELM in comparison to the IPM is that it helps to explain why people do not always pay a great deal of attention to ads. This is, of course, actually the most common way we engage with ads. In this regard, researchers have used the ELM to test the effects of message, source, receiver and channel variables on a consumer's attitude. Petty *et al* (1983), for example,

Figure 6.3   The peripheral route

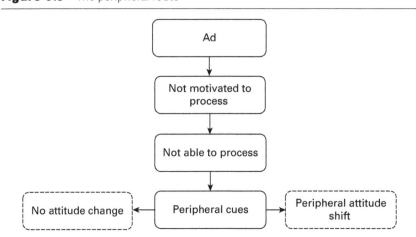

Figure 6.4 The full elaboration likelihood model

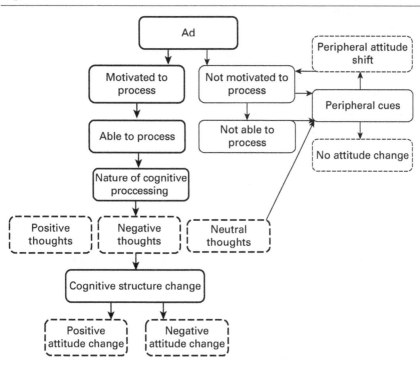

revealed that consumers who are highly involved with a product or brand are more likely to be influenced by a persuasive message. In contrast, consumers with a low involvement in the product or brand were more likely to be influenced by the source of the message – preferring celebrity endorsements over real-life endorsements (see Thought box 6.2).

Social psychology

Cognitive psychology is not the only psychological theory that has been used to explain how advertising works. Although alternative perspectives are less popular within advertising research, it is worth considering them to understand some of the limits with the cognitive approach. Within social psychology, in particular, it is argued that we do not act exclusively on the basis of information stored in our own internal memory banks but also in accordance with the social setting we find ourselves in.

Indeed, social psychology is based on the idea that much more of our behaviour is influenced by our desires to fit in with those around us than we usually admit. It emerged as a research discipline as academics sought to explain the atrocities of the Second World War. Researchers needed to explain how supposedly rational individuals working within large bureaucracies could be convinced to commit horrific acts on other human beings. Social psychologists came to realize that such acts can only be explained if we understand how people are influenced and controlled by others.

Thought box 6.2: Factors that affect the success of advertising in ELM

Message variables include the nature of the argument and the framing of information in an ad. Differences have been found in the outcomes of two-sided and one-sided arguments in ads (Hastak and Park, 1990) and between ads that provide information and those that offer story-based testimonials (Braverman, 2008). Metzler *et al* (2000), for example, study the impact of message variables on HIV social marketing. They found that teenagers were more likely to be persuaded by strong messages with striking images than they were by weaker messages.

Source variables include the credibility of the perceived sender of message. In advertising this can be the brand but it might also be a spokesperson in the ad itself. Sources with a perceived high level of trustworthiness have even been shown to be more important than the message quality. That is to say, viewers believe a highly trusted source more irrelevant than what they are saying. Researchers have found that sources of 'suspect trustworthiness' are recalled quicker by viewers than those with a high level of trust. This may represent a case in which a message is processed through the central route but rejected as unconvincing.

Receiver variables focus on difference between the people exposed to advertising. They include the concept of involvement developed by consumer researchers. Schumann, Petty and Clemons (1990), for example, found that consumers with a low involvement in the product focused on cosmetic changes in an ads appearance across a campaign while highly involved consumers would notice substantive variations in the arguments of different ads. Receiver variables also cover pre-existing attitudes and individual difference. Here, studies show that individuals with a high 'need for cognition' hold attitudes that are more resistant to change than individuals with a low need for cognition (Haugtvedt and Petty, 1992).

Channel variables cover features of the advertising media which affect how people receive ads. Different media allow different types of message and demand different levels of attention on the part of the audience. In this regard, a number of studies have demonstrated that the effectiveness of internet advertising is moderated by the distractions of browsing online.

For example, in the Asch Conformity Experiments, we see how easy it is to get people to agree with something they know is wrong. In the experiment, first conducted by Solomon Asch in 1951, a group is shown a series of lines. Two of the lines are the same length. All the individuals in the group have to do is say which two lines are the same. However, the experiment is set up so that only one person in a group is genuinely giving their answer. The others have been prepared to follow a script. They quickly start to give the wrong answer. This has a notable effect on the one person who is genuinely giving an answer. Typically around three-quarters give at least one incorrect answer that follows the wrong answers given by the rest of the group. The reason for this is that people change their answers so they do not have to feel the embarrassment of standing out.

Social proof and calls to action

Moving beyond an interest in the effects of authority, social psychologists have also come to explore the various mechanisms through which people figure out the appropriate action for a given social setting and how they moderate their behaviour to fit in. We do this, according to social psychologists, by looking for 'social proof' about what counts as appropriate behaviour. Put simply, we look to others to tell us what is 'normal' and then moderate our behaviour to fit in – a process called 'normalization'.

An everyday example of social proof influencing people is canned laughter on television shows. Researchers have shown that when a television show includes a laughter track the audience is more likely to laugh at the show and more likely to rate the jokes as funny (Provine, 2000). The canned laughter demonstrates the correct (or normal) response to the joke. In fact, even if we are sat at home alone watching a show, canned laughter provides us with evidence of what we should be finding funny and, as such, makes us more likely to find it funny.

Behind the notion of social proof lies a different model of learning from that which informs models such as the IPM and ELM. According to social psychologists, learning is not simply a process in which individuals store information in their memory. Instead, it is a process of making sense of an uncertain world. It involves guesswork, theories, heuristics and other people. Learning, put simply, is not something we do alone. It is social learning.

In a pivotal study here Bandura *et al* (1961) showed that learning occurs when we observe what happens to others around us – known as 'observational learning' or 'vicarious learning'. In their study, they asked groups of preschool children to watch adults playing with a toy. One group saw adults playing aggressively with the toy. Another saw the adults playing peacefully with the toy. Later, the children were allowed to play with the toy themselves. Even though the children were given no explicit information about how to behave, the children who saw adults acting aggressively also acted more aggressively. The children who saw adults playing peacefully also played more peacefully. The results of this study illustrate that people learn how to behave by watching what others do. Indeed, this might be why people are more willing to break speed limits when driving if others are also breaking the speed limit. We know that there is a punishment but we think it is okay because everyone else is doing it.

The concept of social proof, then, tells us that people will do whatever seems normal for their social setting and that they will figure this out by looking at what others are doing. Importantly, for advertising researchers, it is not only what other people in our social setting are physically doing that affects us. Later, Bandura and colleagues (1963) repeated the experiment using videos. They found that children would imitate aggressive behaviour irrelevant of whether they had been exposed to a real-life or filmed illustration. Advertisements can, in this sense, provide a form of peer pressure. Media representations of what we should be doing can be equally as effective as any other form of social proof. Cialdini explains:

> Television executives are hardly alone in their use of social evidence for profit. Our tendency to assume that an action is more correct if others are doing it is exploited in a variety of settings. Bartenders often salt their tip jars with a few dollar bills at the beginning of an evening to simulate tips left by prior customers... Advertisers love to inform us when a product is the 'fastest-growing' or 'largest-selling' because they don't have to convince us directly that the product is good; they only say that many other think so, which seems proof enough. (2009: 99–100)

In addition to providing us with social proof that influences our behaviour, ads also motivate us to act through a 'call to action'. Social psychological research suggests that the idea of missing out on something that others have is a powerful motivation for everyone. The sale, the free gift, the special offer all not only indicate what others are doing but suggest we might miss out if we do not act. For example, when you visit the supermarket you might be tempted by an impulse purchase for a product you did not want because you do not want to miss out on a bargain. Consumer researchers have found that such calls to action, added with social proof, can be extremely powerful. So much so that crowds of consumers can run out of control in stores as in the case of 'Black Friday' sales in which there are stampedes, fights and even killings.

So, in contrast to the cognitive models we discussed earlier, social psychologists argue that advertising is effective when it provides social proof about what we should do and motivates us to act. As such, social psychology encourages us to explain how advertising works by contextualizing advertising in a given social setting. This is a crucial contrast with cognitive psychology, which typically focuses on the ways that advertising works on individual consumers.

Depth psychology

The final psychological theory of advertising we will consider is depth psychology. It is based on a perspective on consumers known as 'motivation research'. It tells us that people do not consume things because of information or attitudes but because of inbuilt instinctual drives and desires that are channelled onto particular objects, products and brands. According to this perspective, we must understand the reasons why people value particular products and brands and design ads which help to people channel their desires effectively on those products and brands.

The most influential proponent of depth psychology was Ernest Dichter. He argued that consumers are incredibly complicated and that it is impossible to model how they relate to products through simple step-by-step processes like the IPM and ELM. Consumers, he said, do not really know why they do the things they do. They do not know their own motivations. These can only be uncovered through effective research. As such, Dichter went out and spoke to consumers. He watched them, observed them and listened to them.

Dichter drew on the psychological theory of psychoanalysis. This theory, developed by Sigmund Freud, is based on the idea that the mind is made up of three interrelating parts. The *id* is like the motor of the mind. It is the home of our instincts and desires. Over time, as we grow up, we add an *ego* to manage the relationship between the *id* and the external world. We do this when we discover that the things our *id* desires can get us into trouble with other people. Freud suggests we think of the *id* as a horse and the *ego* as a rider. The *ego* has less power but is able to channel the passions of the *id*. However, like the horse, the *id* cannot be completely tamed. It remains a mystery to us. Later, we develop a third component, the *super-ego*, to manage the *ego*. It is the *super-ego* that makes us critical of ourselves. The relationship between the regions of the mind are shown in Figure 6.5.

Figure 6.5 Freud's model of the mind

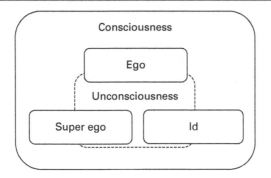

Symbolism

According to Freud, when you ask someone why they do something, their *ego* will tell you what it thinks you want to hear or what their *super-ego* lets them say. It will not tell you the truth. In fact, it probably does not know the truth.

But Freud believed that what we say and how we act reveal the motivations and desires of our *id* even if we were unwilling to admit to them. Freud had argued, for instance, that the images we see in our dreams, which might appear nonsensical to us in waking life, have deep symbolic meaning for our unconscious. When we sleep, he said, our *ego* shuts down and our *id* is allowed to run free.

Thought box 6.3: Making the car a mistress

A famous example of depth psychology is Dichter's work with Chrysler to assist their struggling Plymouth brand of cars.

To understand what motivated car buyers, Dichter spent time in car dealerships watching how buyers made decisions and interviewed hundreds of consumers. He noticed two things. First, when a family went shopping for a new car, the wife was far more important in the decision-making process than was previously thought. Thus he recommended that Chrysler begin promoting the Plymouth in women's magazines. Second, he noticed that a certain kind of man would engage in a standard pattern of behaviour. Middle-aged, married men would typically gravitate to the more racy sports cars in a showroom before turning their attention to the more sedate and practical cars.

Dichter's interpretation of this was that the sports car represented a dream of escape from domestic life for the man. It represented freedom – bear in mind his study was conducted in the United States in the 1950s, a time of 'organizational men' in 'grey flannel suits'. Indeed, Dichter went as far as to equate the sports cars with mistresses and the practical cars with marriage. Dichter observed that these married men had no intention of leaving their wives and, if asked, would deny every considering the thought. This only confirmed that the dream, rather than reality, of escape was a powerful motivating idea of 'tremendous symbolic significance' (Horowitz, 2011: 47). Convertible cars allowed them to act out their fantasy of escape without having to go through with it.

The idea that cars represented mistresses might seem far-fetched but the consequences of Dichter's studies continue to be seen in car ads today. Pre-Dichter car ads competed to offer more features, faster speeds and bigger engines. They provided information hoping to produce a favourable attitude among consumers. Post-Dichter car ads such as Jaguar's 'Desire' campaign focused on where you could go. Cars are now presented as 'objects of desire'. Consuming them is a form of escape. Don't believe me, go and watch a car ad. Chances are it'll show an attractive man or woman driving on their own along an open road. Looks like they are happily escaping to me!

Analysing these images, Freud found that the things people dreamed about actually made sense in terms of their life histories. Indeed, he found he could treat his patients' physical and psychological illnesses by unpicking the symbolic images in their dreams and presenting their motivations to them. Adopting this idea, Dichter believed that advertising could use people's chains of symbolic connections to breathe life into products and services. Advertisers, he argued could speak to consumers' unconscious motivations by using symbolic images that made sense to our ids (see Thought box 6.3).

For example, Samuel (2010) reports on a study by the advertising agency McCann-Erickson concerning the use of insecticides. They found that female users 'were convinced that roach killers which came in little plastic trays worked better and were less messy than sprays, even though they had never tried them' (2010: 152). But they couldn't figure out why the women felt this way. Eventually, they asked them to draw pictures and write stories to try to reveal their unconscious desires. Interestingly, they all drew male cockroaches and wrote stories about demanding men. The roaches, then, 'were convenient surrogates for men who had treated these women badly... "Killing the roaches with a big spray and watch them squirm and die allowed the women to express her hostility toward men and have greater control over the roaches," explained Paula Drillman, McCann-Erickson's director of strategic planning' (Samuel, 2010: 153).

The first step in this process, then, involves exploring the potential motivations at work for a specific group of consumers regarding a specific product type. Here, Dichter used standard psychoanalytic tests such as free association, sentence completion and projection tests and anthropological observations to piece together an account of what motivated particular consumers in relation to a brand or product. But, as depth psychology suggests that consumers will find their own motivations unbelievable and the chains of symbolic connections silly (more accurately, their conscious minds will), Dichter knew people would find his conclusions ridiculous. Consequently, he supported his interpretations with extensive market research. In fact, Dichter was an early adopter of large-scale survey and experimental methods for marketing. Summarizing his approach, Karmasin tells us:

> The essential factor in all of Dichter's research conclusions was that the non-functional values... were the defining factors that drove consumers' decision making. ... He thus advised his clients to build motivational appeals that fueled the flames of desire not so much through exciting words and pictures but through psychological excitement engendered by the promise of dreams coming true. (2011: 115–19)

From a depth psychology perspective, then, advertising works when it creates meaningful objects of desire. One key idea in depth psychology is that our desires need us to invest them in some objects in order to be satisfied. If we do not do this, those desires build up and search for some form of satisfaction – often leading us to do things we might not want to do. Advertising, then, simply helps to channel consumers' desires in ways that, according to Dichter, can benefit consumers, advertisers, the economy and society.

Unconscious, non-conscious and low-involvement models

Curiously, in the 1950s when Dichter was at his most influential, a strand of depth psychology was developed within cognitive psychology: the non-conscious processing of information. Freud's psychoanalysis suggests that our brains operate through conscious mental processes and unconscious mental processes. Each system influences what we do and what we think. But the relationships between them are extremely complex. In some cases, they might even operate independently such as when we dream. Importantly, the idea of an unconscious, though, means that consumers do not know themselves. There is something that they are unaware of.

During the 1950s, marketers started to imagine a world in which they could communicate with consumers unconsciously – that is to say, without the consumers being aware of the marketing. Psychologists had long argued that our perceptual apparatus, in particular our eyes, have notable physical limitations which produce curious psychological effects. For example, psychologists had found that people could be exposed to short visual messages without realizing it. Put simply, they could be exposed to a message subliminally – or below their conscious awareness. Yet, these messages could still have an effect on them.

The idea that advertisers could expose consumers to ads without the consumers knowing it, and being annoyed by them, seemed too good to be true. This was, in fact, put forward as a perfect solution to the growing problem of advertising clutter (Aclund, 2012). Dichter himself was happy to go along with this idea while it looked like there was money to be made, but he never proclaimed to be able to influence consumers unconsciously only to understand their unconscious motivations (see Packard, 1957/1981). Others, though, did explore this idea more seriously.

In a famous case, a US market researcher named James Vicary, introduced to in Chapter 2, reported the results of a study on the effect of subliminal advertising to the press and, in the process, sparked an international debate about the ethics of advertising to consumers without their being aware of it. Vicary designed an experiment to see if advertising messages could be transmitted subliminally and still influence people's behaviour. He thought he could make 'a visible commercial pint-size, even below a whisper, lighter than a feather' (1957).

He placed two extremely short messages in a movie – one reading 'Eat Popcorn' and the other 'Drink Coke'. The messages were imposed over the film every five seconds and lasted 1/3000th of a second – short enough for no one to consciously see them but potentially long enough for them to be processed subliminally.

He arranged for the movie to be shown during a six-week period in a cinema in Fort Lee, New Jersey. It was seen by some 45,699 movie-goers (Rogers, 1992). Vicary claimed that those who saw the movie bought significantly more products. He said he increased the sale of confectionaries at the cinema by nearly 60 per cent!

Before Vicary knew it, the idea of subliminal advertising caught the public imagination. But quickly the initial enthusiasm among marketers evaporated as consumers began to fret about the power of marketers to manipulate them unconsciously. Science fiction writers reflected these concerns in stories such as J G Ballard's 'Subliminal Man', in which characters find themselves buying more and more products they do not need thanks to subliminal influences. As Vicary came under increasing scrutiny, he went missing. The results of his study were never published officially.

However, the effect of this scandal and the subsequent public outcry against subliminal advertising led academic advertising researchers to largely abandon depth psychology, although the idea that ads create powerful association between products and brands and consumer's desires and instincts remains accepted as a universal truth by many practitioners. Bill Bernbach, for example, stated late in his life that consumers are driven by powerful inbuilt instincts and tend to rationalize their behaviours after the fact.

More recently, though, thanks to dual processing models like the ELM, which tell us that advertising can have effects below conscious thought, this topic is again attracting the interest of academic researchers – although few of them are brave enough to talk explicitly about subliminal influences now that term has entered popular consciousness to mean manipulation. Rather, academics – such as Heath (2012) and Bargh (2002) – have attempted to explain the 'non-conscious' or 'subconscious' influence of ads. Indeed, there has been a resurgence of interest in Freud's ideas with marketing theory (Cluley and Desmond, 2015).

Divided or united?

It is tempting to consider each of these models in competition with one another. Indeed, for a long time that is exactly how marketing theorists have treated them. Depth psychology has, in particular, been an unwelcome guest in academic discussions since the subliminal advertising scare of the 1950s. Yet, there are some important similarities among these psychological theories of advertising.

What unites all of them is the belief that the effects of advertising happen inside the consumer's mind (as Thought box 6.4 shows, not everyone agrees with this). As such, rather than measure the success of an ad purely through sales, all of these perspectives posit that 'advertising can satisfy its ultimate objective of affecting demand only by establishing a hierarchy of intermediate effects in its audience' (Scholten, 1996: 97). Where each perspective differs is in how ie sketches out these intermediate effects.

In a sense, this is nothing new. In 1961 two marketing theorists suggested that we think about consumer behaviours through a 'hierarchy of effects' (Lavige and Steiner, 1961). Advertising, they argued, does not necessarily lead to changes in behaviour in the short term but may contribute to changes in the long term in complex ways that depend on the consumer, the context and the choice. Sometimes, they explained, people do make decisions that seem to follow an IPM perspective. They seek information, evaluate it and make an informed purchase. In other cases, people go on their feelings and later rationalize their decisions. In other cases still, people act almost without thinking and rationalize their decisions after. In other cases, people mix and match the rational, emotional and motivational.

They may start with a motivation that leads to an emotion that they later rationalize. Or they may start with a rational problem but become emotionally involved with a brand.

Advertising can influence people at each of these levels. It involves three functions:

- There is a *cognitive* component that deals with intellectual ideas and rational states.

- There is an *affective* component that deals with the emotional of feeling states.

- There is also a *motivational* component that encourages actions.

So, in much the same way as we have seen that contemporary advertising practitioners need the ability to switch between scientific advertising theory and creative advertising theory as their theory-in-use, it may be more useful to think of each of these psychological perspectives as a complementary theory that helps with particular problems. If a product tends to be evaluated rationally, focusing on transmitting information may be the best approach. However, in a competitive market where products are largely identical, depth psychology might help to differentiate what products mean to consumers. It is worth remembering, though, that despite this seeming consensus, not everyone agrees with the psychology of advertising (see Thought box 6.4).

Thought box 6.4: It's what's outside the blackbox that counts

Ehrenberg (1974) argues that when you look at actual consumer behaviours, it is hard to agree with any psychological theories. Unlike cognitive and social psychologists, who started with abstract models and tested them through their empirical work, Ehrenberg analysed actual buying behaviour and found that consumers rarely switch products or brands. He found that the most important variables influencing what someone buys is not advertising, information, attitudes, symbolism or emotions but what they bought before.

For Ehrenberg, when people trial new products it is, essentially, a random process. They are tempted at a specific moment in the store, the store does not have their usual product, someone has made a recommendation and so on. Almost never does someone explicitly plan a decision based on information contained in ads as the IPM suggests and it is highly improbable that people form attitudes about products prior to trying them as the ELM proposes. He argues that all advertising can do is make consumers aware of a brand. Whether a consumer chooses to try the brand, Ehrenberg argues, is up to them.

The primary effect of advertising is, in other words, awareness. Other than this, ads can promote offers that might stimulate a trail such as a 'buy-one-get-one-free' sale. Here, the ad essentially makes consumers aware of an offer, it does not persuade them to do anything. The second effect of advertising is, then, to stimulate a trial. Finally, ads can also have the effect of reinforcing brand awareness for existing customers and stopping them from being tempted to switch to a substitute product or brand. Thus, Ehrenberg put forward what is known as the ATR model of advertising effects (which stands for awareness, trial and reinforcement).

Summary

In this chapter we have reviewed three prominent psychological approaches that have been used in advertising research. We have explored cognitive psychology through the IPM and ELM. We have explored how advertising can normalize behaviours and provide calls to action using social psychological theory. Finally, we have seen how advertising can help to make products meaningful to consumers by using symbolic imagery that links products to consumers' drives and emotions.

Although these perspectives are often treated as competing expla- nations for the effect of ads on us as individuals, I think it is wise to integrate them through some sort of hierarchy of effects. This helps us, for example, to explain how advertising works when it delivers information that is cognitively processed by a consumer and used to inform a later decision. But it also helps us to understand how firms can persuade consumers to value brands beyond the specific features of a product by adding symbolic values through their advertisements.

Put simply, I would say that it is essential to understand each of these perspectives and to learn when it is appropriate to use one as a theory in use and when it is appropriate to use another.

Some other interesting sources

If you are interested in social psychology, there are some very good illustrations and documentaries available concerning the classic Stanford Prison Experiment (https://youtu.be/L_LKzEqIPto), Asch Experiment (https://youtu.be/NyDDyT1IDhA) and Milgram Experiment (https://youtu.be/eTX42IVDwA4)

There is an interesting Frontline documentary about the continuing influence of depth psychology and motivation research available through PBS called 'The Persuaders' (see www.pbs.org/wgbh/pages/frontline/shows/persuaders/)

A prominent contemporary motivation researcher is Martin Lindstrom. He has a series of books, interviews and presentations explaining his approach (see https://youtu.be/fAAihnJEbDE and https://youtu.be/pnxqMZyoDSw) He blends neuroscience, social psychology and depth psychology.

References and further reading

Aclund, C R (2012) *Swift Viewing: The popular life of subliminal influence*, Duke University Press, New York

Ajzen, I and Fishbein, M (1977) Attitude behaviour relations: a theoretical analysis and review of empirical research, *Psychological Bulletin*, **84**, pp 888–918

Bandura, A, Ross, D and Ross, S A (1961) Transmission of aggression through the imitation of aggressive models, *Journal of Abnormal and Social Psychology*, **63** (3), pp 575–82

Bandura, A, Ross, D and Ross, S A (1963) Imitation of film-mediated aggressive models, *Journal of Abnormal and Social Psychology*, **66** (1), pp 3–11

Bargh, J A (2002) Losing consciousness: automatic influences on consumer judgment, behavior, and motivation, *Journal of Consumer Research*, **29** (2), pp 280–85

Braverman, J (2008) Testimonials versus informational persuasive messages: the moderating effect of delivery mode and personal involvement, *Communication Research*, **35**, pp 666–94

Bettman, J R (1979) *An Information Processing Theory of Consumer Choice*, Addison Wesley Publishing Company, Reading, MA

Cialdini, R B (2009) *Influence: Science and practice*, Pearson, London

Cluley, R and Desmond, J (2015) Why psychoanalysis now?, *Marketing Theory*, **15** (1), pp 3–8

Cluley, R and Dunne, S (2012) From commodity fetishism to commodity narcissism, *Marketing Theory*, **12** (3), pp 251–65

Gleich, J (2011) *The Information: A history, a theory, a flood*, Fourth Estate, London

Hastak, M and Park, J (1990) Mediators of Message Sidedness Effects on Cognitive Structure for Involved and Uninvolved Audiences, in M E Goldberg, G Gorn and R W Pollay (eds) *Advances in Consumer Research*, **17**, pp 329–36

Haugtvedt, C P and Petty, R E (1992) Personality and persuasion: need for cognition moderates the persistence and resistance of attitude changes, *Journal of Personal and Social Psychology*, **63**, pp 308–319

Heath, R (2012) *Seducing the Subconscious: The psychology of emotional influence in advertising*, Wiley-Blackwell, London

Heath, R and Feldwick, P (1999) Fifty years using the wrong model of advertising, *International Journal of Market Research*, **50** (1), pp 29–59

Henderson, C (1957) A blessing or a bane? TV ads you'd see without knowing it, *Wall Street Journal*, **13** (September)

Horowitz, D (2011) From Vienna to the United States and back: Ernest Dichter and American consumer culture, in *Ernest Dichter and Motivation Research: New perspectives on the making of post-war consumer culture*, eds S Schwartzkopf and R Gries, Palgrave, London

Karmasin, H (2011) Ernest Dichter's Studies on Automobile Marketing, in *Ernest Dichter and Motivation Research: New perspectives on the making of post-war consumer culture*, eds S Schwartzkopf and R Gries, Palgrave, London

Key, W B (1974) *Subliminal Seduction: Ad media's manipulation of a not so innocent America*, Signet, New York

MacInnis, D J and Jaworski, B J (1989) Information processing from advertisements: toward an integrative framework, *Journal of Marketing*, **53** (4), pp 1–23

Metzler, A E, Weiskotten, D and Morgen, K J (2000) Adolescent HIV prevention: an application of the elaboration likelihood model, *Annual Conference of the American Psychological Association*, pp 3–26

Packard, V (1957/1981) *The Hidden Persuaders*, Penguin, London

Petty, R E and Cacioppo, J T (1981) Issue involvement as a moderator of the effects on attitude of advertising content and context, in *Advances in Consumer Research*, ed Kent B Monroe (8) p 204, Association for Consumer Research, Ann Abor, MI

Petty, R E, Cacioppo, J T and Schumann, D (1983) Central and peripheral routes to advertising effectiveness: The moderating role of involvement, *Journal of Consumer Research*, (10) 135–46

Provine, R R (2000) The science of laughter, *Psychology Today*, 33 (6), pp 58–62

Rogers, S (1992) How a publicity blitz created the myth of subliminal advertising, *Public Relations Quarterly*

Samuel, Lawrence R (2010) *Freud on Madison Avenue: Motivation research and subliminal advertising in America*, University of Pennsylvania Press, Oxford

Schumann, D W, Petty, R E and Clemons, D S (1990) Predicting the effectiveness of different strategies of advertising variation: a test of repetition-variation hypotheses, *Journal of Consumer Research*, 17, pp 192–2002

Scholten, M (1996) Lost and found: The information-processing model of advertising effectiveness, *Journal of Business Research*, 37, pp 97–104

Vicary, J (1957) 'Invisible' ads tested, *Printers' Ink*, 20, p 44

The society   07
of the spectacle
The sociology of advertising

Introduction

In the last chapter we explored how advertising affects consumer
decision making. Harms and Kellner (1997) describe this as an
'administrative' approach to studying advertising because it aims to
help marketing managers control or administrate the market. There
is, though, another area of advertising studies that focuses on the
wider social effects of advertising. Harms and Kellner describe this
body of work as 'critical' advertising studies.

It is inspired by a tradition in social science known as 'critical
theory'. Critical theory tells us that all societies have to address problems that threaten their long-term survival. Within consumer societies
such issues include the high levels of social inequality and environmental destruction that are caused by contemporary consumption.
How, critical theorists ask, can a society continue without addressing
these issues? Their answer is that there is a difference between the
real state of affairs and what we believe to be true. Critical theorists
investigate where this difference comes from, how it continues and
what it does. Here, they have turned their attention to advertising.

Bridging administrative research and critical advertising studies
is another area of advertising studies that explores how advertising remains a socially acceptable business practice. This might seem
obvious but it is worth remembering that advertising has not always
been socially acceptable (see Chapter 1). Indeed, to this day most
societies specify particular products, media and techniques that
advertisers cannot engage with. It is, then, essential to understand the

legal, political and regulatory structures necessary to allow advertising to operate. Through this, we will appreciate the social functions of advertising and how it stays socially acceptable.

Overview

The chapter proceeds as follows. First, will we explore the social theory of advertising. Within this body of work, research suggests that advertising is the 'oil' that helps society run smoothly. Building on this, we will introduce social critiques of advertising inspired by Marxist theory. Second, we will address the sociology of advertising. This area of research questions whether advertising helps to bring societies together or pulls them apart. The chapter will close by discussing how advertising industries have used critical perspectives to design their own systems of regulation. The chapter pays particular attention to the system of regulation in the United Kingdom as this is regularly held up an as example of best practice in academic research.

OBJECTIVES

By the end of this chapter, you should be able to:

- articulate potential social effects of advertising;
- describe the relationship between advertising and social class; and
- explain how advertising remains socially 'acceptable'.

Key questions to keep in mind

- Does advertising have social effects?
- Does advertising treat different social groups differently?
- Should advertisers be able to regulate themselves?

Social theory and advertising

Social theorists attempt to explain how it is that human beings can live and work together. Sometimes, their theories are based on empirical research. They have, for example, explored the importance of informal rules in everyday behaviour by observing actual social interactions (see Becker, 1963). But social theorists also look at the bigger picture. Here, they work on the basis of pure speculation to characterize the workings and peculiarities of a particular society. In so doing, social theorists have identified various mechanisms that they believe help some social groups to attain positions of power over others. Early on in this work, they considered whether advertising is one such mechanism.

The debate here focuses on whether advertising changes society or whether it simply reflects things that are happening already. On one side, we have theorists who think according to a theory of order. They tell us that advertising simply reflects society (see 'Sociology of order' in Figure 7.1). As we will see, this broadly maps on to the view that advertising transmits information to consumers to help them make better choices. Set against them, we have theorists of change. They tell us that advertising can change society (see 'Sociology of change' in Figure 7.1). This perspective supports the social constructionist idea that advertising can persuade consumers to value appearances and reputation over price and product quality. More recently, though, social theorists have put forward the idea of structuration. This tells us that society can shape advertising and advertising can change society (see 'Sociology of structuration' in Figure 7.1).

Without passing judgement on the big theoretical questions between these perspectives, let us start our journey through social theory by looking at one of the earliest contributions to the social theory of advertising. It is based on the sociology of change. Here, some argued that advertising was a necessary solution to the problems that emerged at the beginnings of consumer culture and has had a profound effect on society ever since. But it was a solution that served particular interests at the expense of others.

Figure 7.1   Basic models of social interactions

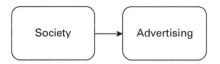

Sociology of order: society shapes advertising

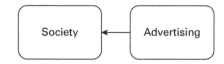

Sociology of change: advertising shapes society

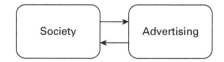

*Sociology of structuration: advertising is shaped by
and shapes society*

The oils that keeps society moving: the political economy of advertising

Modern advertising emerged at a particular point in history and in a particular cultural context. It emerged along with the industrialization of economies in North America and Europe. What was it about these situation that led to the development of advertising?

One of the biggest challenges facing producers during the industrial revolution was managing demand. It turned out that it was easy enough to produce things. It was harder to produce consumers who wanted them. As Williams puts it:

> The critical problem posed by the factory of advanced machines was that of the organisation of the market. The modern factory requires not only smooth and steady distributive channels... but also definite indications of demand without which the expensive processes of capitalisation and equipment would be too great a risk. (1960: 27)

Indeed, early industrialists needed to convince consumers to purchase an entirely new type of object: the mass-produced commodity. Up to the industrial revolutions in North America and Europe people were used to consuming goods they had either made themselves or goods made by people in their local communities. They expected things to be slightly different, imperfect and handmade. When they saw the standardized products churned out by the first factories, they considered them crude, ugly and impersonal. So, to make industrialization work, consumers had to be educated to value these new products (see Thought box 7.1).

Thought box 7.1: Modern advertising in Britain

Williams (1980) provides a political economic analysis of the development of advertising in Britain. For much of the early industrial period, he tells us, advertising was only used on a small range of products. For most goods, advertising was unnecessary because consumers had very limited choices. Where new factory-made goods were in competition with locally produced items they had just one real advantage: they were cheap. As a result, advertising was largely limited to in-store price displays.

Things changed after an economic depression that hit Britain between 1875 and 1890. Williams (1980) explains that after this depression prices dropped across the economy for all goods – including low-priced mass-produced ones. As industries reorganized to protect themselves against future fluctuations, they realized they needed to be able to influence the market and not rely on the 'invisible hand'. In short, there was 'a growing desire, by different methods, to organize and where possible control the market. Among the means of achieving the latter purposes, advertising on a new scale, and applied to an increasing range of products, took an important place.' The Depression, according to Williams, taught producers a lesson. They needed modern advertising to survive.

Different societies offered their own solutions to this problem. At one extreme, some tried to organize demand centrally. For example, in post-Revolutionary France, it was suggested that the best way to organize production and consumption was for a bureaucrat to record all the things producers could make and to invite consumers to describe their needs such that the bureaucrat could match them to a producer's offerings (Fletcher, 2008). Many communist societies organized demand centrally in a similar way.

In consumer capitalist societies, though, people wanted to be free to choose what they could consume. Advertising proved to be an effective technique in these societies as it allowed producers to shape demand without limiting consumers' freedom of choice. As the economist J K Galbraith (1958) puts it, advertising helped to keep these societies 'suitably consumptive'.

This gets us to the heart of the social theory of advertising. Many social theorists argue that modern advertising fundamentally works in favour of advertisers not consumers. In fact, they argue that this is the whole point. Williams (1980) describes advertising as a 'magic system' to get at this. It is advanced administrative practice, drawing on the latest scientific methods and technologies. Yet the effects of advertising on consumers are totally different. As Williams puts it: 'If we were sensibly materialist, in that part of our living in which we use things, we should find most advertising to be of an insane irrelevance.' Rather than inform users about products, advertising relies on emotional, symbolic and psychological appeals that have nothing to do with the objects we consume. Through this, advertising makes economic value out of thin air. It is an administrative science that produces magic.

The problem for researchers like Williams (and Klein, 2000; Jhally, 1991; Ewen, 1976 to name a few) is that this means we live in a society in which fantasy is more important than reality. They all argue that advertising is not just concerned with selling individual products but allowing producers to control demand. Jhally, for instance, tells us that 'Advertising is the main weapon that manufactures use in their attempt to "produce" an adequate consuming market for their products. To this end, advertising works to create false needs in people (false because they are the needs of manufacturers rather than consumers)' (1991: 3).

One of the most famous illustrations here is Listerine mouthwash. The advertising historian James Twitchell (2000) summarizes this case nicely. Listerine, he tells us, did not make their money by producing mouthwash. They did it by making bad breath. They did this through a series of ads in which they presented people failing in love and life because of their bad breath. 'Always the bridesmaid, never the bride', one ad read. 'Halitosis makes you unpopular', another. Of course, Listerine did not literally create bad breath. But they made it into a problem that needed fixing rather than a nasty smell (and they made their product the solution to the problem). The ads were certainly effective. After the campaign, Listerine's revenue rose from just over $100,000 a year to $8 million in seven years. Indeed, even today we tend to make sure we have fresh breath before a first date or job interview! An advertising campaign has not only changed what we buy but also how we think and behave.

The Marxist critique of advertising

Many of these political economic analyses of advertising are, explicitly or implicitly, drawing on a perspective developed through Marxist social theory. In particular, they draw on the idea that capitalist economies can only continue by producing 'false consciousness' among consumers. To understand this concept, it is worthwhile delving a little into Marx's writings.

Marxism is often associated with communism. Yet, in his most famous text, *Capital*, Marx (1976) provides a detailed analysis of the workings of capitalism. He starts with the production of a simple commodity and works through industrial production, markets and then social relations.

From his analysis, Marx observed a fundamental contradiction in the capitalist system: in order to continue generating profits, more and more people have to be exploited for the benefit of an increasingly small section of society. How, Marx asks, is this situation allowed to continue? Why do so many people submit so willingly to their own exploitation? His answer is that the capitalist system obscures it by encouraging us to focus on what objects mean to us. Put simply, it makes us care more about emotions and symbols than facts. It makes us value magic above reality.

According to Marxist thinking, advertising contributes to this in a number of ways:

- *Commodity fetishism.* In order to consume an object, Marx suggests we need to be able to ignore the exploitative relations in which it was produced, the environmental damage its production has caused and the fact that we only want it because of the 'false needs' that Jhally discusses. Commodity fetishism is the name he gives this process of overlooking how an object was made. Advertisers themselves have long been aware of the dangers of showing consumers how their products are made. Ewen quotes a leading advertising executive from the 1920s as saying 'never see the factory in which it was made... when you know the truth about anything, the real, inner truth – it is hard to write the surface fluff which sells it' (1976/2001: 80).

Based on this idea, some critical theorists argue that the more people know about the realities of production, the more likely they are to see through the false consciousness produced by advertising. Yet, more recently social theorists have suggested that, ultimately, when we stand at the cash register we will regress back to commodity fetishists. This explains what marketing researchers call the 'attitude–behaviour gap' in which many consumers state their desire to consume ethically sourced and sustainable products yet continue to purchase goods that are neither ethically sourced nor sustainable (Cluley and Dunne, 2012).

- *The society of the spectacle.* A renowned critical theorist called Herbert Marcuse argued that thanks to advertising we think about ourselves in terms of the things we consume. Advertisers use psychological, emotional and symbolic appeals to give products a soul and eventually consumers start to see themselves through the things they consume too. As Marcuse puts it, people 'find their soul in their automobile, hi-fi set, split-level home, kitchen equipment' (1972: 22). This means that a whole range of human needs and desires are effectively reduced to one relationship. We only care about what we can buy. We become 'one-dimensional'.

This idea lies at the heart of Debord's (1967) influential critique of the society of the spectacle. Debord agreed that advertising makes us one-dimensional consumers. But, unlike Marcuse, he argued that rather than recognize ourselves in the things we consume we come to recognize ourselves through symbolic representations of the things we consume. That is to say, through brands and advertising. The result of this is that we now live in a society made up of images and spectacles. Thanks to advertising and branding, we are more interested in appearances than reality.

For example, we know that consumers care as much about seeming to behave ethically as they do actually behaving ethically. The use of the Fair Trade label in ads and on products, for example, allows consumers to feel as though they are making an ethical consumption choice. But researchers have consistently demonstrated that Fair Trade products provide almost no benefits to the producers of coffee, chocolate and other products (Griffiths, 2012).

- *Simulation and hyper-reality*. Does anyone expect ads to present reality? Of course not. Ads show us things that are not only

---

Thought box 7.2: Making the case for war

Mickey (1997) analyses 'The Hill and Knowlton Case' to illustrate the power of advertising techniques to simulate and eventually shape reality. In this case, a public relations firm, Hill and Knowlton (HW), was hired by an action group called Citizens for a Free Kuwait (CFW) to push the case for US intervention in what later became the Gulf War. As part of their work, they prepared a 15-year-old Kuwaiti girl to testify before the American Congress about supposed atrocities committed by the Iraqis against Kuwaitis. The girl gave an emotional, tearful and compelling account including a description of Iraqis dragging Kuwaiti babies from incubators. This image was picked up by decision makers including President Bush – who publicly mentioned the idea of 'incubator atrocities' six times within a single month after the testimony. Media reports on the testimony also focused on these atrocities, with the *Washington Post, New York Times* and *Wall Street Journal* all publishing stories about the 'tragedies against Kuwait' (Mickey, 1997: 279).

Of course, there were other geo-political reasons that led America and its allies to declare war on Iraq in January 1991. But, Mickey (1997) argues, there is little doubt that the work of CFW had the effect of bringing the issues into the public consciousness and shifting attitudes in favour of Kuwait and against Iraq. Yet a year later investigative reporting by the TV shows '20/20' and '60 Minutes' questioned the validity of the original testimony to Congress. It transpired that CFW had employed HW 'to offset unfavorable publicity about Kuwait's form of government as well as its human rights record' for a $10.5 million fee (Mickey, 1997: 278). CFW was itself something of a contradiction as the group was made up of wealthy members of the Kuwaiti ruling class who had, to some extent, caused the unfavourable impression of Kuwait's government and human rights record in the first place. It also emerged that the girl who testified before Congress was the daughter of the Kuwaiti Ambassador to the United States. HW admitted 'to coaching the young girl as to what to say and how to say it'. Indeed, some questioned whether the girl was in Kuwait at all. Reports later confirmed that no mass slaughters of babies took place although some babies had died 'when medical equipment was moved' (1997: 278).

In this case, Mickey argues, we see how a sign that is produced by advertising practice can become real even if it is completely fabricated. Once it enters into intertextual relations with other texts, it can have real effects. It is used as information in the production of other signs. The testimony, for example, fed into the media accounts which fed into political speeches which fed into the declaration of war which fed into critical analyses of the testimony and so on. Indeed, for Mickey, this case shows us that reality is not the issue when we are dealing with marketing communications. Even the truthful fiction can, in this sense, be 'made real' (1997: 280).

unrealistic but in many cases impossible. The models that symbolize beauty in advertising, for example, are not real. They are selected form a pool of professionals whose job is to maintain particular body images. They are stylized by teams of professionals. Then filmed or photographed by more skilled professionals using specialist technologies to enhance light, contrasts and colours. Finally, the images are processed through computer-based graphics programmes to airbrush imperfections and rebuild their bodies. Through this process it becomes impossible to say what reality the final images represent. They are completely fabricated.

Based on this argument, another French social theorist, Jean Baudrillard (1981) suggests that in the society of the spectacle reality has been replaced by 'hyper-reality'. Through the use of processed images and perfected signs, advertising represents a real world that is even more real than reality itself. It takes details of the real world and amplifies them to unnatural proportions.

The result is that advertising becomes what Umberto Eco calls an 'authentic fake' or, as Scott puts it, ads are 'truth-telling fictions'

(1994: 475). Indeed, though the signs and meanings constructed through advertising are fabricated, they have real world consequences. Every day we measure ourselves against the unreal images we see in ads. Mickey (1997) even argues that we have been led to war on the basis of truth-telling fictions within marketing communications (see Thought box 7.2).

The Marxist critique of advertising suggests, then, that advertising is a central component of consumer societies. Advertising educates us as consumers and allows producers to control demand at a distance. But it has had other effects. It has produced false needs and false consciousness that makes it impossible for people to see the reality of the world they are living in. It has, according to some social theorists, made us one-dimensional commodity fetishists living in a society of the spectacle. Hopefully, you now know what this means!

Does advertising bring us together or pull us apart?

Away from the grand analyses offered by political economists and Marxist critics, sociological researchers have attempted to answer a more specific social question: does advertising make us a stronger society or a weaker one. To answer this, they have investigated whether different social groups are treated differently when it comes to advertising.

Advertising: a bond we all share

In terms of researchers who believe that advertising makes society stronger, Leiss *et al* (2005) argue that advertising creates cultural images that enter the wider culture. This produces a 'social discourse' that 'bonds together images of persons, products and well-being' (2005: 1). As such, they see advertising as bringing different social groups together – it is something we can all share. In fact, it is one of the few products that we can all afford.

Illustrating how advertising can bring people together, Elliott and Ritson (1999) conducted an ethnography focused on the role of advertising in everyday culture. They spent six weeks in schools teaching media studies classes and used this access to gather data about the social uses of advertising. They concluded that ads played an important role in the pupils' lives and formed 'the basis for a wide variety of social interactions' (1999: 273). Indeed, Elliott and Ritson tell us that 'advertising may be consumed independently of the product it sponsors' (1999: 274). Advertising is something people talk about. It is a shared cultural text.

But advertising can also be socially divisive. In Elliott and Ritson's study, for instance, pupils who had missed ads could be left out of conversations. They might not get a joke or a reference to an ad. When this happened they could find themselves becoming the butt of the joke.

Advertising: not in my back yard!

Extending this idea, cultural geographers have examined the distribution of advertising. Focusing on outdoor advertising, they tell us that there tends to be more ads in areas populated by lower socio-economic groups. One study reports that low-income communities are up to three times more likely to be exposed to outdoor advertising! Moreover, the products that are advertised to these groups tend to be skewed towards vice products such as alcohol, tobacco and unhealthy foods. In some cases, areas populated by lower socio-economic classes are up to nine times more likely to be exposed to outdoor advertising for vice products! This body of research is summarized in Table 7.1.

This research suggests that outdoor advertising plays a role in reproducing health, economic and social inequalities – with those communities suffering worse outcomes being targeted with persuasive messages that encourage them to consume more vice products. This is interesting for a number of reasons. First, if we accept the argument that increasing amounts of advertising can have negative psychological effects, the fact that some groups see more advertising is surely problematic. Indeed, some equate outdoor advertising with other so-called NIMBY objects such as rubbish dumps, drop-in clinics and shelters (NIMBY stands for 'Not in my back yard'). Second, if we

Table 7. 1 Research demonstrating how outdoor advertising targets particular social groups

Study	Location	Products	Key predictor of outdoor advertising
Mitchell and Grenenberg, 1991	New Jersey, USA	All ads	Ethnicity
Altman *et al*, 1991	San Francisco, USA	All ads	Ethnicity
Ewert and Alleyne, 1992	L.A., USA	Tobacco and alcohol ads	Urbanization
Lee and Callcott, 1994	Detroit and San Antonio, USA	All ads	Income level
Hackbarth *et al*, 1995	Chicago, USA	All ads	Ethnicity
Stoddard *et al*, 1997	Los Angeles, USA	All ads	Urbanization
Pucci *et al*, 1998	Boston, USA	Tobacco ads	Ethnicity and income level
Luke *et al*, 2000	St Louis, USA	Tobacco and alcohol ads	Presence of schools, ethnicity and income level
Hackbarth *et al*, 2001	Chicago, USA	All ads	Ethnicity
Barbeau *et al*, 2005	Boston, USA	Tobacco ads	Education level, ethnicity and income level
Kwate and Lee, 2006	New York City, USA	All ads	Vacant lots
Kelly *et al*, 2008	Sydney and Wollongong, Australia	Unhealthy food ads	Presence of schools
Pasch *et al* 2009	Chicago, USA	Alcohol ads	Ethnicity
Vavardas *et al*, 2009	Heraklion, Greece	Tobacco ads	Presence of schools
Walton *et al*, 2009	Wellington, NZ	Food ads	Food outlets and social deprivation.
Hillier *et al*, 2009	Los Angles, Philadelphia and Austin, USA	Unhealthy products and lifestyles ads	Child-serving institutions and ethnicity
Siahpush *et al*, 2010	Omaha, USA	Tobacco ads	Income level, gender and commercial outlets

accept that advertising in some way drives behaviours, the fact that lower socio-economic groups are targeted with more advertising for vice products that can directly affect their wellbeing is also problematic. In this regard, research suggests that advertising forms part of the environmental cause of health issues such as obesity.

Implicitly, such conclusions take us back to the social theories of advertising we covered earlier in the chapter. Arguing that advertising shapes the behaviour of certain social groups fits in with a 'sociology of change' perspective. It sees advertising as something that can shape social groups and structure people's lives. Yet advertisers say they are simply using existing social distinctions such as social class and location to target consumers who already consume particular things. In so doing, they rely on a different idea about the relationship between advertising and society. They see advertising as something that is, itself, shaped by society but incapable of changing it in return. They think in terms of a 'sociology of order'.

As an example of the 'sociology of structuration', we can turn to the social analysis of online advertising technologies. It has been argued that these allow advertisers to create their own social groupings out of existing behaviours. Research exploring online targeting, in particular, demonstrates that advertisers can use a range of lifestyle factors to cluster audiences into groups (Cluley and Brown, 2014). In these contexts, we can see how targeted advertising does result in tangibly different experiences for different social groups. Consider this example I have adapted from Turow (2011):

> Two work colleagues who are the same age and gender and have similar lifestyles and attitudes go home and look at the same websites. Thanks to online behavioural targeting technologies, the information they see and their experiences are very different. One is positioned in a cluster related to weight-loss because they had previously looked up some dieting websites. Now they are targeted with ads for weight-loss pills, diet plans and so on. This, no doubt, makes them feel conscious of their body. In contrast, their work colleague is positioned in a cluster interested in luxury lifestyles because of their web browsing history. Their experience online is very different. Rather than being made to feel self-conscious, they are presented with aspirational ads for holidays and home improvements. For this person, the internet would make them feel like a success.

Pariser (2012) takes this further. He argues that targeted advertising can create a 'filter bubble' in which we only see online content that is relevant to people like us. In the process, we will never have our ideas about the world challenged by critics. This, he concludes, produces a society in which different social groups live increasingly fragmented lives and rarely come into contact with each other. These ideas draw on a model of social interactions known as 'structuration'. This model tells us that social institutions like advertising both reflect and shape distinctions between groups (see 'Sociology of structuration' in Figure 7.1).

Creating acceptable advertising: the licence to operate

In many consumer societies it is easy to think that advertising is a fact of life. Yet around the world almost every society imposes some limits on what advertisers can do. These range from outright bans on commercial advertising – as was the case in China up until 1979 (see Thought box 7.3) – to bans on specific forms of advertising. Outdoor advertising is, for example, banned in Sao Paulo, Brazil. Limitations might also be placed on the types of products that can use advertising and the types of techniques advertisers can employ. For example, tobacco products are banned from using advertising in the United Kingdom. Similarly, UK advertisers are banned from using subliminal messages.

What each of these examples represents is an attempt to make advertising socially acceptable. As discussed by Heath and Feldwick (2008), the advertising industry has to maintain a 'license to operate'. It does so by recognizing and respecting what Harker calls 'prevailing social standards' (1998: 104). This involves understanding the social critique of advertising set out by political economists, Marxist critics and others. It is essential, then, to understand how advertisers work together to ensure that advertising remains an acceptable business function.

> ## Thought box 7.3: The history of advertising in China
>
> Although advertising is an increasingly important part of Chinese society, it is has only recently received a full 'licence to operate' in China. It was not until 1979 that commercial advertising was permitted in the post-Mao People's Republic of China. Since then, the industry has grown rapidly. In 1983, the Association of Chinese Advertising was founded. In 2005, it reported that there were officially over 84,000 advertising agencies in China and nearly 10,000 advertising media – employing nearly 1 million people. Wang reports: 'What was once a young, unstable sector has taken big strides... turning into an industry with total billings of $18billion by 2005, up 12 percent from the previous year, making up 0.78 percent of China's gross domestic product (GDP), and accounting for an impressive 1.92 percent of the country's tertiary sector' (2010: 1).

The development of self-regulation: CAP, ASA and ASBOF in the United Kingdom

The United Kingdom offers an interesting case study here. It has a long history of regulating advertising to maintain public trust. Starting in the late 1920s, the Advertising Association, a trade group representing the interests of the advertising industry established the National Vigilance Committee. It 'helped to drive shady operators out of the press, brought pressure to bear on agencies to stop them handling fraudulent advertisers' business, and dealt with 1,169 complaints from the public during 12 months in 1936-7' (Fletcher, 2008: 21).

Later, the 1954 Television Act inaugurated the first commercial television station in the United Kingdom and established the Independent Television Authority (ITA) to regulate the amount of advertising that could be broadcast on commercial TV. Originally, this was limited to six minutes every hour. The ITA stipulated that all ads had to be shown within designated 'commercial breaks' in between programmes or during natural breaks within programmes. Religious and political advertising were not allowed on television and the ITA insisted that broadcasters make provisions for local advertisers to use their media. The ITA also appointed a statutory committee, the Advertising Advisory Committee (AAC), to agree standards for advertisers to follow. The first AAC code was published in 1955 – just a year after commercial television went live.

By the early 1960s, in response to various consumer protection initiatives, the Advertising Association set up a new system around the Committee of Advertising Practice (CAP). This committee was made up of representatives from leading advertising agencies, media providers and advertisers. It produced a rulebook for British advertising – 'The British Code of Advertising Practice' (1961) – and formed the Advertising Standards Authority (ASA). This new body was to act as an independent enforcer of the rules set by CAP (see Thought box 7.4 for discussion of the current punishments the ASA issues). To finance the ASA, CAP established a levy on all non-broadcast advertising. In 1974, the Advertising Standards Board of Finance (Asbof) was established to administer this voluntary levy. It was set at 0.1 per cent on the cost of advertising space (0.2 per cent levy on some direct mail) and continues to this day. Current figures suggest that over 80 per cent of all advertising expenditure that is liable to the levy pays it (Fletcher, 2008: 115).

More recently, the ASA has entered into co-regulatory relations with other media industry and statutory bodies. In each case, these changes occurred in response to wider trends. For example, in 1988, with the passage of the Control of Misleading Advertisements Regulations, the Office of Fair Trading (OFT) provided the ASA with legal backing. After this Act, advertisers who broke rules relating to misleading claims and who would not cooperate with the ASA could be passed on to the OFT for legal action. In 2004, the OFT was joined by Ofcom as the legal backstop for the regulation of the advertising industry (Brown, 2006). Ofcom, the body that grants broadcast media providers their broadcasting licence, allows the ASA to insist that a broadcaster who does not abide by the CAP codes is stripped of their broadcasting licence.

We can see, then, how the regulatory system in the United Kingdom has grown increasingly complex as it has responded to different trends and challenges. Across its history, though, it shows us how seriously advertisers consider their 'licence to operate'. This system is designed to maintain public confidence in advertising and assure law-makers that, as an industry, advertisers are able to regulate themselves

Thought box 7.4: Enforcing the rules

To establish whether an advertisement is acceptable in the United Kingdom the ASA invites complaints from the public. Many complaints it receives are resolved informally in dialogue with an advertiser. Only where this is not possible are complaints passed to the ASA Council for a judgement. This body is made up of public figure from politics, academia and industry.

If the council judges an ad to have breached the CAP codes, they can require the ad to be amended or withdrawn from circulation. They can also refer an ad to other regulatory bodies where appropriate.

For broadcast media, the ASA can request that scheduling restrictions are placed on an ad. These limit the times when it can be shown. The ASA can also request an ad is removed and, through this, they have the power to impose a 'fine' on advertisers. Media space is paid in advance. So advertisers risk wasting their marketing budget purchasing media space they cannot use if the ASA bans their ad.

For non-broadcast advertisers the sanctions the ASA can impose are somewhat different. Ad alerts can be applied to particular advertisers that advise media owners to withhold services and access to advertising space from the advertiser. For example, search websites can be asked to remove an advertiser's paid-for search advertisements if they link to offending pages. The ASA can also ask media providers to ensure that particular advertiser's work is pre-vetted before display.

without the need for formal legislation (Boddewyn, 1989). However, it costs money to run and requires the voluntary compliance of advertisers, agencies and media producers. Fletcher (2008) explains that advertisers, agencies and media providers participate in this system because it is in their interests to do so. He tells us that advertisers do not agree to abide by the regulations 'out of altruism. They believe it increases the public's trust in advertising, and therefore increases the effectiveness of their campaigns' (2008: 115). Put simply, in this case, we can see how important it is for advertisers to understand social criticisms and to respond to them to make sure advertising remains socially acceptable.

Summary: what does critical mean?

In this chapter we have explored critical advertising studies. This body of work attempts to explain the social function of advertising. In so doing, much of this work tends to take a very negative view of advertising. It sees it as producing false needs, false consciousness and so on.

As a result of this negative view, some advertising researchers refuse to engage with these ideas at all. They accuse them of political bias and producing nothing of value for practising advertisers. Hopefully, in our discussion of advertising regulation, we can see how critical ideas can be used productively by practising advertisers to understand their role and responsibilities to their wider society.

However, if you wonder why these discussions are rarely represented in the pages of leading academic journals you need to bear in mind that many advertising researchers simply do not like to consider the negative effects of advertising. They believe it is something you cannot study objectively as a critic. Personally, I disagree with this perspective. We would not expect a cancer researcher to advocate

---

Some other interesting sources

You can see the testimony that forms the basis of Mickey's analysis of the ways that public relations practice can turn fiction into fact here: http://youtu.be/LmfVs3WaE9Y.

For an illustration of hyper-reality, we can look at the controversy surrounding H&M's campaign with Beyoncé. It was reported that she was furious with the retailer for editing her appearance to make her look better. Details of the case can be found here: www.dailymail.co.uk/news/article-2333226/Beyonce-row-H-M-discovering-wanted-downsize-curves-swimwear-campaign.html

If you are interested in understanding how online marketing helps marketers to create new social groups from user behaviour, Vishal Gurbuxani's talk entitled 'Do you really want to be a marketer's wet dream?' is worth looking at. It is available here: https://youtu.be/-e6SX--FDpA.

cancer or a researcher looking at slavery to support slavery. So why should an advertising researcher have to advocate advertising? What I do think is important is that criticism comes from good thinking and robust research. It should not be the starting point for bad thinking. It is essential, I would argue, for us to understand and respond to criticisms rather than ignore them.

References and further reading

Altman, D G, Schooler, C and Basil, M D (1991) Alcohol and cigarette advertising on billboards, *Health Education Research*, 6 (4), pp 487–90

Baudrillard, J (1981) *Simulacra and Simulation*, trans Sheila Glaser, University of Michigan Press, Michigan

Barbeau, E M, Wolin, K Y, Naumova, E N and Balbach, E (2005) Tobacco advertising in communities: associations with race and class, *Preventive Medicine*, 40 (1), pp 16–22

Becker, H S (1963) *Outsiders: Studies in the sociology of deviance*, The Free Press, New York

Boddewyn, J J (1989) Advertising self-regulation: true purpose and limits, *Journal of Advertising*, 18 (2), pp 19–27

Cluley, R and Brown, S D (2014) The dividualised consumer: sketching the new mask of the consumer, *Journal of Marketing Management*, 31 (1–2), pp 107–122

Cluley, R and Dunne, S (2012) From commodity fetishism to commodity narcissism, *Marketing Theory*, 12 (3), pp 251–66

Debord, G (1994/1967) *The Society of the Spectacle*, trans Donald Nicholson-Smith, Zone Books, New York

Ewen, S (1976/2001) *Captains of Consciousness: Advertising and the social roots of the consumer culture*, 25th Anniversary edn, Basic Books, New York

Ewert, D and Alleyne, D (1992) Risk of exposure to outdoor advertising of cigarettes and alcohol, *American Journal of Public Health*, 82 (6), p 895

Galbraith, J K (1958) *The Affluent Society*, Hamish Hamilton, London

Griffiths, P (2012) Ethical objections to fairtrade, *Journal of Business Ethics*, 105 (3), pp 357–73

Hackbarth, D P, Schnopp-Wyatt, D, Katz, D, Williams, J, Silvestri, B and Pfleger, M (2001) Collaborative research and action to control the geographic placement of outdoor advertising of alcohol and tobacco products in Chicago, *Public Health Reports*, 116 (6), p 558

Hackbarth, D P, Silvestri, B and Cosper, W (1995) Tobacco and alcohol billboards in 50 Chicago neighborhoods: market segmentation to sell dangerous products to the poor, *Journal of Public Health Policy*, pp 213–30

Harms, J and Kellner, D (1991) Toward a critical theory of advertising, *Current Perspectives in Social Theory*, **11**, pp 41–67

Jackson, P and Taylor, J (1996) Geography and the cultural politics of advertising, *Progress in Human Geography*, **20** (2), pp 356–71

Jhally, S (1991) *The Codes of Advertising: Fetishism and the political economy of meaning in consumer society*, Routledge, London

Kellner, D (1983) Critical theory, commodities and the consumer society, *Theory, Culture and Society*, **1** (3), pp 66–83

Kelly, B, Cretikos, M, Rogers, K and King, L (2008) The commercial food landscape: outdoor food advertising around primary schools in Australia, *Australian and New Zealand Journal of Public Health*, **32** (6), pp 522–28

Klein, N (2000) *No Logo*, Fourth Estate, London

Kwate, N O A and Lee, T H (2007) Ghettoizing outdoor advertising: disadvantage and ad panel density in black neighborhoods, *Journal of Urban Health*, **84** (1), pp 21–31

Lee, W N and Callcott, M F (1994) Billboard advertising: a comparison of vice products across ethnic groups, *Journal of Business Research*, **30** (1), pp 85–94

Leiss, W, Kline, S, Jhally, S and Botterill, J (2005) *Social Communication in Advertising: Consumption in the mediated marketplace*, 3rd edn, Routledge, Abingdon

Luke, D, Esmundo, E and Bloom, Y (2000) Smoke Signs: patterns of tobacco billboard advertising in a metropolitan region, *Tobacco Control*, **9** (1), pp 16–23

Marcuse, H (1972) *One Dimensional Man*, ABACUS, London

Marx, K (1976) *Capital: A critique of political economy*, Volume 1, trans Ben Fowkes, Penguin, London

Mickey, T J (1997) A postmodern view of public relations: sign and reality, *Public Relations Review*, **23** (3), pp 271–74

Mitchell, O and Greenberg, M (1991) Outdoor advertising of addictive products, *New Jersey Medicine: The Journal of the Medical Society of New Jersey*, **88** (5), pp 331–33

O'Donohoe, S (1994) Advertising uses and gratifications, *European Journal of Marketing*, **28** (8/9), pp 52–75

Pariser, E (2012) *Filter Bubble: What the internet is hiding from you*, Penguin, London

Pasch, K E, Komro, K A, Perry, C L, Hearst, M O and Farbakhsh, K (2009) Does outdoor alcohol advertising around elementary schools vary by the ethnicity of students in the school?, *Ethnicity & Health*, **14** (2), pp 225–36

Ritson, M and Elliott, R (1999) The social uses of advertising: an ethnographic study of adolescent advertising audiences, *Journal of Consumer Research*, **26** (3), pp 260–77

Scott, L M (1999) the bridge from text to mind: adapting reader-response theory to consumer research, *Journal of Consumer Research*, **21**, pp 461–80

Siahpush, M, Jones, P R, Singh, G K, Timsina, L R and Martin, J (2010) The association of tobacco marketing with median income and racial/ethnic characteristics of neighbourhoods in Omaha, Nebraska. *Tobacco Control*

Stoddard, J L, Johnson, C A, Boley-Cruz, T and Sussman, S (1997) Targeted tobacco markets: outdoor advertising in Los Angeles minority neighborhoods, *American Journal of Public Health*, **87** (7), p 1232

Turow, J (2012) *The Daily You: How the new advertising industry is defining your identity and your worth*, New York: Yale University Press.

Wakefield, M A, Terry-McElrath, Y M, Chaloupka, F J, Barker, D C, Slater, S J, Clark, P I and Giovino, G A (2002) Tobacco industry marketing at point of purchase after the 1998 MSA billboard advertising ban, *American Journal of Public Health*, **92** (6), pp 937–40

Walton, M, Pearce, J and Day, P (2009) Examining the interaction between food outlets and outdoor food advertisements with primary school food environments, *Health & Place*, **15** (3), pp 841–48

Wang, J (2010) *Brand New China: Advertising, media, and commercial culture*, Harvard University Press, Harvard

Williams, R (1980) *Advertising: The magic system, materialism and culture*, Verso, London

The magic system

Cultural studies of advertising

Introduction

Advertising is often described as the dominant cultural form of modern times. Dyer, for example, tells us that advertising is the 'official art' of consumer culture (1982: 1). Certainly, if we go by the numbers it is hard to disagree with her. As mentioned in Chapter 1, billions of new ads are produced each year. They vastly overshadow the number of new movies, books or music videos.

It is unsurprising, then, that one branch of advertising studies analyses ads in the same way that we might examine any other cultural text. In this chapter, we will explore this tradition. We will see how researchers have adopted ideas and theories developed in the humanities in order to 'read' ads. We will also see how cultural analysts have looked at ads to understand the dominant values in contemporary consumer cultures. That is to say, we will see how we can read ads culturally and understand culture by reading ads.

Overview

The chapter begins by exploring semiotics and literary studies. These are theoretical perspectives developed outside of advertising studies that have been used to understand how ads express their meanings. We will then move on to consider other meanings-based approaches. Behind each of these traditions lies the idea that consumption is an increasingly symbolic act in which the meanings expressed through ads are a source of value for consumers. This leads us to consider more critical approaches concerning cultural exploitation, consumer resistance and advertising avoidance. Finally, we will turn to advertising research that has attempted to understand culture by reading advertising as a whole. Here, we will turn to communication studies to explain how advertising cultivates particular ideas about the world.

OBJECTIVES

By the end of this chapter, you should be able to:

- use semiotics and literary approaches to read ads;
- describe the process of interpretation;
- analyse cultural values; and
- consider the cultivation effect of advertising.

Key questions to keep in mind

- Is advertising a valuable cultural text?
- Does advertising have a cultural message?
- Do consumers respond the same way to ads?
- Does advertising reflect or shape cultural values?

Reading ads

A range of researchers have approached advertising as an important cultural form. Informed cultural studies – a diverse field that investigates the dynamics, defining characteristics and hidden conflicts of contemporary cultures – have used theoretical and methodological perspectives more typically used to analyse high art, literature and cinema to understand advertising. In this section we will explore three of the main trends here: semiotics, literary analysis and meanings-based approaches.

Semiotics

Semiotics is the study of meaning. It developed from linguistics and communications theory in response to criticisms of the transmission model of communication (see Chapter 2). Theorists recognized that language is often used in ways that do not follow the 'rules'. People make sense to other people even when the things they say do not make technical, grammatical or logical sense. As such, if we want to understand how people create meaning, we cannot simply look at the rules of language.

In this regard, semioticians argue that meaning emerges out of a complex interplay between the words, images and sounds that make up a message. These interact with each other to produce meanings that are not contained in any one element of a message. In order to simplify their discussions, semioticians describe words, phrases, images, sounds and so on as 'signs' and the individual messages that signs appear in as 'texts'.

Ads have been a particularly rich source of inspiration for semioticians (Oswald, 2012). They are interesting because they are both 'densely convoluted webs of meaning' that draw on a range of signs, genres and cultural memes (Stern, 1996: 62), but they have to be read very quickly – in some cases they may even be read subliminally (see Chapter 6).

Indeed, semioticians argue that meaning is also informed by words, images and sounds in other messages as well. What is not in a text can be as important as the signs that are in it. For example, Danesi observes that because ads draw on ideas and images from wider culture such as celebrities, music genres or popular characters, they 'imply an endless chain of meanings from which the viewer can choose some and ignore others' (2013: 473). In order to make sense, these endless chains of meaning have to be anchored together. In ads, they are anchored around the notion of changing demand. This is a starting point which influences how people interpret them. As a result, the signs which make up an ad and could have many different meanings become fixed in place and the ad can communicate a clear message.

But the aim of semiotic analysis of advertisements is not to say what an individual ad means – what we might call the 'perceptual' message that an individual might take from an ad text. Everyone knows the ultimate meaning of ads. No matter what the product or brand, all ads essentially are trying to say 'buy this product'. Rather, the aim is to interpret the 'cultural' messages of ads (Barthes, 1977: 36). In other words, the aim is to understand what else ads say other than 'buy this product'.

For instance, while we know that advertisers are essentially trying to say 'buy this product', we also know that advertisers almost never say this directly. Rather they provide 'reasons why' to motivate us. They differentiate their brand. They incentivize us.

From a semiotic perspective, then, there are always at least two messages in an advertising text: what the ad says (sometimes call the *denoted message*) and what readers know it means (the *connoted message*). These different messages in ads are shown in Figure 8.1. One way to think about this is to say that advertisers always mean something they do not say. What, semioticians ask, does it tell us about culture that people are motivated by the need to get clothes 'whiter than white'?

This form of interpretation is sometimes called decoding. Goffman (1979), for example, attempts to 'decode' the cultural meaning of advertising text in terms of their messages about different genders. What, he asks, does the presentation of different genders in ads communicate about the role of men and women in society.

Figure 8.1   Basic semiotic model of advertisements

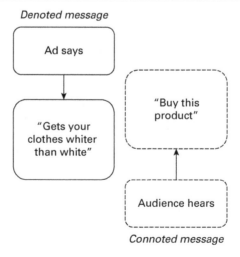

Equally, Williamson (1978) decodes the political and ideological ideas that are disseminated through advertising. These, she argues, are more important than the more obvious promotional messages in ads.

In keeping with this approach, we can consider the role of beautiful models in ads. Advertisers often want to associate their products with beauty and suggest that their product can make a consumer more desirable. To do this, they consistently use certain kinds of models whose meaning is essentially 'beauty'. From a semiotic perspective, such ads also define what we think is beautiful. As well as communicating their commercial messages, they also tell us what a beautiful person looks like.

These ideas were brought together in a pivotal contribution to advertising studies by a French semiotician called Roland Barthes. Barthes (1957/1972) observed that all societies create stories that

Thought box 8.1: Decoding an ad with Roland Barthes

In his book *Image Music Text*, Barthes (1977) provides a detailed reading of a single French print ad for a pasta brand called Panzani. The ad shows packets of pasta, a tin and a sachet all with the Panzani branding. It also shows a tomato, mushroom and onions. Half of the items are in a string shopping bag. The background is a deep red. These are the signs that make up the text of the ad.

Barthes decodes this text into three messages.

The first, he calls the *linguistic message*. This is what the ad says. It comprises the words in the ad. To understand this message, the reader simply needs a command of French. But the ad communicates something beyond the words. Barthes suggests that the sign Panzani itself is meaningful. It is not only the firm's name. It communicates (or connotes) a notion of 'Italianicity'. It sounds Italian.

The second message is a *symbolic message*. Each sign in the ad can be read as a symbol that represents some idea. For instance, the half open bag suggests that someone has just been shopping. It symbolizes an idea of returning home from the market. The vegetables are typical of Italian cuisine and signify Italianicity. But, they are photographed in a particular way. They look tasty, unblemished and healthy. This symbolizes an economy of abundance – one where fantastic food is plentiful. Overall, the arrangement of signs suggests a kind of art. They look like a still life painting. This signifies a kind of timelessness and idea that everyday life can be art.

Finally, there is the *literal message*. Here the tomato represents a tomato. The pepper represents a pepper. This might seem obvious but it is not. The images used in ads are highly edited and processed. In some cases they are completely produced by computers. As such, even at the literal level we must be careful to talk about the representation of the tomato – rather than a tomato itself.

Barthes' point is that the ad works at all these levels simultaneously. That is not to say, though, that individual consumers will necessary understand each of the messages. Rather, the point is that there is a difference between the types of messages we receive as individuals and the types of messages that we receive collectively as a culture.

Thought box 8.2: Deconstructing marketing communications

Stern (1996) illustrates a deconstructionist interpretation of advertising through an analysis of an apparently innocuous coupon for Snausages and PupPeroni dog snacks. It shows a cartoon of two dogs dancing through a field of flowers. Each of them is holding a pack of dog treats.

Stern argues that the 'irrational juxtaposition' of manufactured dog snacks and nature suggests that 'manufactured products are naturally good' and 'kick-start[s] the transformation of a bald "buy now" message into a creative text' (1996: 66). She suggests that the dogs are 'allegorical representations of children at play' (1996: 67). Through this, the over-arching meaning of the ad is constructed: dog snacks provide human-like enjoyment for dogs. Thus, the ad implicitly persuades dog owners 'to treat their pets as children' (1996: 67).

Working behind this message, Stern identifies a key binary opposition between human and animal worlds. Humans, the ad implies, are masters of animals and animals can only be happy when they act like humans. 'This positioning,' Stern tells us, 'privileges human values' (1996: 68).

> As a result, Stern argues that the ad 'hints at an undertone of uneasiness in the culture of affluence, for its form is that of a magical spell articulated to bolster the power structure by keeping animals in their proper place' (1996: 69). Indeed, we might go further to suggest it privileges a particular form of human desires. The ad privileges dynamism over passivity. Happy dogs are not those that lie around doing nothing, as dogs might in nature, but are those that are active, dancing and playing. The ad also privileges being social over being isolated. Happy dogs are sociable.

help them to make sense of the complexities of the world. We call these stories *myths*. His interest was in exploring where myths come from in contemporary consumer societies, as many of the traditional institutions which disseminated myths such as religions have fallen away. He argued that consumer products, brands and ads fill this void. Barthes' point is that the additional messages expressed by ads can serve the same functions as traditional myths. They help us to make sense of the world. This, I think, remains one of the essential ways to think about advertising and one of the essential semiotic accounts of advertising (Thought box 8.1). Indeed, Mick tells us that Barthes 'is perhaps the person most responsible for bringing semiotics to contemporary public light' (1986: 201).

Literary analysis of advertising

The idea that advertising is a modern form of mythology or storytelling which helps us to position ourselves in the world has been accepted in consumer research (Woodside, Sood and Miller, 2008). Taking this idea further, advertising researchers have turned to literary criticism as a way to explore the nature of advertising stories. As Stern explains:

> Analysis of the literary aspects of advertising texts is an additional way of learning about the consumer, for ads simultaneously reflect and influence behavior. They reveal information about consumers and their values, as well as about advertisers, firms, products, media, and messages. (1989: 322–23)

Table 8.1 provides a review of different literary theories that has been used to explore consumers and their relations to advertising. For an example of one of these approaches, we can turn to Scott's (1994) work with reader-response theory. The idea behind reader-response criticism is to explore a text from the perspective of the audience rather than investigate the author's intended meaning. Based on this, Scott (1994) observes that audiences are able to recognize ads as a distinct genre of texts in which a message is 'anchored' to the notion of changing demand. This means that they tend to interpret ads in quite precise ways. She argues that ads make sense, therefore, because readers see them as ads and interpret them accordingly.

Like semiotic analysis, literary perspectives have made a significant contribution in encouraging advertising researchers not only to explore what ads say but also to explore what they leave out. As Stern explains: 'The comprehending reader must realize that what is not explicitly presented in the text is as important as what is on the surface, in that meaning flows from the tension between the unstated and the stated' (1996: 67). To investigate the importance of the unstated in advertising, Stern (1996) turns to a literary theory known as deconstructionism. Deconstruction involves reinterpreting a text by stripping away 'placid surfaces and reveal the subversion, suppression, and hierarchical power struggles that bubble underneath' (1996: 67). Thought box 8.2 shows Stern's analysis in detail.

Meanings-based approaches

Semiotics and literary-based approaches have been accused of ignoring actual audiences. Even Scott's (1994) work on reader responses do not involve speaking to actual readers of ads. In response, other researchers have attempted to 'move beyond conceiving advertising in terms of what it does to people and view it more in terms of what people do with advertising' (Mick 1986: 205). The basic idea here is that ads are not 'fixed stimuli that contain or imply pre-specifiable information' and that audiences are not made up of 'solitary subjects, without identities, who react to ads through linear stages or limited persuasion routes' (Mick and Buhl, 1992: 317).

Table 8.1 Overview of literary studies and advertising studies

Focus	School	Literary domain	Research interest
Author	Biographical	Events in author's life, family and society	Author's context and authorship in advertising
	Editorial	Transmission of texts and revisions	Textual details, history of industry, firm, products or brands and the advertising composition process
	Intentional	Author's intentions	Evaluation of author or text's worth, ethical goals in advertising and social responsibility
Text	New critics	Individual poems or one author's work	Information processing of sounds and imagery
	Archetypal	Myth, rituals and folklore	Fictional forms and traditional themes, emotional appeals, fear and humour responses
	Genre	Forms, techniques and structural patterns	Genre values, themes and consumer traits
Reader	Psychoanalytic	Dream-logic, symbols, therapeutics and sexual fantasies	Sexual fantasy, hidden and vicarious pleasures and identification with ads
	Reader response	Text as interactive dialogue between reader and author	Relationship between author and reader, consumer and brand and emotional response to ads
All	Sociocultural, historical, Marxist and feminist	Humans and society, power relationships and minority voices	Power, values and creativity
	Structuralist	Polysemic meaning, narration and time, social construction of reality	Fictional coding of texts, consumer meanings and values
	Deconstruction	Binary opposites	Hidden assumptions in language

(Adapted from Stern, 1989)

An example of this approach comes from Mick and Buhl (1992). They argue that an audience member's life history plays a key role in shaping the way they interpret an ad. They summarize these ideas through two concepts: life themes and life projects.

Life themes

Life themes 'represent profound existential concerns that the individual addresses – consciously or not – in the course of daily events'. They 'enable and delimit reading experiences, with text meanings being neither inherent to nor about a text, but of about readers' (1992: 318). Examples include the desire to be in control, to be authentic, to find who we really are. These themes are 'pervasive and repetitive in the person's life' (1992: 320).

Life projects

Life projects 'are in constant flux' (1992: 318). They are influenced by where we live and who we are. Mick and Buhl explain that our culture 'establishes the basic alternatives within each sphere that are available to a given individual to develop at a particular stage in life' (1992: 320). Through our life projects, then, we both act out given social roles – parent, teacher, consumer and so on – but also construct those roles in a way that fits in with our life themes. So, when someone whose life theme centres on being in control has a child and finds themselves no longer in control of the things they care about, they will not simply adopt the role of the parent but will construct their own idea of parenthood.

Life themes and life projects synthesize who we are and who we want to be and they provide a frame through which we interpret ads. For this reason, Mick and Buhl propose that advertising researchers work on 'life history analysis' (1992: 336). To illustrate this, they interview three Danish brothers. First, they interview them to determine their life themes and life projects. Later, they interview them about five ads. They then use the first set of interviews to make sense of the second set. They discover, for instance, that the eldest brother's life theme centres on the issue of freedom. This theme feeds into his interpretation of ads. When looking at a Danish Beer ad, for example, the elder brother stated that he felt constrained as a consumer.

He has to drink Danish beer because he is Danish. In contrast, he pointed out that he admires English consumers for their freedom to choose any drink. Relating this to his life projects, when interpreting a second ad, this time for luxury clothing, the elder brother describes the ad in term of the 'freedom to look nice'. He explained how he has now lost touch with one group of friends and has made friends with a more diverse and experimental social group who encourage him to be more fashionable.

Through their work, Mick and Buhl argue that as much as life history shapes how audiences interpret ads, ads provide a useful way to understand consumers. Here, we can relate their argument with the other meanings-based analyses. Researchers in this area agree that the relations between consumers and ads do not work in a single direction.

A prominent model here is McCracken's (1986) theory of the 'movement of meaning' (see Figure 8.2). McCracken argues that we live in a culturally constituted world. That is to say, coming from a social constructionist position (see Chapter 2), he argues that the tools we use to make sense of the world are themselves socially constructed. These include popular culture references, sayings, clichés and stereotypes. The meanings of these references are used

Figure 8.2   Movement of meaning model (adapted from McCracken, 1986)

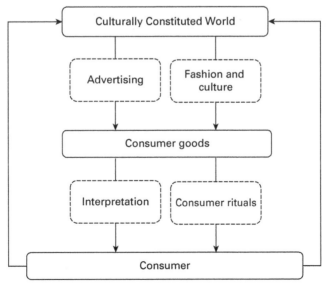

by advertisers. In the process, the meaning of these signs moves onto consumer goods. Then, through interpretation, the social uses of advertising (see Chapter 7) and everyday consumer behaviours, those meanings move onto consumers themselves but are modified and changed through consumers' new interpretations. Finally, these new meanings feed back into the culturally constituted world from which advertisers create their messages and the whole process starts again.

We can illustrate the movement of meaning more specifically by looking at McCracken's (1989) theory of celebrity endorsement (see Figure 8.3). What, McCracken asks, does a celebrity offer advertisers that a generic model or actor does not? They can all represent demographic groups that make sense for a target audience. But celebrities have a unique advantage. They can represent specific lifestyle, personality and symbolic meanings. As McCracken explains: 'Audrey Hepburn delivers "elegance" much more vividly than even the most elegant model. She does so because she has enacted and absorbed this elegance by performing it on stage and screen.' Celebrities, then, first acquire their meanings 'from the roles they assume in their television, movie, military, athletic, and other careers' (1989: 315). After this, those meanings, such as Hepburn's elegance, can be transferred

Figure 8.3   Movement of meaning in celebrity ads (adapted from McCracken, 1989)

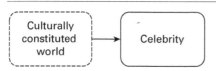

Move 1. Culture gives celebrity meaning

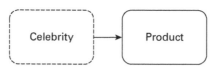

Move 2. Celebrity in ad gives product meaning

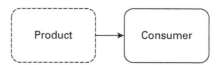

Move 3. Consumed product gives consumer meaning

to a product through an ad before, finally, moving to the consumer through the act of consumption.

One consequence of this movement of meaning is that it is difficult to reuse ads across cultures. Different cultures construct the world differently. They invest different meanings in the same signs and cultural references. As De Mooij explains:

> Advertising has developed its own particular systems of meaning. These are by no means universal across borders but are often culturally defined and frequently vary from country to country. This suggests a difference in the way advertising is composed and read: that is, a difference in advertising codes. It also suggests that where a different language is spoken, there is likely to be a different set of symbolic references, including myths, history, humour and the arts. (2004: 180–81)

So, the cultural study of advertising lets us understand how ads make sense and how they construct meanings. It also lets us understand the ways that people interpret ads and change their meanings. It is essential to know what ads mean – not just what we want them to mean. Otherwise, there is a risk that people creating ads will think they are saying one thing, when they are really communicating something very different.

Symbolic consumption: resistance and avoidance

One consequence of this focus on the meaning of ads has been that consumer researchers have thought more and more about consumption as a symbolic practice. Mick, for instance, tells us that the 'consumer world is a web of meanings among consumers and marketers woven from signs and symbols ensconced in their cultural space and time' (1986: 196). For a range of researchers, then, it is essentially the meanings associated with products and brands through advertising that consumers really consume. The physical things we buy, on this view, are merely a way to deliver these meanings (Goldman, 1992; Wernick, 1991).

This has inspired a range of critical interpretations of advertising and a range of critical responses from consumers. Collectively, they share a belief that advertising exploits culture and consumers but also empowers them to resist.

Resistance

Critics point out that artists and other cultural producers – not just celebrities – shape the culturally constituted world. They provide raw materials for advertisers. Unlike celebrities, though, many of them find their ideas adopted in ads without their permission and, often, without compensation. This is the focus of Frank's (1998) influential work on the 'conquest of cool'. He argues that advertising serves as a cultural safety valve. It takes counter-culture and avant-garde ideas and sanitizes them for the general public.

In response, some counter-culture artists and musicians have directly attacked branding and restricted the extent to which their work can be used within advertising. For example, the US hip-hop group The Beastie Boys refuse to allow their music or images to be used in advertising. They have sued a number of companies who have ignored this restriction.

Critics also point out that if consumers are doing the symbolic production involved in branding, why should they pay premium prices for brands? This has led to a consumer activist movement centred around *Ad Busters* magazine and the Brandalism movement on social media that tries to undermine modern advertising through the practice of 'culture jamming' (Lasn, 2001). This involves activists and artists producing their own ads which, rather than promote products, satirize and mock advertising techniques.

Avoidance

Perhaps more mundane, but no less troubling for advertisers, in this regard is the tendency for audiences to avoid advertising. Even when they are not motivated by counter-culture politics, researchers have discovered that many consumers actively seek to limit their exposure to advertising through various psychological, behavioural and mechanistic techniques (Speck and Elliott, 1997). For example, people might zone out when ads come on. This is an example of what researchers call 'cognitive avoidance'. In addition, they might alter their behaviour to minimize their exposure to ads. For instance, they may walk a different route to ensure they avoid billboards or flip through pages of ads without reading them. These are examples of 'behavioural avoidance'.

Donaton (2004) tells us that advertisers accepted that around 40 per cent of television ads would be behaviourally avoided as audiences would use commercial breaks to stretch their legs, make a cup of coffee or talk to each other. More recently, though, this number has increased. After the adoption of video recorders and digital video recorders, the number of ads that were avoided rose to nearer 80 per cent. The reason for this is that people used these technologies to 'mechanistically' avoid ads. The technologies let them skip ads altogether. Making matters worse, audience members increasing use new technologies such as 'ad blockers' to filter the amount of advertising they see too (Kelly, Kerr and Drennan, 2010).

Freistad and Wright's (1994) 'persuasion-knowledge model' brings together these ideas. It tells us that consumers tend to avoid obvious attempts to influence their behaviours. But, importantly, it tells us that peoples' knowledge about persuasive techniques develops over time. This means that effective advertising techniques tend to get less effective over time because people figure them out and learn how to avoid them.

Reading culture through advertising

Just as some advertising researchers have attempted to understand ads by situating them in their cultural context, others have looked at ads as a way to say something about the wider cultural context. Put otherwise, they have attempted to understand a culture by analysing ads. Mickey, for example, argues that marketing communications are texts through which our contemporary consumer culture 'understands itself' (1997: 272). He explains: 'To look at the cultural meaning of advertising... is to understand how we understand ourselves and how we act in the culture' (1997: 272). Tse,

Belk and Zhou (1989), for example, explore the different rhetorical appeals in advertising in China, Hong Kong and Taiwan to understand differences in these cultures in the 1970s and 1980s. They find that ads in Hong Kong tend to show hedonistic images of consumers enjoying products; ads in China tended to demonstrate how products performed; while those in Taiwanese more often illustrated the ingredients in goods. The key theoretical discussion in this area is whether advertising reflects or causes such cultural changes.

Cultural values

The work of Richard Pollay is foundational in this area. Pollay argues that ads tend to focus on lifestyle issues rather than product features. But the lifestyles they present are chosen with a specific purpose: to sell the product. For this reason, ads present us with an image of 'the good life' that we should all aspire to live. They are not representative of the lives we do live. As Belk and Pollay, put it, ads 'present a picture of the way we would like to see ourselves' (1985: 888). They show us what a happy family looks like and what a happy home-life looks like.

Even when ads do not show us explicit images of 'the good life', Pollay argues that ads transmit 'cultural values'. These are the 'standards that govern what beliefs and behaviours are worth preserving, trying to change, and even going to war and dying for' (Pollay, 1983: 72–73). They are 'determinants of virtually all kinds of behaviour and attitudes, from simple purchasing acts to political and religious ideology' (1983: 72).

Typically, such values are disseminated through a cultural by institutions such as the family, church, military, courts, arts and education. But, echoing Barthes, Pollay argues that in consumer cultures, advertising is also capable of expressing these cultural values. In ads, cultural values are the things that make a product 'good' – that is to say, not just effective but worth buying. As Pollay and Gallagher explain:

> Values are the core of the advertising message, unless the advertisement is a totally unadorned brand name reminder. Typical advertisements endorse, glamorize and inevitably reinforce values. Values are manifest in advertisements in both the art and language. It is the creative task of

art directors and copywriters to imbue the product with a sense of value so that the object becomes a 'good'. It is a value that is displayed in any 'reason why' offered as a rationale for preference. (1990: 364)

Reviewing 2,000 print ads in US magazines, Pollay (1983) suggests there are 48 cultural values that are expressed in modern advertising (see Table 8.2). Many of them are direct opposites such as maturity and youth. Where ads tend to present one side of these dualisms above the other, they shape culture to see it as a valuable aspiration. So, to put it simply, if ads tend to present us with youthful images, they will help to shape a culture that values youth.

Table 8.2   Cultural values in print ads

This product is 'good' because it is:		
practical	or	ornamental
effective	or	ornamental
durable	or	ornamental
cheap	or	dear
popular	or	distinctive
traditional	or	modern
natural	or	technological
This product is 'good' because it promotes a sense of:		
wisdom	or	magic
productivity	or	leisure
productivity	or	relaxation
productivity	or	enjoyment
maturity	or	youth
safety	or	adventure
civility	or	wildness
tamed	or	untamed
morality	or	freedom
modesty	or	sexuality
humility	or	pride
humility	or	security
humility	or	humility

(*Continued*)

Table 8.2   (*Continued*)

This product is 'good' because it is:		
independence	or	affiliation
caring	or	needy
family	or	community
This product is 'good' because it helps consumers to be:		
vain	or	plain
healthy	or	frail
neat	or	casual

(Adapted from Pollay, 1983)

Pollay's attempts to document the changing nature of advertising by conducting large-scale content analyses of print ads has provided a degree of rigour to the discussion of the cultural consequence of advertising. But his work raises a theoretical question concerning the impact of advertising on culture. Across his studies, Pollay repeatedly describes advertising as a 'distorting mirror'. We will look at this in detail in Chapter 10. For now, we can say that what he means by this is that advertising, in general, does not reflect dominant cultural values accurately. Rather, it selectively picks out certain values and, in the process, comes to influence which values dominant in a culture going forwards. For example, Pollay and Gallagher tell us:

> The advertising... provides a chorus of commercial communication, harmonious and consistent in its value basis. The value character of advertising is apparently, at least in the USA, independent of the cultural character of the population on which it operates. (1990: 369)

Others support this view. A number of researchers have observed that advertisers rarely follow all cultural changes. Mick, for instance, summarizes research which shows us that 'widespread sociocultural changes, fuelled especially by the women's movement, have been either ignored or trivialized by many advertisers' (1986: 206). However, as we will see in Chapter 10, while few disagree with Pollay that advertising tends to present a limited set of cultural values, some do disagree with the idea that advertising is a distorting mirror that changes culture. They are particularly critical of Pollay for not adequately explaining how advertising has its effects on cultural values.

How advertising changes culture: cultivation theory

Outside of marketing research, a branch of advertising studies conducted within communications research provides a theoretical explanation for advertising's cultural effects. Across a milestone study of media content known as the 'Cultural Indicators' project, the media studies scholar George Gerbner and his colleagues explored how the news and entertainment media shape our understanding of the world. They tracked media content from the 1960s to the 1990s, paying particular attention to the ways particular types or people, activities and occupations were presented on television. They then compared these representations with reality.

Having identified differences between real world conditions and their depiction in the media, Gerbner and his colleagues would survey audience members to explore whether people who spent more time watching television had a skewed view of the world that was influenced by representations on television. Perhaps unsurprisingly they found such an effect. They called this the 'cultivation' effect of television and describe the 'cultivation differential' as 'the margin of difference in conceptions of reality between heavy and light viewers in the same demographic subgroups' (Gerbner, 1998: 180). As Cohen and Weimann summarize: 'The primary proposition of cultivation theory states that the more time people spend "living" in the television world, the more likely they are to believe social reality portrayed on television' (2000).

The effects of cultivation, Gerbner argues, are not due to any one specific piece of media content. Instead, they are the cumulative effect of systematic trends across media content. As he explains, it is the effect of 'the pattern of settings, castings, social typing, actions, and related outcomes that cuts across program types and viewing modes' (1998: 179). These systematic trends produce a 'mainstream' image of the world and 'mainstreaming' of attitudes, beliefs and actions based on the social world presented on television.

The effects of the mainstream are not simple. They do not affect everyone in the same way or to the same extent. There is a dynamic between the cultivation effect and people's engagement with the media.

If, for example, someone's experiences 'resonate' with the presentation of the world on television, the effects of cultivation are heightened – and vice versa. In this regard, Gerbner describes cultivation as a gravitational process. He states: 'The angle and direction of the "pull" depends on where groups of viewers and their styles of life are with reference to the line of gravity, or the "mainstream" of the world of television. Each group may strain in a different direction, but all groups are affected by the same central current' (1998: 180). Cultivation theory is now widely accepted by media and communications researchers. In fact, it was one of the three most-cited theories in mass communications research published in the most prestigious academic journals between 1956 and 2000 (Bryant and Miron, 2004).

For Gerbner, cultivation theory helps us to understand how advertising specifically effects consumer culture. At a general level, he tells us that the needs of marketers shape the mainstream irrelevant of the types of images they present to us. As Gerbner puts it: 'Humans are the only species that lives in a world erected by the stories they tell. The storytelling process used to be handcrafted, homemade, and community inspired. Now it is the end result of a complex manufacturing and marketing process' (1998: 175). He continues:

> For the first time in human history, children are born into homes where mass-produced stories can reach them on the average of more than 7 hours a day. Most waking hours, and often dreams, are filled with these stories. The stories do not come from their families, schools, churches, neighborhoods, and often not even from their native countries, or, in fact, from anything with anything relevant to tell. They come from a small group of distant conglomerates with something to sell. ...
> The cultural environment in which we live becomes the byproduct of marketing. (1998: 176)

Where cultivation research has been particularly useful, though, is in exploring how the presentation of particular groups in advertising contributes to people's understandings of those groups. This has been particularly useful in revealing stereotypical attitudes towards different genders, ethnicities and sexualities. Lin (1998), for instance, studies the use of sexual appeals in television commercials. Reviewing hundreds of ads broadcast on primetime television, she found that

12 per cent of these commercial featured models in a state of undress and that female models are more often presented as sex objects in comparison to male models. Blaine and McElroy (2002) examine weight-loss infomercials. They find that women are twice as likely to be models in these ads yet the 'scientific expert' in them was always a man. Equally, the infomercials over-represent thin women as they showed three times as many thin women as they did heavyweight women. More recently, Paek *et al* (2011) compare the gender and occupation of prominent characters in over 2,500 television ads from Brazil, Canada, China, Germany, South Korea, Thailand, and the United States. They find that males are featured in the ads in prominent visual and auditory roles but women tend to be portrayed in highly stereotypical ways. Cluley (2016) even turns cultivation theory onto marketing itself and demonstrates how marketing practice is presented as 'men's work' in the news media.

Is advertising culture?

As we have seen in this chapter, understanding advertising as a cultural form has allowed researchers to adapt a range of theoretical perspectives from outside the traditional confines of marketing, advertising and consumer research. They have worked with linguistic ideas through semiotics as well as consumer anthropology. It is, hopefully, clear that few of these analyses would be possible if one simply adopts a 'transmission' perspective on communication. They are all based on a social constructionist theory.

However, whether advertising is truly a cultural form of equal worth to art, music, cinema and so on remains to be answered. Many of the people who claim advertising is a dominant cultural form are hostile to advertising. Indeed, as we will see in Chapter 10, the uncertainty about advertising's role in shaping culture is one of the main ethical issues hanging over advertising practice. For some researchers, critics simply place too much faith in the power of advertising to shape culture.

For me, there is some value in thinking about advertising as a cultural text. But I think it is important to remember that while literary theories or semiotics can be a useful way to think about ads, ads are a very different form of text. In fact, as we will see in the next chapter, some people argue that they are a special type of medium with their own messages.

Some other interesting sources

The documentary *The Illusionists* demonstrates how advertising can shape our ideas of beauty. Details are available here: http://theillusionists.org/

If you are interested in the relationship between advertising and other cultural texts, Morgan Spurlock's documentary, *The Greatest Movie Ever Sold*, is a great place to start. It shows us the mechanics of the movie industry and explores how movie makers work with brands. He summarizes the movie in this presentation: https://youtu.be/Y2jyjfcp1as

If you are interested in the cultivation effects of advertising, Jean Kilbourne's talk 'The dangerous ways ads see women' is well worth a watch. It is available here: https://youtu.be/Uy8yLaoWybk

If you want to see how advertisers talk about different cultural groups when planning their campaign, Veda Partalo's talk on 'Advertising and cultural complexity' offers some insights into the process. It is available here: https://youtu.be/HhzvEBJ9fEA

References and further reading

Bang, H K and Reece, B B (2003) Minorities in children's television commercials: new, improved, and stereotyped, *Journal of Consumer Affairs*, 37 (1), pp 42–67

Barthes, R (1957/1972) *Mythologies*, Jonathan Cape, London

Barthes, R (1977) *Image Music Text*, Fontana Press, London

Belk, R W and Pollay, R W (1985) Images of ourselves: the good life in twentieth century advertising, *Journal of Consumer Research*, 11 (4), pp 887–97

Bryant, J and Miron, D (2004) Theory and research in mass communication, *Journal of Communication*, 54 (4), pp 662–704

Cho, C H (2004) Why do people avoid advertising on the internet?, *Journal of Advertising*, 33 (4), pp 89–97

Cluley, R (2016) The depiction of marketing and marketers in the news media, *European Journal of Marketing*, **50** (5/6) pp 752–69

Coltane, S and Messineo, M (2000) The perpetuation of subtle prejudice, *Sex Roles*, **42**, pp 363–89

Danesi, M (2013) Semiotizing a product into a brand, *Social Semiotics*, **23** (4), pp 464–76

De Mooij, M (2004) Translating advertising, *The Translator*, **10** (2), pp 179–98

Donaton, S (2004) *Madison and Vine: Why the entertainment and advertising industries must converge to survive*, McGraw-Hill, London

Dyer, G (1982) *Advertising as Communication*, Routledge, London

Ford, J B, Voli, P K, Honeycutt Jr, E D and Casey, S L (1998) Gender role portrayals in Japanese advertising: a magazine content analysis, *Journal of Advertising*, **27** (1), pp 113–24

Frank, T (1998) *The Conquest of Cool: Business culture, counterculture, and the rise of hip consumerism*, University of Chicago Press, Chicago

Friestad, M and Wright, P (1994) The persuasion knowledge model: how people cope with persuasion attempts, *Journal of Consumer Research*, **21** (1), pp 1–31

Gerbner, G (1998) Cultivation analysis: an overview, *Mass Communication and Society*, **1** (3–4), pp 175–94

Goffman, E (1979) *Gender Advertisements*, MacMillan, London

Goldman, R (1992) *Reading Ads Socially*, Routledge, London

Jayasinghe, L and Ritson, M (2013) Everyday advertising context: an ethnography of advertising response in the family living room, *Journal of Consumer Research*, **40** (1), pp 104–21

Kelly, L, Kerr, G and Drennan, J (2010) Avoidance of advertising in social networking sites, *Journal of Interactive Advertising*, **10** (2), pp 16–27

Klein, N (2000), *No Logo*, Fourth Estate, London

Lasn, K (2001) *Culture Jam: How to reverse America's suicidal consumer binge – and why we must*, HarperCollins, London

McCracken, G (1986) Culture and consumption: a theoretical account of the structure and movement of the cultural meaning of consumer goods, *Journal of Consumer Research*, **13** (1), pp 71–84

McCracken, G (1989) Who is the celebrity endorser? Cultural foundations of the endorsement, *Journal of Consumer Research*, **16** (3), pp 310–21

Mick, D G (1986) Consumer research and semiotics: exploring the morphology of signs, symbols, and significance, *Journal of Consumer Research*, **13**, pp 196–213

Paek, H, Nelson, M R and Vilela, A M (2010) Examination of gender-role portrayals in television advertising across seven countries, *Sex Roles*, **63** (2–4), pp 192–207

Patterson, M and Elliott, R (2002) Negotiating masculinities: advertising and the inversion of the male gaze, *Consumption Markets & Culture*, **5** (3), pp 231–49

Pollay, R W (1983) Measuring the cultural values manifest in advertising, *Current Issues and Research in Advertising*, **6** (1), pp 71–92

Pollay, R W and Gallagher, K (1990) Advertising and cultural values: reflections in the distorted mirror, *International Journal of Advertising*, **9**, pp 359–72

Speck, P S and Elliott, M T (1997) Predictors of advertising avoidance in print and broadcast media, *Journal of Advertising*, **26** (3), pp 61–76

Stern, B B (1989) Literary criticism and consumer research: overview and illustrative analysis, *Journal of Consumer Research*, **16** (3), pp 322–34

Taylor, T D (2009) Advertising and the conquest of culture, *Social Semiotics*, **19** (4), pp 405–425

Thellefsen, T and Sørensen, B (2013) Negotiating the meaning of brands, *Social Semiotics*, **23** (4), pp 477–88

Tse, D K, Belk R W and Zhou, N (1989) Becoming a consumer society: a longitudinal and cross-cultural content analysis of print ads from Hong Kong, the People's Republic of China, and Taiwan, *Journal of Consumer Research*, **15**, pp 457–72

Wernick, A (1991) *Promotional Culture: Advertising, ideology and symbolic expression*, SAGE Publications Ltd, London

Williamson, J (1978) *Decoding Advertisements: Ideology and meaning in advertising*, Marion Boyars, London

Woodside, A G, Sood, S and Miller, K E (2008) When consumers & brands talk: storytelling theory and research in psychology and marketing, *Psychology & Marketing*, **25** (2), pp 97–145

The medium is the message 09

Media studies and advertising

Introduction

So far we have looked at advertising and consumers, firms, the economy, society and culture. But for an advertisement to have any effect, it must be seen and heard. That is to say it must be communicated to people. For this to happen, advertisers rely on media channels. In this chapter, then, we will think about the effect of different media on advertising.

Media studies is often put forward as the example of a 'useless' academic discipline. But this body of research and theory helps us to appreciate the different effects of media channels. It shows us that media channels are not neutral tools. They shape what and how advertising communicates. In addition, media researchers have focused on the benefits and costs of advertising media – not just in terms of the benefits and costs advertisers face but also wider social and cultural costs. A key question here is whether advertising helps to subsidize the production of other forms of communication such as news journalism or whether advertising undermines these forms of communication.

Overview

The chapter proceeds as follows. First, we will look at the different types of relationships that are 'mediated' by different media and technologies. Then, we will think about the social implication of advertising through a media lens. Here, we review the work of

Marshall McLuhan. Drawing on McLuhan's idea of media ecology, we will explore how advertising changes the media landscape. To develop this, we will pay particular attention to the relationship between advertising and news media. We will also explore the possible tensions between advertising and journalism.

OBJECTIVES

By the end of this chapter, you should be able to:

- characterize different forms of mediation;
- explain the media ecology perspective; and
- recognize the potential impact of advertising on a medium such as the news media.

Key questions to keep in mind

- How are media different?
- Does advertising change a media channel?
- Does advertising support or hinder journalism and other media ethics?

Differentiating media

Media channels do different things. They are not able to transmit the same messages or connect all senders with any receiver. Instead, some are able to communicate a single message, others can transmit multiple messages. Some can reach a single receiver, while others can reach a mass audience. Some allow receivers to communicate with each other, but some do not.

Recognizing these differences is a key problem for advertising practitioners. This became apparent with the growth of the World Wide Web. Originally, many advertising practitioners thought of the web like a magazine. In fact, most of the early websites that displayed ads were magazines. But, in thinking this way, advertisers were slow

Figure 9.1 Models of media relationships

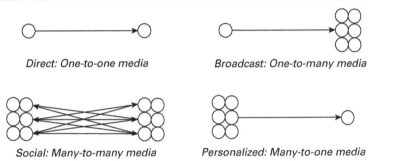

Direct: One-to-one media   Broadcast: One-to-many media

Social: Many-to-many media   Personalized: Many-to-one media

to recognize some of the key powers of the web to engage audiences such as e-word-of-mouth and user-generated content.

In order to separate different forms of media it is useful to recognize four key relationships that media channels can facilitate. The technical name for these relationships is *mediations*. These can be described as one-to-one, one-to-many, many-to-many and many-to-one forms of mediation (see Figure 9.1). Let's look at each model of mediation in detail:

- *One-to-one*. A one-to-one medium allows an individual to communicate with another individual. In other words, it facilitates a direct relationship between a sender and a receiver. The telephone is an example of this type of medium. It allows people to speak to each other across a great distance but is limited, typically, to one speaker and one listener.

- *One-to-many*. A one-to-many medium allows a sender to transmit the same message simultaneously to lots of receivers. It facilitates a broadcast relationship between a sender and multiple receivers. Typically, though, only one message can be transmitted at any given time on a one-to-many medium. A newspaper is an example here. Everyone reads the same stories.

- *Many-to-many*. A many-to-many medium allows a number of senders to communicate with a large number of receivers simultaneously. It facilitates a social relationship between multiple senders and multiple receivers. Indeed, social media platforms offer an example here. On platforms such as Twitter and YouTube people are able to share content with other people simultaneously.

- *Many-to-one*. A many-to-one medium allows lots of senders to simultaneously communicate with a single receiver. This might seem identical to one-to-many channels but there is a key difference. Many-to-one channels are able to transmit many messages at the same time whereas one-to-many media broadcast a single message from a single source. For example, some advertisers deliver personalized mass media content to individual consumers using the powers of social networks. They broadcast multiple messages but each is targeted to a specific user through the same media channel (see Thought box 9.1).

Understanding these different forms of mediation helps us to see how different types of communication can be created through specific tools. If, for example, you want to reach lots of people with

---

Thought box 9.1: Targeting *Straight Outta Compton*

According to the advertising industry blog Digiday, Universal Pictures used Facebook to show audiences very different trailers for the movie *Straight Outta Compton*. Rather than sending a single message to multiple receivers or allowing Facebook users to pick which trailer they found most appealing, Universal designed specific ads for specific groups that were personalized to meet their needs. Digiday reports:

> Universal served a targeted trailer to 'non-black and non-Hispanic' users that almost completely removed mention of NWA, the rap group the entire movie revolves around. Rather, that demographic's trailer focused just on Ice Cube and Dr Dre because the studio believed they were more familiar with them.

This many-to-one targeted advertising campaign was successful but it led to a backlash as audiences were concerned with being targeted based on some questionable cultural stereotypes. Consequently, the advertising campaign received a great deal of press attention for the wrong reasons. However, it shows us how new forms of media allow senders to transmit multiple messages that are tailored to specific receivers on a many-to-one basis.

(see http://digiday.com/brands/universal-slammed-making-different-straight-outta-compton-trailers-facebook/)

the same message, you would want to use a one-to-many medium. If, however, you want to target a specific message to a specific receiver, a one-to-one medium will be more effective. Put very simply, understanding the different forms of mediation alerts us to the fact that media are not equal. Different media let us do very specific things.

The medium is the message: media ecology

Building on the idea that different types of media channels work in different ways, we can turn to a foundational idea in media research. This is encapsulated by the phrase 'the medium is the message'. What this means is that rather than focus on the content of messages that are transmitted on media channels, such as an individual ad, we should consider the meaning of a media channel itself.

This idea was famously set out by a Canadian writer called Marshall McLuhan – an academic theorist who also worked as a consultant for advertising agencies – in his book *Understanding Media*. As McLuhan puts it, to say that a medium has its own message is 'to say that the personal and social consequences of any medium... result from the new scale that is introduced into our affairs' (McLuhan 1964/2002: 7). A medium of any kind – from television to the wheel – is something that extends human facilities and allows us to move ideas or people in new ways. They all help us to transport ideas or things. They do so through a range of techniques, including:

- *Amputation* of a function previously done by humans. For example, the wheel replaces the leg and foot as a medium to transport people.

- *Acceleration* of a function. This occurs when a medium increases the speed with which people and information can move. Email, for instance, vastly increases the speed with which information can travel in comparison to 'snailmail'.

- *Amplification* of a function. This happens when a medium increases the amount of information or people who can move. For instance, a photograph allows higher level of focus than is possible through the human eye.

- *Implosion* of two or more functions. This involves combining two human functions together into one function. For instance, television combines sound and vision. Although we talk about 'watching TV', we listen as well. The two functions are imploded together through the medium of TV.

- *Explosion* of two or more functions. This involves separating out human functions that previously worked together to produce multiple new functions.

- *Fragmentation* of a function. This involves splintering a previously single human function into numerous parts. For example, writing and sending a letter fragments the process of communication into two parts in comparison to speaking where we both compose and transmit a message at the same time.

- *Homogenization* of a function. This involves functions that come to resemble other functions. For example, computers tend to make many tasks look very similar. It is almost impossible to tell the difference between someone shopping, reading the news or working at a computer.

McLuhan's main point is that changing human functions in these ways can have profound cultural and social effects – or 'messages' in McLuhan's words. To illustrate the power of a medium to do more than it seems, McLuhan offers the example of an electric light bulb. Whether a light bulb is on or off has no intrinsic meaning. But the electric light bulb, itself, has a meaning. It eliminates existing relations with time. The electric light bulb allows social life into the darkness. Through this, light bulbs open up industries and increase productivity. They change how and when we sleep. As McLuhan puts it:

> The electric light ended the regime of night and day, of indoors and out-of-doors. But it is when the light encounters already existing patterns of human organization that the hybrid energy is released. Cars can travel all night, ball players can play all night, and windows can be left out of buildings. In a word, the message of the electric light is total change. It is pure information without any content to restrict its transforming and informing power. (1964/2002: 57)

To summarize these cultural and social effects of media, McLuhan sets out a continuum between hot and cool media channels. This distinction is based on the idea that different media provoke different ways of thinking.

Hot media

Hot media are those that magnify a single human faculty. In doing so they provide more information to the receiver than was previously possible. They also transmit a high-definition message. This means the receiver needs to do less work to decode a message sent through hot media. The signal is transmitted very clearly. This, in turn, decreases their participation in the communication process and increases the chances that all receivers will react in the same way. Hot media are capable of firing passions in receivers because the messages can be understood quickly and without much rational scrutiny. Hot media engross us with their messages. A movie, on McLuhan's reading, is a hot medium.

Cool media

Cool media provide less information and transmit low definition messages but their messages typically integrate multiple senses. They require more participation on the part of the receiver and need more time to understand. Cold media, in short, require the audience to interpret the message. But, as receivers have to do more work interpreting a message, the chances are they will react differently. As a result, cool media are less likely to enflame receivers because it takes more time and more rational thought to understand their meaning. A TV show, on McLuhan's reading, is a cool medium. Other examples include cartoons, music and academic seminars.

If you read McLuhan's text now, some of his descriptions of particular media and technologies can seem confusing (see Figure 9.2). For example, McLuhan describes television as a cold medium. Yet, to modern eyes, television is probably much hotter. However, the main point he is trying to illustrate actually helps to explain this confusion.

Figure 9.2   Hot and cool media

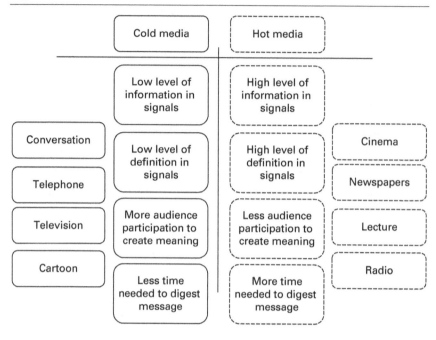

Thought box 9.2: Is TV hot or cool?

When McLuhan was writing, television transmitted black and white, fuzzy images with low production values. Consequently, viewers had to do a lot of work to understand a televised message. They had to compile millions of blurred dots and lines into a cohesive image every second and they had to fill in a lot of missing information between the grainy pictures. The low production values meant they had to imagine more than was shown to them. This involved a shocking amount of cognitive work. For these reasons, McLuhan argued that TV was a cool medium. Now, though, with high definition televisions, huge budgets and special effects, audiences have to do less work when watching TV. So, it might be the case that TV has got hotter.

McLuhan argues that the distinctions between hot and cool media are relative. He talked about this in terms of a 'media ecology'. His idea here is straightforward. We should not think about a medium in isolation but must understand its role by looking holistically at all media that operate in a given context. The hottest media might seem cold to outsiders and vice versa (see Thought box 9.2).

Typically, media ecologies are dominated by a single powerful medium. The light bulb, the newspaper, the radio and, latterly, television have each been put forward as fundamentally shaping the societies they operate in. They are the model which other media are measured against. Now, we are now living in an era in which there is no dominant media channel. The notion of 'media fragmentation' gets at this idea. It suggests that in place of a single dominant media channel we now have a plurality of media working together.

Advertising and the media ecology

What is the role of advertising in regards to the media ecology? There are two ways it can shape it. First, advertising can subsidize and popularize particular media channels. Through this they increase their popularity and decrease the coverage of other channels. Second, advertising can change the meaning of an existing medium itself.

Subsidize and popularize

Advertising has been important in shaping which media people use. Whether it is the growth of the press, radio, television or the internet, once advertisers have adopted a medium as a way to communicate with their markets those media have spread like wildfire. The reason for this is simple enough. It takes time and money to build media infrastructures. Until these infrastructures are in place, a particular medium is unlikely to be adopted by users. There is, after all, no point owning a TV set if there are no TV stations.

So, if advertisers subsidize a media channel, they can expand their reach and make them more attractive to use. Even if a medium does not have many users, when there is a market for advertising through a medium it will grow. Newspapers will invest in printing presses, radio stations will apply for broadcast licences and websites will be created. But, as Hirschman and Thompson explain, advertisers do not just want popular content. They want content that sells: 'As a case in point, the emergence of standard mass media formats such as soap operas, situation comedies, and game shows was intimately tied to advertising interests. Plot lines of soap operas, for example, were often written in conjunction with sponsors' (1997: 43–44). Equally, when advertisers decide to move their funding to a new media, existing infrastructures tend to shrink. In many countries, for instance, the number of local newspapers has decreased as advertisers increasingly concentrate on online outlets.

In addition to supporting particular media infrastructures, advertisers can also support the production of content. Media content is costly to make. But unless audiences find content they want through a particular medium, they are unlikely to adopt it – irrelevant of the reach of the infrastructure. Just as a TV is useless if there are no TV stations, it is also useless if there are no TV shows people want to watch. Indeed, historically, evidence suggests that when advertisers subsidize media content so that it is free for audiences, they vastly increase the size of the audience irrelevant of the quality of the content. As a result, the number of people they can broadcast their messages to increases and the costs of delivering advertising messages go down.

Changing the meaning of a medium

McLuhan actually considers advertising itself as a form of media. Advertising, he argues, is a meta-media. His point is quite difficult to get your head round. But, to put it as simply as possible, what he means is that it is a medium which not only uses other media but also changes their meanings.

As an example, we can return to McLuhan's discussion of an electric light bulb. This medium contains one bit of pure information. It is either on or off. It has no symbolic meaning in and of itself. An electric light bulb begins to express a message once it enters in some kind of social arrangement. For example, when light bulbs are strung together they are capable of spelling out a brand name that has meaning for a particular group of consumers. In this case, the light bulb becomes part of the message of another media such as a billboard. Now it is 'not the light but the "content" (or what is really another medium) that is noticed' (1964/2002: 9).

So, McLuhan tells us that one effect of advertising is to change the way media are used. Light bulbs are no longer means of producing light. They can now be combined with other media to produce billboards. They now change demand. They do not just emit light. They develop a new message. Just as electric lights opened up night-time streets for productive activities, billboards turn public spaces into commercial media than can be used by advertisers to influence our behaviour (Baker, 2007).

Advertising and the news

We can see how advertising can change a media most clearly by looking in detail at what happens in the real world. Up to now, we have been discussing the media in a general sense as the technologies that advertisers use. There is another use of the term though. This is the notion of the *news media*. The effect of advertising on this medium has been the subject of much debate.

There is a cultural assumption in many developed economies that the news media should provide accurate, objectively verified and truthful information on current events. Its aim is to inform the public and encourage free debate. Indeed, where there is less media freedom there tends to be less efficient public bureaucracies (Egorov, Guriev and Sonin, 2009), less social spending (Petrova, 2008) and higher levels of political corruption (Adsera, Boix and Payne, 2003; Brunetti and Weder, 2003). In contrast, even small-scale but independent media can operate as a powerful agent for social change. According to McMillan and Soido (2004), a small independent television station in Peru played a pivotal role as the country's citizens overthrew a corrupt government.

For news media to fulfil its social obligations, news organizations must not be influenced by powerful groups in society. This idea is encapsulated in the notion that the news media is 'the Fourth Estate'. It tells us that the news media is as important as the government in the workings of politics. The First Amendment to the USA Constitution, for example, explicitly protects the freedom of the press from political influence. It states: 'Congress shall make no law respecting an establishment of religion, or prohibiting the free exercise thereof; or abridging the freedom of speech, or of the press; or the right of the people peaceably to assemble, and to petition the Government for a redress of grievances.'

On a practical level, advertising has been a powerful mechanism to ensure that news media are able to operate freely (Petrova, 2011). The reason for this is that, where advertising operates as a primary source of profit for media organizations, it is costly for them to risk alienating their audience by serving narrow interests rather than the public interest. Yet, if we think about *advertising* and *journalism* as types of communication with their own aims, we can begin to see that this seemingly happy marriage of the media and advertising may not be as idyllic as it appears.

If we take the goal of journalism to be *the provision of true information* and the goal of advertising to be *changing demand*, we can begin to see where potential conflicts might arise. For advertisers information is always a means to an end. If true information is not useful, advertisers will use other forms of rhetoric. For journalists, though, nothing else matters but providing true information.

Historically, this marriage between advertising and journalism has been managed through what is known as 'the separation of church and state'. What this means is that news organizations are designed so that advertising and journalism are distinct areas of their business. The 'Church' (journalism) can work according to its own ethical standards while the 'State' (advertising) deals with the day-to-day demands of keeping the organization afloat. *Fast Company*'s editor recently illustrated this separation. He explained:

> CALL ME THE spiritual leader of Fast Company. As editor, it's my job to safeguard our journalistic principles and protect the interests of readers. My partner at the magazine, publisher Christine Osekoski, is tasked with generating revenue. In the magazine business, there is a line between church (me) and state (her), so that advertisers can't extort editorial coverage.
>
> But of course, I need Christine to succeed. Her efforts provide the funding for our journalism. The more ads she sells, the more ambitious we can become in our coverage. Newsstand sales and subscriber revenue

cover less than 20% of our costs; online access to our articles is free. When I say I need Christine to succeed, what I mean is without her ad sales, we're out of business.

But Christine also needs me to deliver high-quality journalism – uncompromised and respected – that attracts a high-quality readership. Without a distinctive product and a distinctive audience, she has nothing special to offer advertisers. It's not in Christine's interest to 'sell' editorial coverage because if she did it once, everyone would demand it. (www.fastcompany.com/1739778/separation-church-and-state)

While it is certainly possible that the division of 'Church' and 'State' helps news organizations produce quality journalism and returns for advertisers. It does not always work. Herman and Chomsky (1988) argue that even with this separation, advertising still affects the news media. They describe the news media as a channel for *propaganda* rather than *information* (see Thought box 9.3). They argue that the organization of the news media has a systematic media bias in favour of powerful interests from government and business. They highlight five features of the organization of the media that, they argue, 'filter out the news fit to print, marginalize dissent, and allow the government and dominant private interests to get their message across to the public' (1988: 2). Of these five filters, advertising and PR comprise two!

Thought box 9.3: Advertising and the propaganda model

Edward Herman and Noam Chomsky (1988) influentially argued that in spite of the desire for the new media to provide free and unbiased information, there are a number of factors that make this impossible. They describe five 'filters' that are built into the structure of the news media – primarily in North America but elsewhere as well – and shape the way that the news is reported. They tell us that these filters work together to make the news more political than we might like to believe. It means that the news is, in their view, more like advertising. It sells particular ideas and ideologies.

Goodwin offers a neat summary of Herman and Chomsky's perspective:

> Like other businesses, the mass media sell a product to buyers who, in effect, 'license' their activities by providing a market for them. However, the buyers of news and information are not individual consumers, who pay at most only a fraction of the operating costs of the media, but big advertisers... [who] not only prefer media that can 'deliver' affluent audiences, but may also overtly discriminate against media or media programming that they find politically incorrect. This sort of conscious discrimination is rarely necessary, given the sort of people who own and manage the media to begin with, but it can have a useful chilling effect, as far as advertisers are concerned, on a much broader range of media than the offending party alone. (1994: 105–106)

The filters Herman and Chomsky identify are:

1 The size, concentrated ownership and profit orientation of media organizations.

2 Advertising as primary income source of mass media.

3 The reliance of news media on information provided by government, business and 'experts' sources.

4 Negative responses from other groups to discipline the media for critical reporting.

5 Political 'strawmen' used as control mechanisms.

Spence *et al* (2011) summarize the situation like this. They tell us that the most striking feature of the media is its relationship with 'the market'. A great deal of media content is produced by large corporations to allow other large corporations to sell their goods. 'Undoubtedly,' they conclude, this leads them to present 'a very market-friendly view of the world' (2011: 51).

So there may be an implicit advertising influence on the news media. Indeed, more recent innovations suggest that advertisers may be expanding the ways they influence the type of news that is reported (see Thought box 9.4). For example, to deal with 'avoidance' (see Chapter 8) contemporary advertisers have explored new ways to integrate advertising into news content. Using 'press releases' that summarize key information that a brand wants to communicate, advertisers attempt to influence the news that journalists report. In this regard, recent cases show that journalists may not seek to verify the information included on the press releases and may even simply 'cut and paste' press releases (this is known as 'churnalism' – see Van Leuven, Deprez and Raeymaeckers, 2013).

Thought box 9.4: Welcome to the 'native age'

While advertisers have long accepted the need to maintain the separation between church and state in news media organizations, this is no longer the case. According to the *Huffington Post*, we have entered a 'native age' in which audiences no longer expect advertising and news content to be strictly divided. They are happy for advertising to be positioned in news content and to decide which content they want to consume themselves.

As a result, we have seen the rise of 'native advertising'. This is defined by the *Huffington Post* as 'sponsored content, which is relevant to the consumer experience, which is not interruptive, and which looks and feels similar to its editorial environment'. The idea here is that the division of church and state was necessary in a media ecology dominated by broadcast media. In such contexts, audiences had few choices about which content they engaged with. But nowadays, consumers have much more choice. They have a range of news outlets to choose from. They can consume content online, through TV or social media. This means that they can edit the content they see in a way that was impossible in a broadcast-dominated media ecology. Moreover, they can cross-reference news reports from a range of other sources.

For 'Generation N', then, if they find that a news organization is promoting questionable content they can easily find out and do something about it. This ensures that advertisers will support quality journalism and also produce quality ads that audiences want to consume. That's the theory at least!

(see http://big.assets.huffingtonpost.com/TheNativeAgeV3.pdf)

In Australia, a pharmaceutical company was accused of specifically targeting regional newspapers that it believed would engage in churnalism. An entire press release for a new drug was even printed verbatim in several Australian newspapers (Spence *et al*, 2011: 106).

This is particular troubling as Australian advertising regulation explicitly prohibits organizations from directly advertising drugs to the public.

You can hopefully start to see, then, how advertising can have both direct and indirect influences on other media. In the case of news media, the 'message' (or purpose) of journalism is to produce true information. Advertisers can help them achieve this aim. But, in so doing, advertisers can change the message. They can turn news media into advertising. It is essential for advertisers to understand this. Media channels are not just things that advertisers can use. Advertisers can change them. The key question that media researchers are still trying to answer is whether there is a point at which advertising not only changes the meaning of the news media but ends up destroying it.

Summary

In this chapter we have looked in detail at media theory. Media are clearly essential tools for advertisers and the theories we have looked at in this chapter can help us to understand what different forms of mediation can achieve. They tell us that media do not exist in isolation but form a media ecology and that advertising has a powerful effect in shaping the form of such ecology. It can support and subsidize particular forms of media but, as in the case of the news media, may also change what a media means.

Yet, somewhat curiously given the importance of media for delivering advertising, differences between media are not a hot topic in advertising and marketing research. Going back to the psychology of advertising, most studies focus on the effects of advertising messages and overlook the differences between media. This may be starting to change. In the advertising industry the lines between agencies and media providers are starting to blur and in academic research we have seen new outlets specializing in advertising through particular media such as the *Journal of Interactive Advertising*, which focuses mainly on online media. Indeed, in the future, I suspect that understanding how different media work will be even more essential for advertisers and advertising researchers.

Some other interesting sources

If you are interested in an advertising perspective on new media, George Nimeh's TED Talk entitled 'What if there was no advertising?' is a good place to start. He argues that without advertising, we simply would not have much of the news and entertainment content we all enjoy. It is available here: https://youtu.be/01PUSrLCvcM.

There are a range of articles, interviews and podcasts that deal with Chomsky's criticism of advertising and its influence on the news media. Some good examples are available here:

- https://youtu.be/N1Wov4use6c
- https://youtu.be/iPI__zs88EU
- https://youtu.be/HI2pgOidn3Q

The British comedian John Oliver has a stinging and hilarious critique of native advertising. It is available here: https://youtu.be/E_F5GxCwizc

References and further reading

Adsera, A, Boix, C and Payne, M (2003) Are you being served? political accountability and quality of government, *Journal of Law, Economics and Organization*, **19** (2), pp 445–90

Baker, L E (2007) Public sites versus public sights: the progressive response to outdoor advertising and the commercialization of public space, *American Quarterly*, **59** (4), pp 1187–213

Brunetti, A and Weder, B (2003) A free press is bad news for corruption, *Journal of Public Economics*, **87** (7/8), pp 1801–24

Egorov, G, Guriev, S and Sonin, K (2009) Media freedom, bureaucratic incentives, and the resource curse, *American Political Science Review*, **103** (4), pp 645–68

Goodwin, J (1994) What's right (and wrong) about left media criticism? Herman and Chomsky's propaganda model, *Sociological Forum*, **9** (1), pp 101–111

Ha, L and McCann, K (2008) An integrated model of advertising clutter in offline and online media, *International Journal of Advertising*, **27** (4), pp 569–92

Herman, E S (2000) The propaganda model: a retrospective, *Journalism Studies*, **1** (1), pp 101–12

Herman, E and Chomsky, N (1988) *The Manufacture of Consent*, Pantheon, New York, NY

Hirschman, E C and Thompson, C J (1997) Why media matter: toward a richer understanding of consumers' relationships with advertising and mass media, *Journal of Advertising*, **26** (1), pp 43–60

Hoffman, D L and Novak, T P (1997) A new marketing paradigm for electronic commerce, *The Information Society*, **13** (1), pp 43–54

Jackson, D and Moloney, K (2015) Inside churnalism: PR, journalism and power relationships in flux, *Journalism Studies*, **17** (6), pp 763–80

Kozinets, R V, de Valck, K, Wojnicki, A C and Wilner, S J S (2010) Networked narratives: understanding word-of-mouth marketing in online communities, *Journal of Marketing*, **74** (March), pp 71–89

McLuhan, M (1964/2002) *Understanding Media: The extensions of man*, Routledge, London

McMillan, J and Pablo, Z (2004) How to subvert democracy: Montesinos in Peru, *Journal of Economic Perspectives*, **18** (4), pp 69–92

Petrova, M (2008) Inequality and Media Capture, *Journal of Public Economics*, **92** (1/2), pp 183–212

Petrova, M (2011) Newspapers and parties: how advertising revenues created an independent press, *American Political Science Review*, **105** (4), pp 790–808

Spence, E H, Alexandra, A, Quinn, A and Dunn, A (2011) *Media, Markets, and Morals*, John Wiley and Sons, Chichester

Van Leuven, S, Annelore, D and Raeymaeckers, K (2013) Increased news access for international NGOs? How Médecins Sans Frontières' press releases built the agenda of Flemish newspapers (1995–2010), *Journalism Practice*, 7(4), pp 430–45

Wright, P L (1974) Analyzing media effects on advertising responses, *Public Opinion Quarterly*, **38** (2), pp 192–205

The distorted mirror 10

Advertising and ethics

Introduction

According to Rory Sutherland (2011), who was writing as President of the Institute of Practitioners in Advertising, 'marketing raises enormous ethical questions every day – at least it does if you're doing it right'. What he meant by this is that everyday marketing practitioners are put into situations where they need to choose between their own morals, their responsibilities to consumers and society generally, and their duty of care for their clients, agency and co-workers. Settling these decisions is not easy.

As we have seen, advertising is regularly highlighted as a negative influence on individuals, markets, societies and cultures. It is thought that it makes us more materialistic, narcissistic and selfish. In this regard, a number of researchers have explored the ethical dilemmas involved in marketing practice and the responses to these dilemmas among practitioners.

The academic debate about the ethics of advertising erupted in a series of articles in the mid-1980s and 1990s. So, in this chapter, we will spend some time reviewing this debate. Following this, the chapter will investigate more recent studies which explore how practitioners reconcile the ethical issues involved in advertising work.

Overview

The chapter opens with a review of Richard Pollay's influential critical analysis of advertising. We then look at Morris Holbrook's response to Pollay and Pollay's own response to Holbrook. This discussion neatly summarizes the two perspectives on advertising's ethics. Following this, we will look at how contemporary advertisers deal with ethical issues in practice. Finally, we will close by considering some of the potential positive effects of advertising on individuals, culture and society.

OBJECTIVES

By the end of this chapter, you should be able to:

- offer a balanced assessment of the ethical issues associated with advertising;
- reflect on the current state of ethics in the advertising industry; and
- show moral imagination concerning new advertising practices.

Key questions to keep in mind

- Does advertising have aggregate effects?
- How can practitioners reconcile the competing ethical demands placed on them by their clients, agency, co-workers and other stakeholders?
- What should responsible advertising look like?

The distorted mirror: ethical criticism of advertising

In 1986, Richard Pollay published a rare paper in the *Journal of Marketing* focusing explicitly on the critical literature about advertising – much of which we have discussed in Chapters 7, 8 and 9. Pollay's argument was simple enough: there is a consensus among thinkers about the negative effects of advertising. Yet marketing and advertising research barely acknowledges it. As Pollay observes, despite 'nearly four decades of prodding from parallel social science paradigms, to date our discipline had produced shamefully little in response' (1986: 33).

He explains that one reason for this is, simply, that marketing, advertising and consumer behaviour researchers 'are by tradition focused on the study of advertising's practical consequence, sales promotion' and that 'the unintended social consequences of advertising, the social by-products of the exhortations to "buy products", is less helpful' here (1986: 19). Indeed, within academic research there is a strong preference for quantitative methods and ethical questions typically cannot be answered using this approach. It is not, for instance, 'clear how to separate cause and effect when discussing the relation between advertising and social character' (1986: 30).

For Pollay, though, this gap in knowledge concerning advertising's unintended side effects does marketing, advertising and consumer behaviour students a disservice. As he puts it: 'Clearly it is not acceptable for our entire discipline to avoid addressing questions merely because certain constructs are difficult to measure. Most of the most important aspects of life elude simple measurement' (1986: 21).

However, he acknowledges that there is a wider tendency in culture to underestimate the full effects of advertising. Pollay calls this the 'myth of personal immunity' (1986: 23). We see so much advertising, this myth tells us, it cannot all be effective – perhaps even none of it is. This gets generalized into an attitude that advertising is not worthy of serious analysis. As Pollay puts it: 'It is ironic that it is advertising's very omnipresence that contributes to its being taken for granted' (1986: 24). In contrast, Pollay tells us:

Advertising is without doubt a formative influence within our culture, even though we do not yet know its exact effects... It surrounds us no matter where we turn, intruding into our communication media, our streets, and our homes. It is designed to attract attention, to be readily intelligible, to change attitudes, and to command our behavior. Clearly not every advertisement accomplishes all of these aims, but just as clearly, much of it must – otherwise, advertisers are financially extravagant fools. (1986: 18)

To counteract this lack of understanding and critical analysis in marketing, advertising and consumer research, Pollay provides a detailed summary of the criticisms of advertising produced by a range of North American thinkers. He highlights two approaches:

- There is a small collection of advocates. They draw to the idea that advertising provides information that improves consumer decisions making.

- There is a much larger group of critics. They highlight the negative social and cultural effects caused by 'the overall system' of advertising (Pollay, 1986: 18). These researchers reject the idea that advertising informs consumers and focus on its persuasive powers.

Pollay identifies a number of common themes among this second group of researchers:

- *Advertising has aggregate effects.* Individual advertisers might not intentionally want to harm other people. But this does not mean that advertising as a whole does not have unintended harmful consequences. Pollay (1987) suggests we think of this through the metaphor of rain. The negative effect of rain is getting wet. But this is not caused by an individual raindrop. Getting wet is an aggregate effect caused by the presence of lots of single and otherwise harmless drops of rain. The raindrops have not set out with a coordinated goal to make you wet but they still have that effect. So it is with advertising. It is not a single ad that is the problem. It is advertising as a whole. Pollay explains: 'No matter what the problems facing the individual advertiser, one cannot conclude that there are no effects whatsoever from relentless, intrusive repetitions of diverse exhortations to consume' (1987: 107).

- *Advertising makes us more irrational.* One thing all advertisers share is a need to get the attention of people who, largely, do not want to read, hear or watch ads. This forces advertisers to adopt more intrusive tactics. This produces a cat-and-mouse game in which consumers constantly figure out advertisers' tricks, causing them to develop even more sophisticated means to communicate with consumers and to adopt more and more media into advertising. The side effect of this game, Pollay argues, is that consumers start to filter out more and more of the information that surrounds them.

Advertising as a whole can, therefore, be accused of 'producing hypnoid states of uncritical consciousness' (1986: 26).

- *Individual ads may be offensive but advertising as a whole is offensively inoffensive.* In order to communicate effectively advertisers draw on socially acceptable images. Often, as we have discussed in Chapter 8, this takes the form of stereotyping particular people, activities and occupations. These stereotypes are then disseminated back into culture through advertising. In this way, advertising not only mirrors society but acts as a 'distorted mirror' which presents us with very selective images of reality. As Pollay explains: 'Simplistic, symbolic stereotypes, chosen for their clarity and conciseness, serve as poor models and inhibit sympathetic understanding of individual differences. ... To the extent that these images are disrespectful or unworthy of emulation, they are social divisive' (1986: 27). More generally, advertising also presents cultural values – family, beauty, happiness and so on. But, Pollay explains, 'it does so on a very selective basis, echoing and reinforcing certain attitudes, behaviors, and values far more frequently than others' (1986: 33). As a consequence, advertising as a whole ends up reproducing some questionable views, images and values. The history of racist and sexist imagery in advertising is a case in point.

- *Credibility, cynicism and community: Advertising weakens community.* Another result of advertisers' tendency to use particular words and images is that certain signs are anchored to advertising and end up losing their true meaning (see Thought box 10.1). In this way, advertising 'affects the credibility of language, and so simultaneously cheapens its own currency' (Pollay, 1986: 29). When we hear something is 'free', for instance, we might wonder about hidden charges. As a result, critics argue that ads make us cynical and paranoid and weakens our ability to trust, relate and communicate with others. Indeed, advertising shapes the kinds of issues we care about. It fills our heads with concerns about our own feelings and failings – the kinds of things we can solve for ourselves by purchasing products and brands – rather than general social problems. As such, advertising unintentionally reduces our concerns with the plight of others. As Pollay puts it: 'The intent of advertising, especially in the aggregate, is to preoccupy society with material concerns, seeing commercially available goods or services as the path to happiness and the solution to virtually all problems and needs. In so doing, advertising makes consumption a top-of-mind behavior' (1986: 21).

Driving all of these criticisms is a belief among social critics that advertising does not simply provide us information or reflect our culture back to us. Rather, it shapes our culture. Advertising, they say, is not a mirror. It is a mirror maker.

But it works in particular ways. Advertising is not representative. It selects particular images and values and holds these up as the 'reason why' consumers should want products and brands. So, advertising is a distorted mirror. It is distorted by the challenges which face advertisers as they seek to communicate to a mass audience. But it is also distorting because, through its sheer volume, advertising cannot help but communicate some arching cultural messages. It creates 'distortions through "selective feedback"' (Pollay, 1986: 27).

Thought box 10.1: Advertising English

The author David Foster Wallace explained how words changed their meaning as a result of advertising. Technically, a word like 'unique' refers to an 'absolute, non-negotiable' state and cannot be combined with 'comparatives like more and less or intensives like very'. But, in reality, this does happen.

Foster Wallace tells us that we 'can blame the culture of marketing' for this. He explains that as 'the number and rhetorical volume of US ads increase, we become inured to hyperbolic language, which then forces marketers to load superlatives and uncomparables with high-octane modifiers (special – very special – Super-special! – Mega-Special!!), and so on'. Consequently, Foster Wallace argues that we distinguish between Standard Written English and Advertising English. He observes: 'Sentences like "We offer a totally unique dining experience"; "Come on down and receive your free gift"; and "Save up to 50 per cent... and more!" are perfectly OK in Advertising English – but this is because Advertising English is aimed at people who are not paying close attention' (www.telegraph.co.uk/culture/books/9715551/What-words-really-mean-David-Foster-Wallaces-dictionary.html).

For Pollay, the consensus among serious social theorists on this point demands we pay more attention to advertising's unintended social effects in advertising studies. Indeed, 'the veritable absence of perceived positive influence' is, Pollay concludes, 'shocking' (1986: 19). We must 'take these assertions about advertising unintended consequences seriously. Despite the relative lack of data based research to date and despite the challenge this indictment represents to our own vested interests and ideologies, the charges are much too serious to dismiss cavalierly' (1986: 31).

Sticking up for advertising

Despite this consensus, it would be wrong to think that everyone agrees with Pollay's arguments. In response to Pollay's work, a well-respected consumer researcher called Morris Holbrook (1987) published a short criticism called 'Mirror, Mirror, on the Wall, What's Unfair in the Reflections on Advertising?'. In order to mark the distinction between Pollay's personal opinion and the ideas he summarized in his paper, Holbrook levels his response at what he calls Conventional Wisdom or Prevailing Opinion about advertising – which he abbreviates as CWOPO.

Holbrook's first line of attack against CWOPO concerns its logical coherence. Holbrook argues that, while CWOPO makes intriguing reading, 'the logic by which CWOPO arrives at such conclusions seems rather obscure and lends itself better to enumeration than to coherent argumentation' (1987: 96). Specifically, CWOPO lacks 'the kind of structure that might convey a logical progression from premises or assumption to deductions or inferences to conclusions or implications' (Holbrook, 1987: 96). As a result, it is impossible to prove whether CWOPO is true according to the standards of scientific enquiry dominant in marketing, advertising and consumer research.

Aside from these methodological issues, Holbrook argues that all social criticisms of advertising suffer from three questionable theoretical assumptions. First, they 'adopt a tacit view of advertising as a monolithic institution that somehow (whether intentionally or unintentionally) acts in concert to pursue certain shared ends via a set of common means' (1987: 96). Second, there is an 'assumption of a mass audience characterized by innumerable homogenous receivers of its promotional message' (1987: 96). Finally, there is an assumption that advertising relies too heavily on emotional impact and rarely informs consumers with useful information.

Holbrook provides a telling response to each of these assumptions:

- *Is advertising a monolithic institution?* Regarding the view that advertising is a monolithic institution, Holbrook points to empirical research about advertising agencies. This research shows us that most advertising is produced in a 'climate of jealous competitive secrecy and internecine business strategizing' (1987: 98). Rather than working in 'perfectly synchronized harmony' there is 'a vast particularistic assortment of atomistic elements, each engaged in a sort of communicational random walk' (1987: 98). So, according to Holbrook, it is not a monolithic institution (see Chapter 4).

- *Do audiences think alike?* Regarding the assumption that there is a mass audience, Holbrook points out that marketing researchers have repeatedly highlighted 'the fallacies of assuming the existence of a mass market of homogenous customers, all of whom will respond favorably to some offering or marketing mix' (1987: 98). Indeed, as we have seen in Chapter 8, in cultural studies and communication research the notion that there is a homogenous audience that passively responds to advertising in the same way is largely discredited. For Holbrook, then, audiences do not think alike.

- *Is advertising too emotional?* In terms of the focus on emotion appeals in advertising, Holbrook argues that much advertising attempts 'to supply reasons as the basis for action' but even when advertising does rely purely on emotional appeals this is not necessarily a bad thing (1987: 101). It is, he argues, 'somewhat churlish to single-mindedly attack the negative aspects of emotional advertising without giving balanced attention to the capacity of ads for evoking happiness' (1987: 102). Much of CWOPO, he contends, focuses on the worst aspects of advertising – the use of slogans, catchphrases and jingles – and overlooks 'the tremendous creative talent and energy' that goes into producing much advertising.

Indeed, adopting a similar logic but arguing from a different perspective, one could say that that because 'some advertising masterpieces endure' all advertising is a noble cultural form (1987: 99). As Holbrook explains, CWOPO would lead one to think that 'reading print ads or watching TV commercials is the moral equivalent of sticking one's head in a toilet' (1987: 100). For Holbrook, this is simply not the case.

Summarizing his analysis of these fundamental assumptions, Holbrook concludes that CWOPO is based on 'the weakest thread of logic, which tends to break from the burden Pollay places upon it' (1987: 98). He explains that advertising is, in his opinion, a mirror. If we do not like what we see in it, we should not smash the mirror. That would be like saying that the news has unintended social effects because it reports bad news. 'Ask yourself,' Holbrook ends, 'which would leave you feeling more cheerful, watching two hours of randomly selected television commercials or viewing 10 minutes of the evening news' (1987: 102).

The last word: Pollay's response

Pollay offers a response to Holbrook's critique. He suggests that Holbrook's perspective as a powerful insider in marketing research and his defence of advertising might be linked. He claims there is a widespread desire on the part of marketing researchers 'to see ourselves as virtuous' (1987: 108). This, Pollay continues, can 'blind us to the truth' (1987: 108). Indeed, Holbrook (2015) himself has recently documented the struggles he encountered when seeking to publish controversial and challenging ideas about consumer behaviour.

Either way, Pollay tackles each of Holbrook's defences against CWOPO head on:

- *Logical coherence*. Pollay tells us that Holbrook's claim that CWOPO lacks logical coherence misses the point. As he explains: 'Our current failure to have an explicit theory of advertising acculturation does not imply that advertising has no such influence, or that the views of others are mistaken' (1987: 107). For Holbrook, CWOPO is too unwieldy to be empirically tested using the accepted research methods in marketing, advertising and consumer research. But, Pollay argues, the tendency for particular forms of empirical research in marketing, advertising and consumer research contribute to the knowledge gap about the social consequences of advertising in these areas. Moreover, he contends that the convergence of opinions in CWOPO which come from a range of different research traditions 'suggests robustness, not frailty, of the hypotheses' (1987: 105).

- *Pluralism.* Holbrook argues that advertising is too heterogeneous for us to make valid claims about advertising in general. Pollay's response to this is that one can simply look at ads in the real world to see how much repetition there is. As he explains: 'Given the common products, goals, and cultural premises of clients and agencies, some notes and themes are echoed by multiple voices. Many ads echo basic behavioral suggestions on who (You!), what (Indulge!), how (Buy!), when (Now!), and where (Here!). The why's (eg Pretty, Durable, and Cheap!) vary, but repeat a short list of ideas' (1987: 105).

- *Audiences and effectiveness.* Holbrook suggests that audiences are too heterogeneous for us to make valid claims about the effectives of advertising in general. Pollay agrees that 'the creation of successful ads is still an artful, craftsman's activity without total predictability or control' (1987: 107). But, he points out this does not mean that advertising as a whole does not have predictable effects. Indeed, he highlights a fundamental inconsistency in discussions of advertising effectiveness: 'Industry spokespersons often claim ineffectiveness when faced with criticism and effectiveness when selling their services to clients, talking their skills up or down to suit their self-interest' (1987: 107). This brings us back to Sutherland's (2011) comments about the ethics of marketing practice. He tells us that, as a practising advertiser, he would rather be thought of as being evil and effective than ethical but useless.

In an attempt to summarize the points of agreement among critics and advocates of advertising, Pollay sets out four basic points which, he claims, everyone roughly agrees on. First, he says that everyone agrees that advertising as a whole has some kind of effect. Researchers just disagree on the precise nature of it. Second, everyone agrees that advertising communicates values as well as information. Whether everyone receives these values is open to debate. Third, Pollay tells us that everyone agrees that advertising does not accurately reflect society or culture. The debate centres on whether we think it should. Finally, everyone agrees that over time advertising changes how we think about society and culture. This, though, need not be negative. Some argue that advertising makes us collectively happier.

Advertising ethics in practice

While Pollay's argument is levelled at the ethics of advertising as a whole, researchers have also explored the ethics involved in 'the conduct of the advertising function' within commercial organizations (Cunningham, 1999: 500). This body of research draws on the corporate social responsibility agenda and the growing area of research in business ethics. It explores how practising advertising workers approach the ethical concerns of their work.

Broadly speaking, researchers distinguish two forms of ethical concerns involved in advertising practice:

- *Message ethics*. Message ethics relate back to the types of concerns Pollay and Holbrook discuss. They address ethical problems that emerge in creating and delivering commercial messages. These include long-standing issues with truthfulness and moral issues such as sexual, racist or offensive content and exaggeration. However, new media are bringing up new ethical questions here. For example, thanks to the rise of online behavioural targeting, advertisers have to deal with privacy and data protection issues that were simply not relevant in the broadcast era of advertising. Equally, social media allow advertisers to engage in a whole new range of ethically questionable activities. They can, for instance, create fake product reviews or sponsor bloggers to produce favourable videos. But whether they should do this is another matter.

- *Business ethics*. Business ethics relate to ethical issues that arise thanks to the organization of advertising work. They are not focused on the ads themselves but, rather, the relationships, working practices and responsibilities of advertising organizations. Issues such as conflicts of interest, which we have discussed in Chapter 4, represent a business ethics decision – as do issues around advertiser control of media content. Other business ethics involve sexual discrimination and diversity in the advertising industry. As we have also seen in Chapter 4, top positions in many agencies are dominated by white men. Researchers such as Alvesson (1998) suggest that this has produced an industry in which everyday sexism is rife. More recently, there have been concerns that the industry discriminates against older workers. Fortune reported that the preference for 'digital natives' has reduced the opportunities in the advertising industry for older workers.

The most commonly discussed message and business ethics problems that advertising practitioners have to deal with are summarized in Table 10.1. Research suggests that most advertising workers encounter at least some of these issues in their everyday practice. Hunt and Chonko (1987), for instance, report that 85 per cent of the respondents in their survey-based study claimed they encountered ethical problems in their daily work. Chen and Lui (1998) report that 67 per cent of Taiwanese advertising workers claimed that ethical problems were commonplace in their work. Moon and Franke (2000) found that 55 per cent of advertising workers in Korea reported that advertising poses ethical question every day.

Where individual advertising workers sit on these issues is determined by personal background, industry position, organizational context and their cultural background. Singhapakdi and Vitell (1993), for instance, explore some of the personal value systems that underlie the moral judgements individual practitioners make. In this regard, in an attempt to provide consistency among practitioners, organizations such as the 4A have set out explicit codes of conduct for the industry. The 4A states that accredited agencies will not knowingly create false or misleading statements; exaggerations; testimonials that do not reflect the real opinion of the individuals involved; misleading price claims; untrue or unsupported professional or scientific opinions; or offensive content. Equally, corporate social responsibility researchers

Table 10.1 Key ethical questions raised in advertising textbooks

Message ethics
Should advertisers use shock tactics and controversial content?
Should advertisers rely on gender and racial stereotypes?
Is there such a thing as too many ads?
Should advertisers use offensive content (eg sexual imagery)?
Should advertisers tell the whole truth?
Should advertisers deceive or manipulate consumers?
Should advertisers encourage people to want things they don't need?
Are there products which shouldn't be advertised?
Should advertisers target vulnerable consumers (eg children or the elderly)?
Does advertising socialize us as consumers?
Should ads be clearly identifiable as ads?

Business ethics
Should advertisers only follow the law or should they follow other moral codes?
Who is the more important stakeholder for an advertiser: themselves, their clients, their agency, their co-workers or society at large?
Should advertisers edit media content (eg news or entertainment shows)?
Should advertisers promote diversity in the workplace?

(Adapted from Drumwright and Murphy, 2009)

have attempted to create standards and protocol to support ethical behaviour among advertisers (see Table 10.2).

In general, Drumwright and Murphy (2004) highlight three positions that advertising workers adopt when faced with ethical questions: moral muteness, moral myopia and moral imagination.

- *Moral muteness.* Moral muteness occurs when advertising workers ignore ethical issues altogether. For instance, they might attempt to serve their clients no matter what and, assuming that their 'client is always right', they will never stop to critically question what they are doing.

- *Moral myopia.* Moral myopia is linked to moral muteness. It involves a distortion of an individual's moral vision such that moral issues do not come into focus. An individual advertising

Table 10.2 Checklist for responsible ads

Main property	Constituent properties
Does no harm to any stakeholder while benefiting at least one stakeholder	Avoids advertising that could induce harmful behaviours within vulnerable populations Uses potent emotional appeals cautiously Addresses unintended consequences immediately
Encourages behaviours consistent with long-run social welfare	
Maintains consumers' dignity and autonomy	Avoids deception, which may include puffery Avoids non-consensual persuasion techniques Avoids shallow/inane ads Avoids condescending and paternal ads Accommodates individual differences in perspectives and preferences
Respects consumers' egos	Avoids psychoactive ads with problematic appeals (eg appeals that induce shame) Placement avoids unintended exposure to vulnerable groups

(Adapted from Hyman, 2009)

worker might, for example, deny that their messages are effective in changing what people do or think. As a result, they may claim that it does not matter whether they use offensive content or questionable tactics. Moral myopia occurs, then, whenever advertising workers find ways to stop themselves from having to confront the ethical issues involved in their work.

- *Moral imagination.* Moral imagination is the opposite of moral muteness. It describes advertising practitioners who consciously tackle ethical issues in their work and are willing to consider new ethical challenges, to question others and to act on their ethical positions. For example, some advertising workers refuse to work on tobacco advertising accounts. Their moral imagination encourages them to question whether an agent should be willing to promote any product no matter what their personal feelings are about it. This has led some agencies to put formal systems in place to make it easy for workers to opt out of work that goes against their ethical positions.

We can see, then, that irrelevant of the academic debates, practitioners have to find ways around ethical issues in their everyday practice. These do not simply address the ethics of advertising but the ethics of advertising work. There is, of course, no right or wrong in this regard. We might think, for instance, that practitioners engaged in moral muteness are acting unethically. However, they are simply practising a different ethics – one that puts the needs of their clients above others. We might agree or disagree with this but, from the perspective of advertising studies, the key issue is to understand which ethical issues advertisers face and how they deal with them.

Advertising for good

Before closing this chapter, it is worth reflecting on some of the potential benefits of advertising to culture and society. As we have seen, Pollay (1986) points out the most vocal defence of advertising is based on an economic justification. Advertising advocates argue that it educates consumers and helps them to make better use of their resources. It lowers barriers to entry and improves the operation of markets. But advertising has some other advantages, which Pollay and Holbrook overlooked.

Advertising makes us happy

The influential motivation research Ernest Dichter (1960/2012) argued that advertising helps us to make the world meaningful and interesting. Advertising, he explained, helps us to relate to mass-produced goods and this, ultimately, is what makes us happy. Without advertising, if we were to simply relate to things as material objects without emotions the world would be drab and boring. This view is neatly summarized by Leo Burnett, the founder of the Leo Burnett advertising agency, when he stated that, without advertising, the world 'would be much the poorer – not merely in material commodities, but in the life of the spirit' (Belch and Belch, 2012: 704).

Advertising supports culture

While critics point out that advertising holds too much influence over cultural institutions such as the entertainment industry and the news industry, the other side of this argument is that advertising pays for much of the entertainment and news content we enjoy. For example, it is estimated that a Google search costs around 10p. We do not have to pay this because the service is subsidized by advertisers. Equally, economic historians tell us that societies which sponsor news content through advertising accrue notable benefits. They tend to have less corruption and more efficient governments. The reason for this is that the main other way of paying for news content is for governments to subsidize it. When this happens news organizations lose their abilities to hold government officials to account (Petrova, 2011).

Advertising is a tool

Perhaps most importantly, it has been argued that advertising is just a tool and does not have any ethics in and of itself. The ethical questions only arise when people start to use advertising. Here, they might try to use it for evil ends or good ones. In this regard, some of the advertising industry's leading figures have displayed great moral imagination. Prominent practitioners such as Bill Bernbach, discussed in Chapter 3, argued that advertisers could use their creative and persuasive powers for good as well as evil. He explained: 'All of us who professionally use the mass media are shapers of society. We can vulgarize that society. We can brutalize it. Or we can help lift in onto a higher level.' Indeed, in a speech to the advertising industry former US President Bill Clinton urged advertising workers to follow Bernbach's advice. Clinton pointed out that many of the problems the world faces can only be solved by persuading people to change their behaviours. It is not enough to tell people facts about economic inequality, environmental destruction or disease. As Clinton put it, we need people 'to fire our imagination and fill our brains as well as our hearts. You know how to overcome people's inherent resistance to hearing a set of facts they hadn't imagined were true, yet are'.

Whose side are you on?

Whether or not advertising is inherently evil we will, most likely, never know for certain. Equally, whether advertising is a mirror or mirror-maker, as Pollay and Holbrook debated with some aplomb, we will never know for certain either. However, for advertising practitioners and researchers alike, it is dangerous to ignore ethical issues.

Clearly, there are ethical issues in advertising practice and practitioners require advertising studies to help highlight those issues. That is to say, advertising studies can support practitioners' moral imaginations. Moreover, where practitioners adopt mute and myopic ethical

---

Some other interesting sources

Rory Sutherland, whose quote opened the chapter, offers an interesting and hopeful perspective on the role of advertising for good in his TED Talk. He argues that the symbolic values created through advertising could allow us to create a world in which we all feel more prosperous without having to consume more material goods. His talks are available here: https://youtu.be/audakxABYUc

Another example of a pitch for advertising for good comes from Emil Wilk in his presentation 'The future of advertising is good'. It is available here: https://youtu.be/nvt1Cgy0FsA

Jerry Seinfeld offers a wry look at the ethics of advertising. 'We know the product is going to stink,' he says. But between the commercial and purchase, he says, ads make us happy. His speech is here: https://youtu.be/uHWX4pG0FNY

In contrast, Jacob Östberg draws on the 'myth of personal immunity' to argue that we need to be far more critical of the role of advertising in our lives, societies and cultures in his TEDx Talk entitled 'The Stockholm syndrome of advertising'. It is available here: https://youtu.be/bEULSwE5GEk

In this short talk to the NABS Tuesday Club, Jonathan Wise reflects on business ethics of advertising for individual advertisers: https://youtu.be/aENq_wNEIbo

Highlights of Bill Clinton's speech to advertisers are available here: https://youtu.be/Rc7rTLZNhd0

stances, advertising studies can help to explore where and why this is the case. We may discover, for example, that far from being an ethical decision made by individual practitioners, these perspectives are forced onto practitioners by problematic business practices. Indeed, advertising researchers can help advertisers not only to react to moral criticisms but also to explore and maximize the benefits of advertising to individuals, advertising workers, clients, society and culture.

Ethical considerations are never easy. While it is comforting to follow the kinds of protocol and codes of conduct corporate social responsibility researchers offer. I would, in closing this chapter, offer caution here. I am deeply sceptical of the idea that there is a right and wrong ethics per se. It seems to me that what is right and wrong changes in different contexts. What is troubling for me is having researchers and practitioners who simply refuse to think about what they are doing in ethical terms. For me, moral blindness could hide moral inconsistencies. The truly unethical position is to know something is wrong but do it anyway... or to know something is wrong, pretend it is not an ethical issue and do it anyway.

References and further reading

Belch, G E and Belch, M A (2012) *Advertising and Promotion: An integrated marketing communications perspective*, McGraw-Hill Irwin, London

Bishop, F P (1949) *The Ethics of Advertising*, Robert Hale, Bedford Square

Chen, A W and Liu, J M (1998) Agency practitioners' perceptions of professional ethics in Taiwan, *Journal of Business Ethics*, **17** (January), pp 15–23

Dichter, E (1960/2012) *The Strategy of Desire*, Martino Fine Books, New York

Drumwright, M E and Murphy, P E (2004) How advertising practitioners view ethics: moral muteness, moral myopia, and moral imagination, *Journal of Advertising*, **33** (2), pp 7–24

Drumwright, M E and Murphy, P E (2009) The current state of advertising ethics: industry and academic perspectives, *Journal of Advertising*, **38** (1), pp 83–108

Hackley, C E and Kitchen, P J (1999) Ethical perspectives on the postmodern communications leviathan, *Journal of Business Ethics*, 20, pp 15–26

Holbrook, M B (2015) Some reflections on psychoanalytic approaches to marketing and consumer research, *Marketing Theory*, **15** (1), pp 13–16

Holbrook, M B (1987) Mirror, mirror, on the wall, what's unfair in the reflections on advertising?, *Journal of Marketing*, **51** (July), pp 95–103

Hunt, S D and Chonko, L B (1987) Ethical problems of advertising agency executives, *Journal of Advertising*, **16** (4), pp 16–24

Hyman, M (2009) Responsible ads: a workable ideal, *Journal of Business Ethics*, **87**, pp 199–210

Moon, Y S and Franke, G R (2000) Cultural influences on agency practitioners' ethical perceptions: a comparison of Korea and the U.S., *Journal of Advertising*, **29** (Spring), pp 51–65

Nairn, A and Fine, C (2008) Who's messing with my mind?, *International Journal of Advertising*, **27** (3), pp 447–70

Petrova, M (2011) Newspapers and parties: how advertising revenues created an independent press, *American Political Science Review*, **105** (4), pp 790–808

Phillips, B J (1997) In defense of advertising: a social perspective, *Journal of Business Ethics*, **16**, pp 109–118

Pollay, R W (1986) The distorted mirror: reflections on the unintended consequences of advertising, *Journal of Marketing*, **50** (April), pp 18–36

Pollay, R W (1987) On the value of reflections on the value in 'the distorted mirror', *Journal of Marketing*, **51** (3), pp 104–109

Singhapakdi, A and Vitell, S J (1993) Personal values underlying the moral philosophies of marketing professionals, *Business & Professional Ethics Journal*, **12** (1), pp 91–106

Sutherland, R (2011) 'Foreword,' in Jon Alexander, Tom Crompton and Guy Shrubsole (2011) Think of me as evil? Opening the ethical debates in advertising, Public Interest Research Centre and WWF-UK

Waller, D S and Lanis, R (2009) Corporate Social Responsibility (CSR) disclosure of advertising agencies: an exploratory analysis of six holding companies' annual reports, *Journal of Advertising*, **38** (1), pp 109–122

Where next?   11

The new essentials of advertising

This brings our journey through the essentials of advertising to a close. Although we have explored a range of different perspectives on advertising, it is hopefully clear that there are some overarching concerns that relate to almost all advertising research. Hopefully you are now in a position to understand what interests you and how it relates to the broad range of perspectives that make up advertising studies.

To tease out some of these essential questions on advertising studies, I would encourage you to think about the 'big questions' I put forward at the start of the book:

- How does advertising communicate with consumers?
- Is advertising an art of a science?
- Is the advertising industry well organized?
- What is the relationship between advertising and consumer behaviour?
- Does advertising help consumers make better decisions or not?
- Does advertising have social and cultural effects?
- How can advertisers balance their moral duties to their own ethics, their clients and their organizations?

I do not think these questions can ever be answered conclusively. Indeed, the fact that we are still asking these questions over 100 years after Hopkins claimed to have discovered the 'fundamental laws' of advertising only makes me more sceptical. I think it is okay for us to all have our own answers to these questions and to respect and understand those who think differently.

But, in listing these questions, it is clear to me how many of them are related to each other. In fact I actually think that there are just two essential questions about advertising. First, is advertising good or bad? Second, can advertising be managed or not?

Answering these questions takes us back to the main point of this book. Our ideas about advertising are shaped not only by different disciplines and research methods but also by our own perspective and desires. People who want to think, for instance, that advertising is a force for good are able to argue this point. But people who want to think that advertising is damaging can do so too.

For me, and I feel I am starting to repeat myself, this is not a problem. Uncertainty creates opportunities for creativity and innovation. Away from advertising research in cultural sociology, for instance, it has been argued that new cultural genres emerge out of the tension between freedom and constraint. When a style of music or writing becomes too formulaic, people innovate a new way to express themselves. We can think of it as if there is a pendulum. When things move too far in one direction, it provides momentum in the opposite direction.

In this regard, I think we are currently seeing the pendulum swing towards the idea that advertising is good and can be managed. We have seen the return of scientific advertising in a big way – although not too many of the enthusiasts seem to have read Hopkins' or Reeves' work. Instead, the 'new scientific advertising' draws on neuroscience, behavioural science and data science for support. These approaches promise to make advertising predictable. Neuroscience, for instance, promises to uncover a 'buy button' in the brain that advertisers can press with their executions. Data science, in contrast, says that through machine learning and A/B testing, we can find the most effective messages and target consumers with highly engaging ads. If history shows us anything, though, it is that advertising has never been predictable. So I am sceptical of these approaches and I am looking forward to advertisers rediscovering their artistic sides!

INDEX

4A organization 206

ability factor, elaboration likelihood
    model 112
acceleration of function, media
    ecology 181
acceptability of advertising 131–2,
    145–8
acceptance, information process
    model 107
account managers, advertising
    agencies 57, 69, 70
account planning, advertising
    agencies 69–70, 78
account reviews, agencies 68–9
activist consumers 166
ad villages 75
administrative approach 131, 136
advanced administrative practice 136
advertisers' role, production of
    advertising 65
advertising
    amount of 4–5, 10
    as a bond 141–2
    bringing together/pulling
        apart 141–5
    defending 201–3
    defining 2, 3–5
    development over the years 5–8
    discussions about 1
    new essentials of 215–16
    thinking about 1, 3–4, 12, 16
    as a tool 210
advertising agencies
    contemporary advertising 57
    creative advertising 52, 56
    organizational perspectives 63–83
    scientific advertising 48
advertising industry 64–71, 81–2
    awards 73
    development 66
    diversity 74, 80
    importance of 15
    networks 76–7

numbers employed in 8
restructuring 74–5
scientific theory 46
self-regulation 146–8
structure 63
uniqueness 41
advertising research 105, 154
Advertising Standards Authority
    (ASA) 147, 148
Advertising Standards Board of
    Finance (Asbof) 147
advertising studies
    appreciating 2
    'big questions' 12, 215–16
    knowledge development 11–12
    new essentials of 215
    overview 161
    reasons for 8–10
advertising theories 6, 8
    see also theoretical approaches
'adverts in the world' 8
affective component of advertising 125
agencies see advertising agencies
agency's roster 68, 80
agglomeration, ad villages 75
aggregate effects of advertising
    198, 199
AIDA model 44–5
Alka Seltzer campaign 55–6
amplification of function, media
    ecology 181
amputation of function, media
    ecology 181
ancient civilizations 4, 32–3
antecedent factors, information process
    model 109
Aristotle 32–3
art, advertising as 13, 41–2, 50–6, 57,
    59, 153
    see also creative advertising
ASA see Advertising Standards
    Authority
Asbof see Advertising Standards Board
    of Finance

Asch Conformity Experiments 115
associations of advertising 29–30
ATR model *see* awareness, trial and
        reinforcement model
attention, information process
        model 106
attitude – behaviour gap 138
attitudes 110–13, 115
audience size, subsidization
        of media 186
audiences
    effectiveness of advertising 204
    homogenous 202
    meanings-based approaches
        160, 162
    see also consumer...
Australia 191–2
avertissement 6, 7
avoidance of advertising 166–7, 190
awards 73
awareness of advertising 126
awareness, trial and reinforcement
        (ATR) model 126

bad advertising
    cost of 49
    value and 91–2
BAME *see* black, Asian and minority
        ethnic agents
bans on adverts 145
Barrett, Thomas 50–1
Barthes, Roland 157–9
beauty 140, 157
behavioural avoidance 167
behavioural basis
    Ehrenberg's theory 125
    information process model 106
behavioural change
    'monologue' view 36
    psychology of 124
    studying 8–9
benefits
    firms' adverts 93–5
    marginal 88–9
    media channels 177
Bernbach, Bill 51–4, 59, 72, 123, 210
billboards 186–7
black, Asian and minority ethnic
        (BAME) agents 74
body images 140
brain-scanning imagery 49

brands
    awareness of 126
    as codes 25
    creating 14
    creative advertising 51
    cyclical model 32, 37
    'dialogue' view 31
    economic research 88, 97
    information 89–90
    psychology and 110
Britain, 'modern advertising' in 135
    see also United Kingdom
'Bubbles' (Millais) 50–1
built-in redundancy 26
Burnett, Leo 209
business ethics 205–6, 207
buying department, agencies 70
'bytes', information storage 26

calls to action 115–18
canned laughter 116
CAP *see* Committee of Advertising
        Practice
capitalist societies 136, 137
car advertising 53, 119–20
celebrity endorsements 164–5
    see also endorsements
central organization of demand 135
central route, elaboration likelihood
        model 110–11
change theories 133, 144
changing demand
    meaning and 155
    reader-response theory 160
    through advertising 3–4, 14
channel variables, elaboration
        likelihood model 115
'chemistry meetings' 68
'A Child's World' *see* 'Bubbles'
        (Millais)
China, history of advertising 146
Chomsky, Noam 189–90, 193
Chrysler Plymouth campaign 119–20
church–state separation 188–9, 191
churnalism 191
client–agency relationship 67
Clinton, Bill 210, 211
clusters of words 29–30
codes of conduct 206, 212
codes, information as 25
cognitive avoidance 167

cognitive component of
        advertising 125
'cognitive load' 108
cognitive psychology 103, 104,
        106–13, 126
combative advertising 96
commission rates, media space 78
Committee of Advertising Practice
        (CAP) 147
commodity fetishism 137–8, 141
communication
    changing demand through 3–4
    defining 19
    marketing 158–9
    'medium is the message' 177, 180
    role of 13
    social constructionism 20, 25–30,
        31, 36–7
    transmission model 20–4, 31, 46
community effects 199–200
competition
    economics 86, 90–2, 93–4, 97, 99
    increasing 14
    sales and 49
complaints 148
concentration effect 89
concepts, definition 69
conclusion tools, rhetoric 34
'conduit' perspective, meaning 25
conflict 76
connoted messages 156
constructionism see social
        constructionism
constructive advertising 96
consumer activist movement 166
consumer culture 133, 172
consumer societies 136, 141
consumers
    creative advertising 55
    economics of 85–93, 95
    psychology 103, 118, 124–5
    see also audience...
consumption 90, 165–7
container theory of language 25
contemporary advertising 56–7
    see also 'modern advertising'
content providers see media producers
context of advertising 58
Conventional Wisdom or Prevailing
        Opinion (CWOPO) about
        advertising 201–4

cool media 183–5
corporate social responsibility 205,
        206–7, 212
cost-accounting, agencies 79
cost per thousands (CPM)
        of audience 66–7
costs
    bad advertising 49
    firms' adverts 93–5
    marginal 88–9
    media channels 177
    persuasive advertising 88–9
counter-culture 166
coupons 45, 46
CPM see cost per thousands
        of audience
creative advertising 50–6, 57–8, 67,
        71–4, 125
    see also art, advertising as
creative boutiques 77
creative briefs 68
creative department, agencies 69
creative identity, agencies 72
'creative revolution' 54
credibility 199–200
critical advertising studies 131,
        149–50, 154, 166, 196–201
critical theory 131, 138
cues, peripheral attitude shift 111
cultivation theory 171–4
cultural change 171–3
cultural context of advertising 167–70
cultural form, advertising as
        173–4, 203
cultural safety valve, advertising
        as 166
cultural sociology 216
cultural studies 153–76
cultural values 168–70, 199
culture
    advertising as a bond 141–2
    advertising studies 9
    advertising supporting 210
    associations of advertising 29
    effects of advertising 15
    mirroring 200
CWOPO see Conventional Wisdom
        or Prevailing Opinion about
        advertising
cyclical model, brands 32, 37
cynicism 199–200

data-driven marketing 79
data science 47, 216
    see also information
DDB *see* Doyle Dane Bernbach
Debord, G 138
decoded signals 23
decoding adverts 156–8
deconstructionism 158–9, 160
demand
    central organization 135
    changing through advertising 3–4,
        14, 155, 160
    elastic 90, 93
    industrial revolution and 134
    inelastic 88
    markets and 96
    rational model 89
    reality and 136
denoted messages 156
dependency effect, persuasion 92
The Depression, Britain 135
depth psychology 103–4, 118–19, 121,
    123–4, 127
desire 121–2
'dialogue' view of communication 13,
    19, 25–30, 31, 36
Dichter, Ernest 118, 119–20, 209
differentiation of media 178–81
'The Direct Era', advertising
    industry 65
direct information 89–90
direct value 91
discounts 46
distorting mirror, advertising as
    170, 195–214
diversity, advertising industry 74, 80
division of audience, rhetoric 34
Doyle Dane Bernbach (DDB)
    52, 53, 72
Doyle, Ned 52
drama in advertising 34–5, 55
dreams 119, 120
dual processing models 123
    see also elaboration likelihood
    model

economic depression, Britain 135
economics
    of advertising 85–102,
        134–7
    changing demand 14

communications process 23
    defence of advertising 209–10
effectiveness of advertising 204
ego 118–19
Ehrenberg's theory 125–6
elaboration likelihood model
        (ELM) 109–15, 126
elastic demand 90, 93
Elliott, R 141–2
ELM *see* elaboration likelihood model
emails 22
emotions 55, 110, 202–3
empirical research 203–4
encoded signals 22
endorsements 50, 113, 164–5
engagement, elaboration likelihood
        model 109
English language 200
entertainment industry 210
entrepreneurs, advertising
        industry 65–6
escape theme, car advertising 120
espoused theory 42–3, 56–7, 59
estimates, amount of advertising 4–5
ethics
    advertising studies 9
    distorting mirror 195–214
    effects of advertising 15
    in practice 205–9
    sociological perspectives 139
    subliminal advertising 123
ethnicity, agents 74
ethos, rhetoric 33, 35
everyday ethics 209
'executions' 69
exhibitions 16
explosion of functions, media
        ecology 182
exposure to adverts 10, 106, 110, 167

facts provision 47
Fair Trade label 139
false consciousness 137–8
feedback loops 22, 24
feedback mechanisms
    communication models 23, 26
    cultural messages 200
figures, providing 47
filters, news media 189–90
firms, profit improvement 93–5
Foster Wallace, David 200

fragmentation of function, media
    ecology 182
    see also media fragmentation
framing, linguistics 29
freedom of the press 187–8
Freud, Sigmund 118–20
full service agencies 70–1
'the funnel' theory 44

gender basis, advertising industry 74
gender differences
    cultivation theory 173
    decoding 156–7
    symbolism 120–1
generalities in advertising 47
Gerbner, George 171–2
good advertising
    science 216
    value 91–2
good, advertising for the 209–10
government subsidies 210
gravitational process, cultivation 172

happiness 209
harm 198
Hegarty, John 53
Herman, Edward 189–90
heterogeneous audiences 204
hierarchy of effects 124, 126
high-definition messages 183
'Hill and Knowlton Case' 139–40
historical aspects
    advertising studies 11–12
    Chinese advertising 146
    development of advertising 5–8
History of Advertising Trust 16
Holbrook, Morris 195–6, 201–4, 211
holding companies 76
homogenization of media
    functions 182
homogenous audiences 202
Hopkins, Claude 44–50, 54–5, 67
hot media 183–5
humour in advertising 46
hyper-reality 139–41, 149

id 118–19
'idea factories' 69
The Illusionists documentary 174
Illustrated London News 50
images in advertising 34

imperfect consumer information 90
implosion of functions, media
    ecology 182
incentives 89
independent agencies 77
Independent Television Authority
    (ITA) 146–7
indirect information 89–90
individuals, psychology 103
    see also audience...; consumer...
industrial revolution 7, 134
industry, advertising as part of 15
    see also advertising industry
inelastic demand 88
inelastic segments 94
information
    as codes 25
    communicating 13, 19, 21, 23
    economic research 89–90, 92–3,
        97, 99–100
    meaning of 26–7
    news media 188, 192
    non-conscious models 122
    see also data science
information asymmetries 14
information process model
        (IPM) 106–9, 124, 126
infrastructures, media 185–6
innovation 73, 74
instincts 123
Institute of Practitioners in
        Advertising 81
intelligence, transmission of 21
intermediaries, agencies 78–81
intermediate effects, psychology 124
international agencies 76
interpretation of messages 183
introduction tools, rhetoric 33
intrusive tactics 198
inventory, agencies 66
involvement concept 114–15,
        122–4
IPM *see* information process model
irrationality 198–9
ITA *see* Independent Television
        Authority
iterative approach,
        communication 19

journalism 188, 192
    see also news media

keyed adverts 45
knowledge gap, ethical issues 197

language
    communication models 23–5
    meaning and 200
    semiotics 155
    social construction 30
Lasker, Albert 46, 50
learning models 116
legal aspects 147
license to operate 145–8
life projects 162–5
life themes 162
lifestyle adverts 168
light bulb example, media 182, 186–7
Lindstrom, Martin 127
linguistic context, communication
        28–30
linguistic messages 157
Listerine mouthwash campaign 136–7
literal messages 158
literary studies 153, 159–60
location, advertising agents 73
logical coherence, CWOPO 203
logos, rhetoric 33, 35
loss-leaders 97
low-involvement models,
        psychology 122–4

McCracken, G 163–4
McLuhan, Marshall 178, 181–4,
        186–7
magazines 5, 35
'the magic system' 153–76
'mainstreaming' 171–2
management research 63, 81
management theories 43
manipulation 124
many-to-many media 179
many-to-one media 180
Marcuse, Herbert 138
marginal benefits/costs 88–9
market leaders' reputation 95
market research teams, agencies
        70–1
market segmentation 94
marketing communications 158–9
marketing needs, account
        management 69
marketing practitioner ethics 195

marketing research perspective 203
marketing theories, psychology
        and 124
markets
    competitiveness 86, 90–2
    creative advertising 50
    effect of advertising 96–8
    media relationship 190
    welfare view 98–100
Marshall, A 89
Marxist critiques 137–41
mass audience, assumption of 202
mass-produced goods 7, 50, 134–5
mathematical calculations,
        communications process 23
meaning
    changing meaning of media 186–7
    construction of 31
    of information 26–7
    media channels 181
    movement of 163–5
    semiotics 155
    theories of 25
    of words 27–30, 200
meanings-based approaches 153–4,
        160–5
media
    changing meaning of 186–7
    communications process 20
    effects of advertising 15
    'modern advertising' 7
    relationship models 179
media-buying agencies 77
media channels
    advertising changing 192
    meaning 181
    nature of 177
    subsidizing 185
media ecology 181–7, 192
media fragmentation 185
    see also fragmentation of function
media planning 70
media producers/providers 65–6,
        70, 71
media space 78, 148
    see also space, advertising
media studies 177–94
'The Mediated Era', advertising
        industry 65
mediations differentiation 179–81
'medium is the message' 177–94

memory 107, 108
Mesopotamian civilization 4
message ethics 205, 206–7
message, medium as 177–94
meta-media 186
metaphors 29
Mick, D G 162–3, 170
Mickey, T J 139–40, 141, 149, 167
microeconomics 88
Millais, Sir John 50–1
mirror
    advertising as 203
    of culture 200
    see also distorting mirror
'modern advertising'
    birth of 6
    in Britain 135
    'rhetorical devices' 34
    see also contemporary advertising
monolithic institutions 201–2
'monologue' view of
            communication 13, 19,
            20–4, 31, 36
moral imagination 208–9, 210–11
moral muteness 207, 209
moral myopia 207–8
motivation research 118, 127
motivational aspects
    of advertising 125
    depth psychology 121
    elaboration likelihood model 112
movement of meaning model 163–5
movies 174, 180
museums 16
'myth of personal immunity' 197
myths 159
    see also story-telling

narration 34
'native advertising' 191
negative view
    critical studies 149, 198
    ethics and 195, 196
    markets/advertising 98–9
networks, advertising industry 76–7
neuroscience 49, 216
new entrants, economics 95
news media 179, 187–92, 210
NIMBY see Not in my back yard
Nimeh, George 193
noise, signals 22, 23, 24

non-conscious models of
            advertising 122–4
normalization 116
Not in my back yard (NIMBY)
            142–5
Nyilasy, G 57–8

observational learning 116
offensive adverts 199
one-to-many media 179, 181
one-to-one media 179, 181
online advertising 144–5, 149
opportunity costs 88
organization theories 43
organizational perspectives 63–83
Östberg, Jacob 211
outdoor advertising 142–3, 145

paper, salesmanship on 5, 50
pathos, rhetoric 33, 35
Pear's soap campaign 50–1
peer pressure 117
penetration, adverts with 47–8
perception, information process
            model 107, 108
perceptual messages 155
peripheral attitude shift 111–13
personalization 180
persuasion
    advertising as 13–14, 19, 32–6, 52,
            87–9, 92, 100, 210
    elaboration likelihood model
            109–10, 113
persuasion-knowledge model 167
picture theory of language 25
the pitch 67–8
planning function, agencies
            69–70, 78
pluralism in advertising 204
political economy of advertising
            134–7
Pollay, Richard 168–70, 195–201,
            203–5, 211
polysemic words 25–6
popularization of media 185–6
positive view
    ethical issues 196
    markets/advertising 98–9
practitioner-author perspectives 41
Pratt, A C 75
press releases 190–1

pricing
  markets and 96–7
  persuasive advertising 87–8
  value advertising 91
print
  cultural values 169–70
  'modern advertising' 7
  salesmanship in 5, 6, 43, 46
production of advertising 65, 68
products
  economics 87–8, 90
  scientific advertising 46
professionalism, agencies 72
profits
  improving 93–5
  price/advertising and 96–7
project-form of working 57, 80
proof
  rhetoric and 34
  social psychology 115–18
propaganda 189–90
psychoanalysis 118
psychology 11–12, 23, 103–29
'pulled' consumers 48

quantitative methods 197

rational model, consumers 88–9
rationalization of decisions 124–5
reader-response theory 160
reading adverts 154–65
reading culture through adverts
        167–70
reality
  cultivation theory 171
  demand control 136
  simulation 139–41
  society of the spectacle 138
Reality in Advertising (Reeves) 47
recall tests 109–10
receiver variables, elaboration
        likelihood model 114–15
receivers, media 178–81, 183
recognition tests 110
redundancy, communication
        messages 23, 26
Reeves, Rosser 47–50, 67
reflexivity, advertising industry 81
refutation, rhetoric and 34
regulation 132, 146–8
Reid, L N 57–8

repetition in adverts 204
reputation, market leaders 95
resistance to advertising 166
Resnik, A 92–3
responsibility checklist 208
restructuring advertising industry 74–5
retailers, reorganization 7
retention, information process
        model 107, 108
rhetoric 19, 32–6
rhetorical triangle, Aristotle 33
risk-taking, linguistic context 28–9
Ritson, M 141–2
Rosenblum, Jeff 100
roster, agencies 68, 80

St Lewis, Elmo 44
sales brochures 67
sales effects 96
sales pitches 54
salesmanship
  on paper 5, 50
  in print 5, 6, 43, 46
  see also selling
samples 46, 50
'saying what has to be said' 53–4
schemas, information process
        model 107–8
science, advertising as 13, 41–9, 51,
        54–5, 57, 58–9, 67, 125, 216
Scientific Advertising (Hopkins)
        44, 54–5
Scientific Management (Taylor) 55
'search products' 90
segmentation see market segmentation
Seinfeld, Jerry 211
selective feedback 200
self-regulation of industry 146–8
selling
  advertising as 7
  scientific theory 43–4, 49
  see also sales...
semiotics 153, 155–9
services
  agencies 66, 69, 70
  economics 87–8, 90
  offering 46
sexism 206
Shannon, Claude 21–5, 26
'shops', agencies as 65–6
signals, noise 22, 23, 24

signs in semiotics 155
simulation 139–41
situational variables, information
          process model 109
social advertising studies 9
social constructionism
    communication 20, 25–30, 31,
          36–7
    cultural studies 173
    meaning 163
    psychology 109
    word power 30–1
social context, communication 27
social effects of advertising 15
social groups
    advertising bonding together 141
    outdoor advertising 143
    targeted advertising 144
    vice products 142, 144
social interaction models 134
social media 179, 180, 205
social proof 115–18
    see also proof
social psychology 103, 113–18, 126–7
social theory 133–41, 201
social welfare 98–100
socialization, agencies 72, 75
socially acceptable advertising 131–2,
          145–8
sociology of advertising 131–52, 216
source variables, elaboration likelihood
          model 114
space, advertising 66, 73, 78
specialist advertising agencies 77–8
spectacle, society of 138, 141
speech 24, 25
sports cars 120
statistical processing,
          communication 23–4
stereotypes 199
Stern, B L 92–3, 158–60
story-telling 34–5, 172
    see also myths
structural organization of industry 63
structuration, sociology of 133,
          144, 145
subjective perspectives 98
subliminal advertising 122–4
subsidization of media 185–6, 210
super-ego 118–19
Sutherland, Rory 101, 195, 204, 211

symbolic consumption 165–7
symbolic messages 157–8
symbolism 119–24, 126, 153–4

targeted advertising
    movies 180
    online 144–5
Taylorism 55
telephones 21, 179
television 171, 183–4, 186
Television Act, 1954 146
test markets, scientific theory 45–6
texts, semiotics 155–6
theatrical performances 55
theoretical approaches
    advertising research 105
    communication 19
    contemporary advertising 56–7
    meaning 25
    'modern advertising' 6, 8
    sociology 133–41
    types 42–3
theory-in-use 42–3, 55, 57–9
'Think Small' advert 53
'third person effect' 9
trade-offs, consumers 88
'transmission of intelligence' 21
transmission model of
          communication 20–4, 31, 46
trials 125–6
tripartite industries 64, 77
true information 188, 192
trust 114
'truth-telling fiction' 140–1

U-shaped benefits/costs 94–5
UK see United Kingdom
uncertainty 59, 216
unconscious models of
          advertising 122–4
Unique Selling Proposition (USP)
          48, 49
United Kingdom (UK)
    bans on adverts 145
    self-regulation development 146–8
    see also Britain
USP see Unique Selling Proposition

value
    advertising as 91–3, 101
    products/services 87

values
    advertising changing 205
    cultural values 168–70, 199
vicarious learning 116
Vicary, James 29–30, 122–3
vice products 142, 144
Volkswagen Beetle campaign 53

war, power of advertising 139–40, 141
Weaver, Warren 21, 25
welfare view 98–100
Wells Lawrence, Mary 54–6

white spaces 35–6, 53
wholesalers, agencies as 65
Wilk, Emil 211
Williams' analysis 135, 136
Wise, Jonathan 211
women 173
    see also gender...; sexism
words
    meaning of 27–30, 200
    polysemic nature 25–6
    power of 30–2
working practices 67–8, 74, 80, 206